More Praise for

WHO GETS IN AND WHY

"A fascinating, useful, and important book—fascinating because of its wealth of vividly reported detail on how the college admission system works (for instance, why little Amherst College admits more athletes than mighty University of Alabama); useful because of its clear-eyed view of how students and families can calmly get through the winnowing process; and important because higher education has become so central to American opportunity and mobility."

—James Fallows,
national correspondent for
The Atlantic

"Timely and engaging . . . details how college admissions is rigged in favor of the privileged and how it came to be gamed even further. . . . *Who Gets In and Why* speaks to the current political moment."

—*The New York Times*

"An invaluable tool for college-bound students and their families, guidance counselors, and college admissions personnel."

—*Library Journal*
(starred review)

"For nearly twenty years, Jeff Selingo has been one of America's most trusted voices on higher education. This is his finest work. He pulls back the curtain on all the code words, awkward secrets, and noble hopes associated with college admissions today. Each chapter can help college-bound families turn confusion into clarity."

—George Anders,
Pulitzer Prize–winning author of
You Can Do Anything and *The Rare Find*

"A searing and sensitive look into the world of college admissions. Informed by a remarkable front-row view from the very rooms where it happens, this eye-opening book offers insights that will inspire, enrage, and enlighten."

—Ned Johnson,
coauthor of *The Self-Driven Child* and
president and founder of PrepMatters

"An illuminating and multisided view of admissions work . . . eye-opening and insightful."

—*Booklist*

"Jeff Selingo has done it again. . . . Selingo has managed to lift the veil from the 'inner sanctum,' showing how admission officers deal with the challenges presented by talented and diverse applicants."

—Robert Massa,
former dean of enrollment,
Johns Hopkins University

"A valuable outsider-as-insider's-eye view of the college admission process, spotlighting what applicants will never see. For the tireless, dedicated professionals who do this work, the students and parents trying to understand it, and anyone in between, there are great lessons to be learned here."

—Emmi Harward,
executive director of the Association of
College Counselors in Independent Schools

"Selingo addresses the tyranny of selective admissions and its inordinate social and emotional impact on the more than 90 percent of students who enroll in nonselective schools. Bravo!"

—Deborah Quazzo,
managing partner of GSV Advisors

"An important book that shines a clarifying light into the mystifying corners of the college admissions process."

—Jill Madenberg,
author of *Love the Journey to College*

"For students and their parents grappling with questions about how grades and testing may be considered by colleges in the midst of Covid-19, Jeff Selingo offers readers a seat on the admissions committee and explains how 'getting in' is about much more than just a student's GPA or test score."

—Andrew B. Palumbo,
dean of admissions and financial aid,
Worcester Polytechnic Institute

"Very accessible and quite accurate . . . A great resource for parents."

—Rick Hazelton,
director of college advising,
The Hotchkiss School

Also by Jeffrey Selingo

*College (Un)bound: The Future of Higher Education
and What It Means for Students*

*There Is Life After College:
What Parents and Students Should Know
About Navigating School to
Prepare for the Jobs of Tomorrow*

WHO GETS IN AND WHY

A YEAR INSIDE COLLEGE ADMISSIONS

JEFFREY SELINGO

SCRIBNER

New York   London   Toronto   Sydney   New Delhi

Scribner
An Imprint of Simon & Schuster, Inc.
1230 Avenue of the Americas
New York, NY 10020

For Heather

Contents

Preface   xvii

Introduction: Steering the College's Agenda   1

PART ONE

Fall: Recruitment Season

1. Selling a College: The Endless Pursuit of Students   19
2. Defining Prestige: The Buyers and Sellers   47

PART TWO

Winter: Reading Season

3. Understanding Merit: Look at All the Bs   83
4. Playing the Odds: Early Decision   117
5. Finding an Edge: Athletes and Legacies   145
6. Comparing Grades: High School Matters   163
7. Finding Diamonds: Regular Decision   181

PART THREE

Spring: Decision Season

8. Shaping a Class: The Final, Close Calls   201
9. Paying for College: The Best Class Money Can Buy   221

Contents

10. Making the Final Decision: May 1   237

    Conclusion: Charting the Future   253

    Appendix: Beyond the Rankings: 269
       Finding Unsung Schools

    Acknowledgments   277

    Notes   281

    Index   291

Preface

As COVID-19 upended the college search for students during the 2020–21 application cycle, I found myself speaking several times a month over Zoom to groups of parents and high school counselors worried about how the selection process might change as a result. The college search was already so different for Generation X parents compared to their own search thirty or forty years ago. Now they feared it was about to change again—just as their children were embarking on the journey.

Rest assured that the book you hold in your hands describes a college admission selection machine that will largely remain in place long after the coronavirus subsides. Admissions deans like certainty even more than applicants do. The rule in the enrollment profession is: however you alter your process of recruiting or admitting students, do it gradually. That way you know—or, at least, can guess—which of the levers you pulled caused a shift.

That said, the pandemic reshaped almost every facet of admissions—and did so all at once. SAT and ACT tests were canceled at hundreds of sites around the world over multiple months, forcing more than six hundred colleges to waive their testing requirements (some permanently). Online learning became the norm in high schools, making pass-fail grades more prevalent and altering the traditional cadence of courses. Sports and extracurricular activities were also wiped out, taking away a critical component of the application. What's more, prospective students were left to "kick the tires" of the colleges on their lists through *virtual* campus tours and events, as in-person recruiting was mostly put on hold.

While high schools and college admissions will veer back closer to normalcy, a few changes will stick. It's clear, for instance, that the SAT and the ACT won't return to their former prominence. Even ACT's CEO conceded that in a blog post. Other changes from the pandemic year will be seen in retrospect, though, not as the beginning of a trend but as one-time anomalies.

One blip that will likely fade away is the boom in applications to selective colleges. While the number of applications received by elite institutions will continue to grow, they'll mostly do so from their pre-pandemic levels. The unprecedented surge in applications in 2020–21 was the result of two rare events: highly selective colleges making test scores optional for the first time, and students finding themselves unable to take in-person campus tours or meet with college representatives who in the past would have visited their high schools.

So students hedged their bets and applied to more colleges than usual. While application volume for spots in the Class of 2025 rose by 10 percent, the number of unique applicants remained nearly flat, according to the Common Application, a standard form used by more than nine hundred schools. Most of the increase in applications went to selective private colleges and big public universities, while smaller and less-selective universities were left begging for students. In other words, the rich got richer. The University of California at Los Angeles received a staggering 160,000 applications, a jump of 25 percent over 2019–20 Colgate University saw its applications more than double. Penn State was up 11 percent; Emory, 19 percent; and Harvard, 42 percent.

Test-optional policies undoubtedly played a significant role in the tsunami. In the admissions cycle prior to COVID-19, 77 percent of students self-reported a test score on their Common Application; that share dropped to 46 percent during the pandemic.

Not only were there more applicants, but admissions deans described them as different applicants. Before the pandemic, teenagers usually scoured the *U.S. News & World Report* rankings looking for the column that listed the middle 50 percent of test scores for admitted students to each college. For prospective students, that "mean range" was like a flashing red sign: don't bother applying if you're below these numbers. Once COVID took hold, test-optional policies almost guaranteed that many of those students would apply. After all, why *not* take a shot at Harvard?

"Testing is a specter out there for certain students," said John Latting, Emory University's dean of admissions. "It's a deterrent. It's much more powerful than I ever realized."

At Emory, nearly half of the applications for the Class of 2025 arrived without test scores. Overall, Emory admitted 13 percent of its applicants. But the admit rate for those with test scores (17 percent) was higher—about twice as high—as those without (8.6 percent). The same was true at Colgate (25 percent vs. 12 percent). At Georgia Tech, the admit rate for those with test scores was 22 percent compared with 10 percent without a score. The gap was much closer at Vanderbilt (7.2 percent vs. 6 percent).

In general, about half of applications to selective schools arrived without test scores. But admissions deans said those applicants were usually less competitive across the board and were accepted at a lower rate. Many top colleges new to the test-optional club, however, were tight-lipped about the applicants they accepted without test scores. Given that many colleges have extended their test waivers for another year (or more), admissions deans were cautious about saying too much, worried about future applicants trying to game the system.

Where does that leave applicants who wonder if test-optional *really* means test-optional? At highly selective colleges, a test score is another signal in an application full of them. The more positive signals you can send in your favor, the better your chances of getting in. If you can take a test and achieve a high score, by all means submit it. That said, admissions officers know that the rigor of high school courses and the grades earned in them are the best measure of success in college, and test scores are highly correlated with family wealth. So this was the year many admissions officers focused on "institutional priorities"—such as increasing the number of students who are the first in their family to go to college—or they advocated for their favorite applicants without worrying about a borderline test score that in any other year might have knocked them out of the admit bin.

By and large, my reporting found that admissions officers expected higher-income applicants or those from top high schools to send test scores; if they didn't, it was assumed the number was sub-par. It didn't mean they didn't get in, but either the rest of the application was exceptional or it came from a high school that had a history of sending good students.

It's difficult to make blanket recommendations for the future based on the experiences of a single pandemic-fueled admissions cycle. While there's overlap in the applicant pools at highly selective schools, they aren't the same. One public flagship university, for instance, found that their test-optional admissions depended largely on the major: the acceptance rate was ten percentage points higher for business and engineering majors with test scores while it was nearly even for everyone else. At Georgia Tech, most applicants who submitted scores had high ones to begin with, skewing the averages and rendering courses and grades more useful. Case in point: 93 percent of test-optional applicants to Georgia Tech took calculus in high school, which isn't covered by the SAT's math section per se.

Without test scores, colleges relied more on historical data for students who, in previous years, enrolled from the same high school as the applicant. When colleges accumulate a significant number of graduates from a particular high school—say, ten students over the course of several years—they can track the grade-point averages and eventual degree completions associated with that school. The data indicate to those reviewing applications how grades in one high school translate into grades at the university.

Even as enrollment staff grappled with finalizing their Class of 2025, they were looking ahead, wondering if the tweaks they made in the evaluation process this cycle will work in the ones that follow. Students in the high school Class of 2022 were only sophomores when the pandemic disrupted their education. They were just finding their footing in high school.

For them, the long tail of the pandemic won't end with the college admission cycle. Many parts of applicants' files are baked long before they begin the college search—from activities they start in elementary school, to the courses they take (or don't take) in eighth grade, to the teachers they get to know as freshmen. As long as students make choices about what they do or don't do in school based on their experience of the pandemic year, the effects of COVID-19 will live on, affecting college applications for years to come.

Jeffrey Selingo
April 2021

WHO GETS IN
AND WHY

Introduction

Steering the College's Agenda

The three admissions officers huddled in a windowless conference room are on a mission. Ahead of them awaits probably the most unpleasant part of their jobs: dashing the dreams of 242 applicants to Emory University's prospective Class of 2023 before official acceptances go out in just a few weeks. Here in early March, the high school seniors have been admitted, tentatively, but statistical models the university uses to predict who will actually enroll indicate that too many of the record thirty thousand applicants for regular decision have been accepted so far.

This team of three is responsible for the southeast region. Of the five regional committees reviewing the high school seniors conditionally accepted to the freshman class, they must make the biggest cuts. While the Southeast team meets behind closed doors, so, too, do the other committees trying to move one thousand applications from the thin admit stack to the much larger deny or wait list piles, a process they call "shaping down." The students will never know just how close they came to getting an offer for one of the 721 seats remaining in Emory's freshman class.

"I wish we could tell kids they were an admit until like March 5, which is huge," says Will Segura, his voice becoming ever so slightly higher-pitched as he turns to his two colleagues sitting at opposite ends of the table under the glare of fluorescent lights. "They don't even know how we loved them."

Will is an associate dean and chair of the Southeast committee.

1

He needs to move eighty applicants out of the admit bin by the end of the day. That's sixteen applicants an hour. The day before, the group made its job more difficult by "moving up" thirty-five applicants who were high priorities in this region to the accept pile.

The group agrees to divvy up the work to move quickly. They don't want to readjudicate an applicant's entire file; they want to see the applicant through a wider lens now that the admissions staff has a better idea of what the class as a whole looks like. Their first cut a few months ago was a rough sketch of the class; this one puts finer lines on the edges. And the following week, an even finer sorting will occur when they craft the final class. This process of shaping is a step at the very end of the admissions process that most teenagers and their parents are unaware of: for a tiny slice of applicants there isn't just one look, but many.

The Southeast team starts with the hardest group of majors: natural sciences. These admission spots are among the most competitive at the university because they represent the most popular majors on campus: computer science, biology, and economics and mathematics. Will works from a spreadsheet of applicant names, arranged from lowest academic ratings (a combination of test scores and GPA) to highest.

The group moves swiftly through the docket fueled by Cheez-Its, bananas, and M&M's scattered on the wood-paneled table in front of them like the remnants of a child's candy bag dumped out on Halloween night. First up is a girl already marked as a "low admit" by the original reader—a breadcrumb left to identify applicants who barely cross the line and can easily be dropped later on. She scored a 1310 on the SAT and wants to major in biology. While she has taken eight of the twenty-three Advanced Placement courses offered by her high school, her midyear grades include a C in AP Environmental Science, a course considered the easiest of senior-level advanced science courses. After three minutes, the group moves her to the deny pile.

The admissions officers don't spend much time talking about any one file. Most of those moved go from admit to deny, bypassing the wait list. They move one boy to deny after looking at his senior-year grades—lots of Bs—and note that they've already rejected four other academically stronger students in his school. They switch a legacy applicant—meaning a parent earned a degree from Emory—to deny because of his light extracurricular involvement. The original readers gave him a score of 2 out of 5 in that category, observing he wants to major in pre-med, "but we don't see activities to support that."

A half hour into their meeting, the group lands on a file that has multiple "tags." The applicant is both a legacy and a child of an Emory employee. Because Emory employees receive tuition benefits for their children, moving an applicant from accept to deny at this point in the process would come at a steep cost for a family with a child so close to the line. The applicant has strong grades and a rigorous curriculum, but the overall file was described as "lackluster" by the original reader with ratings of 2 out of a possible 5 for both recommendations and intellectual curiosity.

"I'm sure there is plenty of goodness in the file," Will says, "but in terms of natural sciences and what we're looking at, I don't believe this is that student."

Someone else in the room pulls up the applicant's midyear grades. They are all As. While the student lists neuroscience as a major, "there is no example of neuro in the file" in terms of activities or in the essays, the admissions officer says. She suggests they move the applicant to the wait list.

Another admissions advisor digs deeper into the applicant's other interests. As she flips through the application, she struggles to find enough to keep the applicant in the admit pile. "I'd move to deny," she says.

Will describes himself as "torn," and turns to one colleague asking her why she's in favor of the wait list. "The two tags are pretty significant," she says. A wait list would be "a softer landing," she adds. The applicant comes from a high school that's a busy one for Emory. The other admissions officer looks at where the student ranks among the applicants from the school, a list that is a page and a half. This applicant is near the bottom of the first page. "If we're looking strictly at natural sciences, it's not there."

Will calls for a vote, a rare occurrence this morning when they have usually agreed on most files. He wants to shift the file from accept to deny, while another admissions officer prefers the wait list. Their third colleague hedges. Will reminds her that this file will come back around for another review the following week because of the multiple tags. "From the perspective we're supposed to be coming at now," the wavering staff member says, "it's a deny."

The three admissions officers had debated the file for twelve minutes. It will be their longest deliberation about any applicant that morning. The following week, the student lands back in the admit pile after a review of hundreds of files with special tags like this one, and the week after that, the applicant receives an official acceptance to Emory University's Class of 2023. The high school senior will never know how close he came to a rejection and how much the college's priorities, in this case for children of employees—rather than any particular aspect of his academic and personal life—played a role in getting him ultimately over the finish line.

For more than two decades, I've written about colleges and universities as a journalist for the *Washington Post*, the *Atlantic*, and the *Chronicle of Higher Education*. Higher education is a wide, fascinating world, and I've written about many parts of it: college presidents, new financial aid policies, changes to the curriculum.

But admissions was a world I knew only from the outside. Never before had I been inside a room as a freshman class was selected. For this book, I got an inside look at three very different institutions. I was with the staff at the University of Washington as they were trained to read admissions files. I went to Davidson College in North Carolina to see counselors debate, applicant by applicant, whom to admit for early decision. And I examined the details of applications alongside pairs of readers in their offices at Emory and listened as they weighed their choices. Over seven months, as

Introduction

I sat with dozens of admissions officers in their offices and conference rooms, and joined them for early morning coffees, casual lunches, and late-night drinks, I started to slowly pull back the curtain on what it takes to get into a selective college today. In the pages ahead, I'll give you that same backstage view of probably the most mysterious, misunderstood, and debated aspect of American higher education, and maybe its most important function.

This is a book about college admissions, and how it has become so ingrained, so entrenched in our culture of success and our winner-take-all society that we will do anything to play the game. As we all know, even the rich and famous, arguably people who already have the most power and opportunities in this society, are willing to break the law to get their children into a top college. We believe that the college we go to frames everything else that follows, from our careers and overall health to our friendships and even our romantic life. At times it seems we've bought so fully into this belief that we often make decisions about college—where we apply, how much debt we're willing to take on, looking for back doors in—that are detrimental to our future.

It's worth reminding you in these first pages that it's much easier than you probably think to get into college these days. Yes, if you're applying to a handful of elite colleges, seats are scarce and the demand for them excessive. And yes, if you're a parent who graduated from one of these campuses, it's definitely more competitive to get in than when you went. But there are plenty of seats available at U.S. campuses for the two million high school graduates each year who plan to go to college. Part of the aim of this book is to reveal the smoke and mirrors that have made applying to college a kind of mythical quest to get into the right schools at any cost when, in fact, plenty of good schools offer a top-notch education and have high acceptance rates.

I didn't grow up in a place where people talked about colleges incessantly nor did I go to a selective college. So I'm both astonished and frustrated now by the preoccupation over what seems to be an ever-shrinking club of elite colleges—whether I'm with fellow parents at home in Washington, D.C., or with colleagues in the media or higher education. My alma mater, Ithaca College, accepted half of its applicants when I applied. My roommate of three years ended up as anchor of *ABC World News Tonight*. In a world of Fortune 500 CEOs with their MBAs from brand-name universities, Bob Iger, the former long-term CEO of Disney, has only a bachelor's degree—from Ithaca. I sit on the Board of Trustees with alumni who are former CEOs, lawyers, health-care executives, accountants, and entrepreneurs. We talk often about how we received a high-quality education with engaged professors who worried as much about students as their own research and were surrounded by classmates more interested in learning from and supporting each other than what the sticker on the back window of their parents' car said about them as an individual. There's more to life than a job title, of course, but if the career success of graduates defines the worth of a college, I can point to tens of thousands of prosperous people who went to hundreds of different colleges that are rarely mentioned in the national media. Success in college is about *how* you go, not just *where* you go.

That said, whenever I write about admissions, messages from anxious parents and frustrated high school counselors inundate my email box. They complain that the college search, rather than a milestone, has turned into a nightmare for too many teenagers. Wherever I go, I hear the same conversation among parents, on airplanes and in coffee shops, comparing their children's college options and fretting that their list of achievements is just not quite good enough to get in. Gen Xers who went to college in the 1980s and early 1990s in record numbers are beginning to send their own kids to college. As I make my way around my community in Washington, D.C., and speak to groups around the country regarding the findings in my previous books, I hear these parents say they'd never get accepted to their own alma mater if they had to apply now.

To many, college admissions has turned into a zero-sum game. People assume one student gets in because another is left out.

When I talked with Eric Furda, the dean of admissions at the University of Pennsylvania, the week after acceptances were released, he was replying to emails, phone calls, and letters about the decisions, mostly from parents whose children were denied admission. The inquiries themselves are nothing new, he told me, nor is the fact that sometimes parents question the qualifications of another teenager they know who was accepted. But in recent years, Furda has noticed a trend: now parents start their letters wondering about the accomplishments of those who were accepted rather than trumpeting the merits of their own children.

The reality is that two applicants are rarely, if ever, pitted side by side. Even when that single applicant to Emory was shifted from the admit pile to the deny pile and then back again, another applicant wasn't simultaneously moved. Hundreds of applications to Emory were shuffled between the admit pool, the wait list, and the reject bin in the weeks before final decisions were released, and in the previous months, tens of thousands of other applications were either accepted or rejected. The truth is that competitive institutions like Emory turn down ten highly qualified applicants for every one or two they accept. Nonetheless, the belief that admissions is an "us vs. them" game is strong especially among applicants at more selective institutions, where seats in the freshman class are few and the application numbers more abundant each year.

At its core, this anxiety reflects a broader concern about the world we live in today—it's harsher, more cutthroat, and more stratified than when the parents of today's high school seniors applied to college. Stability is increasingly scarce. For well-off and middle-class parents, their economic state is a precious position to be preserved for their children.

It's why we buy homes near top schools, sign our kids up for travel soccer teams and piano lessons, and, when it comes to the college search, pull out as many of the stops as we can afford. We do that because we believe that a degree from a fancy institution is the best insurance policy we can buy for our children's future. Never mind that we don't know what a prestigious degree really means in terms of quality. But we do know this: the last five U.S. presidents attended a highly selective college, as did the nine Supreme Court justices, and one-third of Fortune 500 CEOs. We believe going to one of these colleges buys access to a certain set of careers, at a select class of employers, and an alumni network of connections for life, so we do everything we can to get into this handful of schools. We don't want to take a chance that our kids will end up on the wrong side of the economic divide. Compounding this anxiety about admissions is then how to pay for the ever-rising sticker price once our child gets in.

The admissions policies of the nation's most selective colleges have an outsize influence not only on high school seniors but society as a whole. As a result, the discussion about who gets into elite schools and why remains at a constant boiling point. The month I started visiting campuses to research this book, a closely watched federal trial was wrapping up in Boston in an admissions lawsuit against Harvard University. At issue was whether the Ivy League institution discriminated against Asian American applicants by holding them to a higher standard than other ethnic groups. Three months later, the same group that sued Harvard filed a similar lawsuit against the University of North Carolina at Chapel Hill.

Then just as the selection cycle I was following was ending, a massive admissions scandal broke, making front-page headlines and leading television newscasts for days. Dozens of people— among them Hollywood actresses and business executives—were charged by the U.S. Justice Department for their alleged roles in a scheme in which millions of dollars in bribes were paid to get applicants into elite colleges by boosting test scores and paying off coaches to admit applicants as recruited athletes in sports they didn't even play.

Sure, the idea of unqualified kids getting into Harvard, Stanford, or Georgetown angers many of us. We like to talk about our higher education system as the linchpin of meritocracy. But as the stories in this book will show, it never was that, and likely never will be. A confluence of often conflicting priorities for schools, driven in part by how they rank in the pecking order of higher education and compete to improve their positions in that hierarchy, means that questions about fairness will be debated for a long time to come.

I got my start writing about higher education as an intern for the *U.S. News & World Report* college rankings in the summer of 1994, before my senior year at Ithaca. One of the editors of the rankings, Alvin P. Sanoff, became a mentor and a friend, and when he died more than a decade later, his widow gave me a set of the rankings dating back to the first annual guidebook published in 1988. As I was thinking about writing this book, I came across that box of *U.S. News* guides. I grabbed the 1990 edition, the one I would've read as a high school junior when planning my own college search. Flipping through the pages offered a window into a much different era. What was most revealing to me was a list of acceptance rates. Many of the numbers seem like typos when compared to today. Johns Hopkins University accepted 53 percent of applicants back then; now it accepts 11 percent. The University of Pennsylvania admitted 38 percent of applicants; now it takes just 9 percent. Washington University in St. Louis, which accepted 62 percent back then, was as selective as my own alma mater at the time. Today, Washington University admits 14 percent of applicants.

The shift in selectivity was inevitable, as more high school graduates began going to college and the number of applications that students submitted increased. Whereas in 1995, 10 percent of high school students applied to *seven or more* colleges, by 2016, some 35 percent did, thanks partly to the ease of online applications. But colleges also encouraged more applications through increased marketing via email and social media, outreach to high schools, and a new focus on drawing students from overseas. They did so to show off their popularity and boost their selectivity and out of the conviction that more applications could help them fulfill an ever-expanding list of institutional priorities.

And that's where you, the applicant, enter the picture. College admissions is not about you, the prospective student or parent of a student, it's about the college. It's not about being "worthy," per se, it's more about fitting into a college's agenda, whatever that might be. Every school has different needs that change over time, sometimes even from year to year. Goals for the admitted class are set by university leaders and then left to the admissions staff to carry out. In a given year, that might mean more full payers, humanities majors, and students from the Dakotas. Sometimes the goals are narrower: a pitcher for the baseball team, a goalie for the soccer team, or an oboist for the orchestra. Many colleges give special consideration to applicants with deep and lasting connections to the school, such as the children of alumni and employees. (Recall the applicant to Emory who was the child of an employee *and* a legacy.)

A rejection then is not about you; it's about what a college needs the year you apply. Just because a college accepts 25 percent of its applicants doesn't mean you have a one in four chance of getting in. This reality, however, is hidden from applicants beneath impenetrable layers of reviews, rendering it open to criticisms of favoritism or outright discrimination.

The cloak of "holistic admissions," a procedure that considers factors beyond grades and test scores is nearly ubiquitous among selective schools. This approach, which attempts to measure qualities that aren't quantifiable and are usually gleaned from an applicant's extracurricular activities, essays, and recommendations, is loved and hated in equal measure by parents and students. Both favor a method that focuses on the "whole student" until they discover that applicants who had lower GPAs or test scores were accepted and they weren't.

Human beings like certainty and admissions procedures provide anything but. They're seen as unfair because they lack precise signals and information for both the applicant and the school to make timely and knowledgeable decisions. While both applicants and colleges like to pretend that the decisions they each make are rational, the system as a whole is ambiguous because the main players are constantly defining and redefining their agenda. There are many things you can do to increase your chances—which this book discusses—but it's important to know that the baffling process you face is ultimately not a judgment about you or your potential.

Right now, one priority for highly selective schools is attracting students from all backgrounds in order to better reflect the racial and socioeconomic diversity of the United States and shed their reputation as havens for well-to-do students from mostly white and Asian families. It's a perception not far from reality. Most of the growth in the enrollment of black and Latino students and low-income undergraduates over the last three decades has come at less selective schools. Black students, for example, account for about 6 percent of freshmen at elite schools, a proportion that has remained virtually unchanged since 1980. Meanwhile, the most selective colleges enroll more students from the top 1 percent of the income distribution than from the entire bottom half, fueled in part by the admissions preferences given to athletes and legacies, who tend to be overwhelmingly affluent and predominantly white.

That this focus in admissions among selective schools comes at the same time as anxiety about the future among white, upper-middle class, and wealthy communities is rising makes for a combustible combination. Many parents have always assumed that as long as their kids went to good schools and worked hard, a spot at a top college was waiting for them. When that doesn't happen, parents want someone to blame. It's why even in politically left-leaning communities support for affirmative action in college admissions has fallen in the last two decades.

If you're a parent who lives in a privileged community, I don't blame you for trying to make sure your children had the best schooling and access to every opportunity growing up. I live in one of those towns and I'm doing the same things for my kids. But sitting inside the admissions system for a year, I came to understand just how much the traditional selection process continues to favor families like mine with its focus on high school courses, test scores, and extracurricular activities, while sustaining the barriers that have long existed for low-income and first-generation students.

What I hope to do in this book is show you that college admissions is a business—a big one—that you have very little control over. Top colleges are inundated with more well-qualified applicants than they can accommodate. You may not agree with the admissions priorities of schools, but as a parent you need to accept the reality early on in the college search that getting into a top school is more difficult than when you went. Encourage your children to start with a wide-open list (and mind). The fact that your kids had a great high school education and access to your social and professional networks means they'll be fine at any one of hundreds of colleges that every year turn out successful graduates and have reasonable admissions requirements.

Indeed, for all the anxiety, the money spent on extracurricular activities and test prep, the time and effort expended touring campuses and perfecting essays, a puzzling contradiction continues to exist in admissions: it's actually never been easier to get into college. The average four-year college in the United States accepts 6 in 10 applicants. Only 46 out of nearly 1,400 four-year colleges accept fewer than 20 percent of their applicants. Every year, hundreds of colleges are still accepting applications after the traditional May 1 Decision Day for high school seniors.

Yes, a majority of colleges have a seat for most of their applicants. Indeed, slightly more than three-quarters of college freshmen nationwide reported in the fall of 2018 that they were enrolled at their *top-choice* college. Yet many teenagers continue to apply to seven, ten, or twelve colleges every year. Even if a student is accepted by all of them, she can still enroll in only one. So why don't more students apply to colleges that will actually accept them?

This book is about the modern admission system—though that's an imprecise way to describe admissions; it's anything but a system.

The ways to admit students are almost as numerous as the colleges and universities in the United States. When I first started to search for a college that would let me inside their admissions office as it evaluated applications, my goal was to find just one. As I talked to high school counselors and admissions deans to find that school, however, I realized that embedding myself on several campuses would provide a clearer picture of the various pathways to choosing a class and give applicants and their families a sense of how a school's priorities drive selection.

My criteria for choosing those schools were in some ways as subjective as the admissions process itself. I wanted colleges and universities that were selective, meaning they accepted fewer than half of their applicants. Yes, despite my frustration with how we obsess over selective colleges, I still chose to focus on these schools because I wanted to see how admissions offices at such places grapple with sometimes impossible decisions. While some schools I considered were among the ultra-elite, I hoped to expand my reporting beyond that rarified world. Given that 80 percent of American students attend a public university, I also wanted to include at least one state flagship institution.

Over the summer and early fall of 2018, I approached two dozen campuses with my request. Nearly every one refused. Their reasons varied, but most told me that, given the influx of applications, they didn't have time for an outsider to audit the process. Later on, some admitted they didn't want their inner workings revealed to the wider world especially when schools like Harvard were in the midst of discrimination lawsuits. With conversations about inequity a major issue in the political sphere, a few worried about exposing how they shaped their class based on the financial need of applicants.

In the end, three institutions agreed to let me in. One was public, the University of Washington, known as UW. One was a small liberal arts college, Davidson. And the third was Emory, a major urban private research university. There are lessons to be learned from how these colleges run their admissions offices no matter where you decide to apply. The point in featuring them is to give you a window into three major types of selective four-year campuses that exist in the United States.

I asked the three colleges to let me observe the admissions proceedings during various moments in the fall of 2018 and throughout 2019. I visited the campuses regularly during the height of the reading and selection period between November and March. All three schools agreed I could review applications and listen to conversations between admissions officers about applicants on the condition that names and identifying details remained confidential (including the application readers, if they so chose).

At the same time I was embedded in these three admissions offices, I followed a group of around three dozen high school seniors throughout the year. I met them with the help of high school counselors, independent counselors, and parents, as well as two national groups that help students in the college application process, College Possible and the College Advising Corps, the latter an organization that is modeled after Teach For America and places recent college graduates in high schools to increase the number of low-income students entering higher education. The three students you'll get to know throughout the book—Grace, Nicole, and Chris—are not meant as stand-ins for all kids applying to college, nor do their high-school experiences reflect the realities of the millions of students who go through the college search. Their stories are meant to illustrate the numbers and nuance of college admissions. Given that these students were just teenagers going through an emotional experience full of ups and downs, I decided only to use first names, or in some cases if they requested, to change their names. All other details of their lives, unless they would reveal their identities, are true. I let these students' college search play out as if I wasn't following them; I asked questions about the decisions they made throughout the process but, at every turn, I avoided providing advice.

The third group of major characters in this book consists of outside players who exert a significant influence on the college search, including both the well-known—the College Board and *U.S. News & World Report*—as well as people who are invisible to applicants but instrumental to how colleges admit a class.

Before we go inside the admissions offices to see just how colleges select a class, I want to start in a spot that might seem surprising: the admissions world outside college campuses. I'm talking about the marketing machine and Internet data industry, the testing companies, and magazine rankings. In countless ways, they're shaping the playing field that you're going to be stepping onto as you start your college search. They manage which colleges send you mail, influence when you get it, and maintain the hierarchy of university brands that drive so much of the national conversation—and angst—about admissions.

My hope throughout this book is that you can get a sense of what I learned during a year inside the admissions process. It's messier than I realized, with no one pass at an applicant necessarily the final one. It's more arbitrary. It includes deeper and wider pools of qualified applicants than any one person can imagine. It's driven by money and agendas from so many directions. It's making students lose perspective as they constantly try to figure out what colleges want rather than doing what makes them happy. But it's also filled with people trying to do their best while being buffeted by a system that few can control. More understanding of the forces at play, I believe, can help us all navigate the admissions journey and ultimately find the right fit.

PART ONE

FALL:

Recruitment Season

1

Selling a College

The Endless Pursuit of Students

The glossy college brochure. It's become a rite of passage for American teenagers. So many over the years that they weigh down the mail carriers, fill boxes in bedrooms, cover kitchen tables.

Colleges would eventually have found their way into our mailboxes—and later into our email boxes—no matter what, but every innovation needs its Thomas Edison, the person who sees around the corner and speeds change up. For college marketing that man was Bill Royall.

The moment that changed everything took place on a spring day in 1988 at a conference having nothing to do with colleges. Bill Royall's direct mail firm in Richmond, Virginia, didn't have any higher education clients back then; he worked with politicians and with nonprofit organizations that needed to raise money. He had come to Washington, D.C., to talk with people who ran New England summer camps.

The camps wanted to expand their geographic reach, and they invited Royall to the meeting to talk about how direct mail might help in attracting new families. While political campaigns were Royall's focus, he told the summer camp leaders that direct mail was increasingly an effective tool for selling all kinds of products. There was no difference between hawking a candidate for Congress and peddling a summer camp to parents. Better data and technology, he said, allowed mailing lists to be correlated with demographics and statistics from a variety of sources.

But Royall's pitch that day fell flat. "They weren't interested, at all," he remembered.

After the speech, as Royall waited for the elevator at the Capital Hilton, a man approached him. He introduced himself as Robert Jones, the admissions director at Hampden-Sydney College, a private all-men's college in Virginia. He had heard Royall's speech and asked if he had ever managed mailings for colleges. "We didn't have any clients in higher education," Royall recalled telling him, "but there was no reason we couldn't."

A few months later, Hampden-Sydney hired Royall & Company. When Bill Royall started digging into the college's marketing strategy, he was stunned not only by how the Virginia campus recruited students but also by what seemed to be common practices among many other schools, as well. Colleges purchased names of high schoolers much as they do today, but they were buying what Royall considered tiny quantities, limited to the names of juniors. Hampden-Sydney, for instance, bought only the names of students enrolled in private high schools. Most of all, Royall found that too many colleges waited for students to contact them instead of flooding the market with mailings to gin up interest.

The campus brochure, of course, existed long before Bill Royall signed up Hampton-Sydney as his first college customer. What Royall perfected was making the colorful college "viewbook," as it's known, as commonplace in the mailboxes of American teenage homes as an L.L.Bean catalog—and then ensuring the colleges he represented were on the top of the pile. Whether you call it junk mail, spam, or propaganda, generations of high school students and their parents have been inundated with images of perfectly manicured campuses and poetic promises of supportive professors because Royall and those who followed his lead persuaded impressionable seventeen-year-olds that a college actually wanted them.

But what the schools really desired were students to apply in order to boost application numbers and make the colleges look popular to other teenagers, alumni, and the rankings. Sure, some applicants would get accepted, but the more who applied and the fewer who got in, the better for the school's reputation.

If you're a high school student or a parent of one, don't be easily enamored or swayed by all the mail colleges send to your home or your email box. As you'll come to see, while there is a science to why you're getting so much, some of the mail is purely random. What colleges are really doing with that mail is filling the top of their "recruitment funnel," hoping that further down the pipeline they'll receive enough applications to send enough admits to get enough Yeses from seniors to fill their dorm beds and classroom seats.

For you, the would-be applicant, the first brochure or email message you get is only the beginning of how a college's agenda ultimately drives the admissions process.

College admissions is a big business. Colleges and universities spend an estimated $10 billion annually on recruiting students—mostly with old-fashioned direct mail and email, using tactics not much different than those of credit card companies and clothing retailers. Yet at its core, college admissions remains defined by rituals developed in the middle of the last century for a far smaller undergraduate population and for students who tended to stay closer to home than their modern counterparts. If you're a parent and marvel at how different your kid's college search is from your own, consider that it's based on a system designed primarily for their grandparents' generation.

In the years around World War II, students typically applied to one school, and most colleges admitted anyone who graduated from high school. Colleges we refer to today as elite depended heavily on feeder high schools, usually boarding schools, where officials understood the academic standards and knew the student body. Until the 1950s, colleges didn't have an admissions office to speak of. There were no admissions deans. No viewbooks the size of catalogs mailed unsolicited to would-be students. No official campus tours. Instead an administrator split his time between admissions and academic duties with the help of a clerical worker.

By the 1960s, the modern admissions infrastructure started to take shape, the result of more high school students knocking on the doors of colleges. The number of undergraduates more than doubled in the decade baby boomers arrived on campuses, to 8 million by 1969. In response, states expanded public campuses, turning former "normal schools" and "teachers' colleges" into regional universities and building new college campuses to accommodate the growth. The University of California alone opened three new campuses in the 1960s.

With increased choices for students, public and private colleges began competing for them, shifting the admissions conversation from *recruitment* to *selection*. In 1959, the College Board published for the first time what had been previously a closely guarded secret: how many applications a school received and how many students it accepted. The term "selectivity" entered the lexicon of college admissions. "Once admissions statistics became public," Elizabeth Duffy and Idana Goldberg wrote in *Crafting a Class*, a history of college admissions, "they came to signify a college's quality."

As high school students learned about acceptance rates, they began applying to multiple schools to play it safe. Such shopping worried admissions officers. They were concerned about the "growing hysteria over getting into college," as the director of admissions at Ohio's Hiram College put it in 1961—a laughable statement today since even the most elite colleges then weren't as selective as they are now. But the truth is that colleges were concerned with their own sanity rather than that of the applicants. Multiple applications prompted unease within admissions offices, which until then had never developed models to predict which applicants would enroll because usually everyone accepted came.

But even as admissions officers complained about the rising application volume, they stoked the fire to keep fueling the numbers. They did so by going on more high school visits to woo counselors who they worried would start discouraging students from applying to colleges with declining acceptance rates.

Even so, one tactic remained largely unused by colleges until the 1970s: direct marketing.

To admissions officers, unsolicited mail and even advertising were dirty words, corporate approaches used to lure customers. Colleges were even reluctant to use the term "recruiting," since that indicated they might be desperate for students. They preferred to call it "school visiting" instead. In general, colleges tended to wait for students to come to them.

When Jack Maguire started as Boston College's admissions dean in the fall of 1971, he sat with his secretary to watch what she did when a prospective student called requesting information about the school. "She took out an eight-and-a-half-by-eleven envelope, dictated the name and address on it from the phone, stuffed the envelope and put it in the out-basket," he recalled. "I said, 'Wait a minute, aren't you going to keep a record of that name?' and she said, 'No, if they're interested, they'll apply and then we'll have a record.'"

That same year, the College Board offered a new service to campuses that would, over the subsequent decades, revolutionize how millions of high schoolers searched for colleges. It was called the Student Search Service, and it sold the names and addresses of test takers—in other words, prospective students—to admissions offices. The service got off to a slow start. Colleges didn't think they needed to market to students. But as the 1980s began, attitudes shifted. "Ten years ago schools that were actively marketing were seen as hucksters," Lee Stetson, the dean of admissions at the University of Pennsylvania told the *New York Times* in 1984. "Now everyone has to do it."

The last wave of the baby boom generation was leaving higher education. Demographics are destiny for colleges, and analysts projected that the number of U.S. students graduating from high school would shrink for much of the next decade and beyond. Schools needed to fill the classrooms and dorms they had built for the baby boomers, and marketing consultants such as Bill Royall were ready to help them do it.

⧉

When Bill Royall got to work at Hampden-Sydney College, he took a page from the playbook he was already using to raise money for politicians and nonprofits.

The first approach he suggested was to add a P.S. to the letter to prospective students. Hampden-Sydney's admissions director resisted the idea, worried it would look as if he hadn't thought through what he'd written. Royall finally persuaded him to try it out with an A/B test. The P.S. letter performed better; more students who received that letter ended up applying.

Other new ideas followed, each one validated with a randomized experiment. One-page letters instead of two. Sending to juniors in high school as well as seniors. Window envelopes to speed up the mailing process so envelopes didn't have to be matched with letters. An "offer" of free admissions tips if students returned the reply card.

"Everyone was resistant to the offer," Royall told me. "It sounded cheesy, they said. It wouldn't generate good inquiries from students. We told them more inquiries could get them better inquiries."

Later, Royall convinced his clients to allow teenagers to mail those cards to a centralized facility run by his company to speed up the process even further and to better track responses. This was after Royall discovered some colleges stored inquiries from high school sophomores in a closet for up to a year before entering them in their databases because they couldn't keep up with the responses. Most colleges were accustomed to using small consulting firms headed by former academics to run their marketing campaigns, and some colleges even mailed their own materials. Speed often wasn't a priority until Royall came along.

Royall was first intrigued by direct marketing as an advertising tactic when he was a college student in the late 1960s and vol-

24

unteered for statewide political campaigns in Virginia. By 1976, he was running the statewide election effort for President Gerald Ford in Virginia, the only southern state Ford won. The following year Royall helped elect the state's new Republican governor by pioneering a segmentation analysis that sent materials to voters based on the issues that most appealed to them. Such data-driven segmentation was beginning to permeate every facet of marketing consumer products. By the end of the 1970s, Royall left the governor's office, where he was working as a senior aide, to head up a direct mail company in Richmond.

By July 1992, Royall had about a half dozen higher education customers. Politics was still his passion, however. On July 16, 1992, he sat in a hotel suite in New York City, watching Bill Clinton on television accept the Democratic nomination for president. On a table in front of Royall was a letter he'd written hours earlier with excerpts from the speech that the Arkansas governor had signed. The following morning, that letter with a New York City return address was mailed to millions of Clinton supporters around the country. It would become one of the most successful political fund-raising appeals of its time.

If he had wanted, Royall could have cornered the political fund-raising market. But in the early 1990s, colleges were facing even deeper enrollment troubles than during the previous decade, the result of a decline in American births in the 1970s. Schools needed outside help to run their admissions marketing operations, and increasingly they were turning to consultants. In 1995, Royall decided the future of his business wasn't in politics, but higher education.

If you're a high school student deluged with mail from colleges on a daily basis, it's because the College Board has your name. Most people know the College Board as the owner of the SAT. Founded in 1900, the organization counts some six thousand colleges, high schools, and nonprofit groups among its members. While legally a nonprofit, it often feels and acts like a giant corporation. It collected one *billion* dollars in revenue in 2017, according to its federal tax forms, mostly in fees for the SAT and AP tests.

The idea of selling the names and addresses of test takers started with a noble intent—to increase access to college by putting information in the hands of students who historically didn't go. But as campuses competed aggressively for new undergraduates in the 1980s, peddling names turned into a moneymaker. By then, the College Board was selling 30 million names a year, at 14 cents a name and grossing $4 million.

In the 1990s, marketing consultants urged colleges to cast wider nets to find would-be applicants, upping the number of names purchased yet again. Then in the last decade, as email marketing and year-round outreach was introduced earlier in students' high school careers, the College Board expanded further, selling names as many times as it could. "There might be 100 of us all paying for the same name," said Michael Sexton, the former dean of admissions at Oregon's Lewis & Clark College.

In 2006, the College Board sold 60 million names. By 2010, 80 million names were licensed, even though only 5.2 million students took the SAT and PSAT that year. Exactly how much name-selling has grown since is unclear. The College Board refuses to disclose how many names it now sells through "search," as the practice is commonly called in the world of admissions.

Here's what the College Board *would* tell me: search is bigger than ever. It sells names to nearly 2,000 colleges and scholarship organizations, up from 1,600 a decade ago. A student's name is sold, on average, 18 times over her high school career, and some names have been purchased more than 70 times—all at a cost now of 45 cents a name, each time it's requested among those test takers who opt in (students have the choice to participate). While the College Board was the first to sell names, they are far from the only one doing so these days. One survey of admissions officers found that they buy prospects from over a dozen sources, although the lists from the College Board remain the most popular, with the PSAT typically supplying freshman, sophomore, and junior names, and the SAT senior names.

In the pre-Internet days, the College Board released names twice a year; now it offers new names fifteen times during the year, turning the pursuit of students into a year-round effort. Years ago, the fall of junior year was early enough for most colleges to start their outreach. But for competitive reasons, schools now want to scope out students even sooner. As a result, schools have stepped up recruitment of high school sophomores. Today, 9 out of every 10 colleges purchase names of sophomores.

When colleges buy names, they can filter the purchase by a variety of factors. An admissions office, for example, might order the names of men with PSAT test scores above 1200 who live in Pennsylvania and want to major in the humanities. This again is where a college's agenda—and not the talent or accomplishments of students—drives the search buy. A college isn't looking to send mail only to straight-A students who scored a 1500 or higher on the SAT. Campuses have certain needs—more men, more minority students, more English majors, more students from five states away—priorities they attempt to fulfill by buying names fitting those criteria. The information used to compile the search order is gleaned from questionnaires students complete when they register for a test.

The search business has allowed the College Board to add millions to its bottom line each year without doing much more than pressing a button to send names to colleges and their marketing consultants. While the College Board governs the use of the names under licensing agreements with colleges, the group hasn't curtailed the endless stream of marketing to students—marketing that ultimately whips teenagers into a frenzy every year and warps the eventual value of the college search.

In the late 1990s, Royall & Company had plenty of competitors. Twice a year, all the firms would all ramp up staff and wait for FedEx boxes to arrive from the College Board with nine-inch reel tapes embedded with names of test takers.

For Bill Royall, even FedEx wasn't fast enough anymore.

One summer afternoon in 1997, he sent a twin-engine Beechcraft Baron to New Jersey to intercept the tape delivery from a FedEx processing center near Newark airport. What was in those boxes was gold for the colleges that were Royall's clients. Every minute mattered. The sooner he pulled those tapes out of the boxes and got those personalized letters in the mail the sooner those students would know that these colleges wanted them to apply.

In New Jersey, two men—one the Beechcraft's pilot and the other a Royall executive—loaded 150 boxes into the back of their aircraft, the seats removed to make enough room. As the sun set, the prop-plane was cleared for takeoff on its return to Richmond. When it landed, Bill Royall met the aircraft and its precious cargo on the tarmac. The men transferred the boxes into a waiting truck and the group sped off on the thirty-minute drive to Royall's headquarters.

Despite the late hour, the office was full. Workers opened each box revealing the stacks of tapes, each with a slice of student names purchased by a specific client. There were female students with an interest in engineering and SAT scores above 1500 designated for MIT. Seniors from New York City, Philadelphia, Washington, D.C., and Boston marked for Washington University in St. Louis. Yale wanted teenagers keen on the humanities, the University of Miami family incomes above $100,000 and GPAs above a 3.5.

Royall employees confirmed the names on each of the tapes and repacked them for a short trip to a mail-processing firm in nearby Lynchburg. There, workers fed the reels into a machine that spit out letters addressed to each of the students by their first name. The letters included other personal details—their intended major, interests in school—and the all-important tear-off reply card. If students returned the card, they would get some sort of gift, usually a list of admissions tips (*10 Questions Other Admissions Deans Hope You Don't Ask*).

A few weeks later, Bill Royall's phone started to ring steadily with calls from clients, letting him know his strategy had succeeded—mountains of reply cards were arriving on their campuses every day.

For several years, admissions consultants like Royall had pressed colleges to get mail out to prospective students ever faster. In an increasingly competitive market for students, speed was obviously more critical than ever before. From now on, Royall told his team, he wanted his schools to be first in the mailboxes of students— before they had a chance to fall in love with another college.

Line up students in a high school who performed similarly on the PSAT or SAT and ask about the letters, postcards, or emails they've received from colleges and you'll immediately see how arbitrary the search business is. For one, colleges can't buy a list of names sorted by high school. The College Board has never permitted that—it didn't want colleges to essentially replicate in their search what they were already doing with visits to feeder high schools.

If who gets mail and who doesn't seems so random it's because it often is. A typical college's search request usually exceeds how much it can afford to buy. An admissions office might want all the students in Colorado who scored better than a 1300 on the SAT— a request that might generate 12,000 names when the school can afford only 5,000 of them. As a result, the college receives an arbitrary selection of 5,000 names fitting its criteria. This haphazard process for fulfilling orders is why two high school students living in the same town, attending the same high school with similar interests, grades, and test scores might receive mail from different colleges. So while this marketing feels personal to many students who have little experience being sold to, it's often no more personal than the Internet ads that chase us around the web trying to sell shoes.

No matter the medium, however, teenagers ignore the vast majority of marketing from colleges: only 11 percent elicits some sort of response (that's considered good by comparison to direct mail for consumer products where the response rate is even lower). The consensus among the high school students and parents I met while researching this book is that colleges send way too much mail—and most of it ends up in the recycling bin or ignored in email boxes.

So why send so much?

Schools flood the market with mail for many different reasons. They want to make themselves look more selective to the outside world. They're uncertain about who is actually going to apply, so perhaps they want you to get a brochure but their interest has declined by the time your application is reviewed. What's more, selective colleges are always looking for that needle in a haystack— the talented student from a middle-of-nowhere high school that they hope will be among a stack of search names they buy. Most of all, colleges want students able to pay, so schools tend to overbuy names of test takers from wealthy zip codes.

Among top schools, the mind-set is the same as it was fifty years ago when B. Alden Thresher, the former director of admissions at the Massachusetts Institute of Technology, wrote in a seminal book about admissions that selective colleges "want the best and only the best, we are never satisfied." Although a random piece of mail from a faraway college is highly unlikely to make the sale, admissions officers keep trying anyway.

One mother texted me a picture of three milk crates of unopened mail she collected over the course of her daughter's junior and senior years. Another joked she planned to wallpaper her son's room with the discarded mail when he left for college. A Reddit user tallied 2,374 marketing emails he received from more than 100 colleges—an average of 19 *unsolicited* emails from each school. Louisiana State University alone sent him 102 messages.

While occasionally a letter, a brochure, the offer of college swag, or just something different might grab the attention of a teenager—Harvey Mudd in a recent year sent a deck of cards for a scavenger hunt—the mail students told me they most often opened was from schools already on their radar.

Nevertheless, it seems everyone can recall receiving *that* surprise letter or email from an Ivy League school or another name-brand college, even when their stats were below freshman averages for the campus. "I got an email from Princeton," a senior proudly told me when I visited her Maryland high school. The student with a 3.7 GPA and a 1350 SAT score showed me the message, which encouraged her to apply to take advantage of "the tremendous opportunities" Princeton offered to students like her. She sent her application because she thought she was being recruited. She was denied. "It seems some schools recruit you," she said later, "just so they can reject you. Why do they bother if we don't have a chance?"

The name-buying and resulting direct mail are both a cause and symptom of our national obsession with selective schools. Sure, selectivity was a measure of a college's brand well before the College Board ever sold a test taker's name, but the ease and frequency of direct mail changed the dynamics of student recruitment. It allowed colleges in every corner of the country to flood the mailboxes of high school students nationwide, enticing them with pretty pictures to new locales. Suddenly, a high school student in Massachusetts could know about a college in Minnesota or imagine herself walking across a campus in California.

The result was an uptick in applications to colleges, everywhere. Back in 1975, 60 percent of students applied to just one or two colleges. That was the norm. Now those students are in a distinct minority—only 18 percent do that. When I applied to college in the early 1990s, fewer than 1 in 10 students applied to at least seven colleges. Now that number, thanks to marketing and the growth of the Common Application, has exploded: some 1 in 3 students apply to seven or more places. That shift—the marketing behind it, the nationalization that drove it, the uncertainty it's created for institutions, and the anxiety it's fostered for students—is now at the core of what we mean when we talk about college admissions.

When Grace started her college search, she had one wish: a campus on the East Coast, a world away from her tight-knit Chinese American community in San Francisco where she'd grown up. Unlike some of her friends with older siblings who provided a head start on the college search, Grace was the oldest of three. She didn't have the experience of tagging along as a middle schooler on campus tours. Nor was she given a dog-eared *Fiske Guide to Colleges* from an older brother. Her mom, a schoolteacher, had randomly applied to the University of California and ended up at the Davis campus, seventy miles northeast of San Francisco; her dad, who works for the city, didn't graduate from college.

Grace was unsure of the effort it would take to find the right "fit." What was a reasonable number of schools to have on her list? Should she visit campuses before she applied? How long would it take to write her essays? Although the start of senior year was still nine months away, she was already making commitments that would add to the strain of application season: taking four Advanced Placement classes, running cross-country, leading the environmental club, and volunteering at her church.

In December of her junior year, as Grace was preparing to take the SAT for the first time, her fall PSAT results arrived. She scored a 1340 out of 1520, a little more than a 100-point gain from the time she took the test a year earlier. A few days later, she met with her school counselor to talk for the first time about the college search and how to get started. "I want to go to a top school," Grace announced after telling her counselor she also wanted something on the East Coast.

The counselor asked what schools she was interested in, but beyond the brand-name places everyone knew about—Harvard, Yale, and Princeton—Grace struggled to name any. This was how many junior-year meetings started at this high school, or any high school for that matter, where nearly every graduate goes to college. For these students it seemed there were only twenty colleges in the entire country even though most of them were out of reach for them academically. The counselor pressed Grace on why a "top" school was so important. "I want to be around smart, driven people," she told her.

Grace was already getting letters and email from colleges, the result of her sophomore PSAT scores. They were mostly from schools she had never heard of. She ignored the emails and opened the letters and brochures "to read what they had to say because they took the time, effort, and money to send something," she told me with a smile. Still, unless she recognized a college's name, she didn't research it further. "I know that shows my bias toward a brand, even if the school looked good to me in the brochure," she said later.

With a round, open face set off by straight, jet-black hair, an enormous smile, and animated eyes, Grace displays an unshowy self-confidence. But when her counselor asked how much a college's price was a consideration in her search, she hesitated. Grace had broached the subject of paying for college a few times with her mom and dad, but only in the vague terms that parents use to talk about a subject they're uncomfortable discussing. She knew her parents had been putting away money in a 529 college savings plan, but she had no idea how much was there.

Unlike when we buy a house or a car and check out the price tag first, cost doesn't initially factor into a student's decision about where to apply. Research has shown that parents focus on selectivity and reputation more than cost when discussing colleges with their kids. Parents usually avoid the money conversation as long as they can because they don't want to deny their child the chance at a dream school. For Grace, the prices of different colleges seemed like abstractions. That's the case with most teenagers when it comes to college. After all, most haven't bought anything pricier than clothes, a pair of sunglasses, or maybe a video game console in their lives.

After a few more minutes, Grace's counselor recommended she check out the College Board's BigFuture website before they met again. That night in the bedroom of her home in San Francisco's Sunset District, Grace opened her laptop's web browser and signed on to the interactive college-planning tool.

You have 3,825 college options. Choose a category on the left to find the right ones for you. The message on the opening screen was meant to pry open the minds of teenagers as they developed their college lists; instead it just induced anxiety in Grace. "There's just so many colleges to look at," she said later. "It's such a crazy, randomish process." Marketing consultants like Bill Royall were supposed to help students sift through those colleges, but all they did was add to the noise.

For high school students, the college search is likely the first time in their lives they are confronted with so many choices and swamped with so much information as they try to make a momentous decision. It's a classic case of what psychologists and economists refer to as choice overload and information overload. An abundance of college options paralyzes teenagers or makes them doubt their subsequent decisions compared to those who had fewer options. Comparing colleges requires students to digest hundreds of data points. As a result, they tend to retreat to what is familiar or simple. They glance at the rankings, follow their friends' lead, or look for the nicest dorms or the universities that dominate the March Madness basketball tournament.

Savvy applicants typically approach the college search by breaking it down into smaller, manageable parts. First, they figure out what they're looking for in a college—a particular major, research opportunities, location, size—before they ever even start a list of schools. Using those attributes as filters in online search tools, they begin to build their list. Then, they slowly pare down the list over many months by comparing colleges two or three at a time.

As Grace perused BigFuture and clicked on filters randomly for the next hour, her eyes were drawn to the college logos that appeared. She scrolled down the computer screen to see names she recognized. Amherst was first, then a few others she couldn't recall, then Dartmouth. "I was like, I heard of that one," she told me. She added Dartmouth to her list along with a few other names that were familiar: Harvard, Yale, Tufts, Wellesley, and Wesleyan.

Every few weeks, she'd visit her counselor or stop by the school's college center, where a few years earlier the parents' association donated money to help hire a full-time counselor. "I kept asking them what they thought of the schools that I had on my list, how many I should have," she said. Their rule of thumb was similar to what I heard from many school counselors, that is, put together a list of ten to twelve schools overall, with three to four colleges in each of three categories: *likely* or *safety* schools, where she's above the school's ranges for GPA and test scores; *target* or *foundational* schools, where she's solidly in the middle; and *reach* or *dream* schools, which would be a stretch for her. Remember, many students start their college search in the fall with aspirational dreams that end in the spring with a cold reality: you might only get into your "likely schools," so be sure they're colleges you'd want to attend and not just placeholders on a list.

After Grace narrowed her possibilities to a dozen, she drew up a chart, with rows for cost, size, and average SAT scores. There was Yale and Columbia, Brown and Barnard, Skidmore. Just one college, Pomona, was on the West Coast. By the time I met Grace early in her senior year, the list had evolved, but her search was still largely driven by brand-name schools on the East Coast. Grace was wise to start her search in the middle of her junior year because it was her family's first time through the process. However, rather than use that extra time to start with a list wide open with possible schools then tailor it later on, she limited her choices right from the beginning. Her initial list, for instance, didn't have any University of California campuses on it, or any public college options at all. For Grace, UC campuses were too big and too close to home.

In those first months of her search, one factor Grace failed to fully consider was exactly how she would pay for college. I found in my interviews that many middle-income—and especially upper-middle-income and even wealthy families—rarely discuss finances early on. They either believe they can cover tuition from their income or from savings or, more likely, they think they'll secure a merit scholarship in the form of a tuition discount from some college. After all, they hear at parties about family friends whose children received such scholarships, and the media remind them constantly that no one really pays full price for college anymore. The problem for students like Grace who consider only very selective colleges is that financial aid there is usually based on family need, not merit. When looking at top schools, Grace never took into consideration whether her parents' earnings put her above the cutoff for need-based aid.

By comparison, one of Grace's friends had winnowed out costly colleges on the front end, using the net-price calculators colleges are required to display on their websites. If her projected financial aid package was inadequate, she took the school off her list. Grace had looked at the calculators, too, but because she used estimates based on her limited knowledge of her family's finances, the dollar amounts never fully sunk in.

"I still don't think I have a grasp of what $40,000 of debt really is," she said later. She believed what the college experts often said was true, that with aid, the cost of a private degree might not be more than going to a public university. "If people would have told me that for sure I wouldn't have gotten any aid, I wouldn't have been optimistic," she said later. "It would have been good to know that reality."

Grace ignored her counselors' suggestions in those early months to add some less selective colleges that probably would offer merit aid for high-achieving students like her no matter her family's income. As spring break approached and she was making plans to visit colleges, Grace reluctantly added a few campuses of the University of California to her list, at the insistence of her mother. But in Grace's mind, she was still going to school three thousand miles away.

⊞

I first met Grace in the college center at her high school. Draped along one wall were college pennants and a map with pushpins showing where last year's senior class ended up. A quick look at the map showed that Grace's determination to leave is pretty common: in their cross-country recruitment rush, admissions officers most often strike gold in California.

The number of students crossing borders to go to college has more than doubled in seven states since 2008. No one had a higher number of students leave their home state than California (the other six were Arizona, Georgia, Mississippi, Nevada, North Carolina, and Texas). In admissions circles, California students are known not only to leave the state, but also to travel long distances. Fifteen percent of California students travel more than 500 miles for college; the national median is just over 100 miles. No wonder so many colleges send full-time recruiters to the Golden State. The Regional Admissions Counselors of California, which represents recruiters for out-of-state colleges, now has more than 130 members, double what it had in 2008.

Just as all politics is local, so too was higher education throughout much of its history. Few high school graduates went to college. Among those who did, their choices were usually limited to a small set of local institutions they knew of through their network of friends, parents, and teachers.

Over the last half century, the admissions market began to shift. The concept of distance changed in the minds of college-going students and their parents. In the past three decades, in particular, places that once felt far away now feel as if they are one town over, thanks to the Internet, the ease of interstate travel, and the proliferation of discount airlines. High-achieving students—rather than settling for their local institution—started to jump into applicant pools at schools with national brands. This phenomenon was described by Stanford University economist Caroline Hoxby in a 2009 paper published by the National Bureau of Economic Research. She described it as a "re-sorting" of students, where their choices were driven less by distance and "far more by a college's resources and student body."

The re-sorting accelerated in the 1980s when a handful of colleges with well-timed marketing campaigns repositioned their campuses from regional and even local brands into national names. Duke University, the University of Pennsylvania, and Rice University all saw their rankings go up as they expanded the geographic breadth of their incoming classes. Several urban universities, including New York University, Boston University, and the University of Southern California, also transformed themselves from locally focused commuter schools to international brands. This re-sorting is largely why today's admissions process seems so intensely competitive and anxiety-ridden to parents who went to college in the 1980s. It's not that there are so many more top-notch students applying to college; it's that the top ones from Los Angeles and Chicago and Atlanta and Buffalo are now all applying to the same selective schools. And they're applying to way more of them.

There's no denying that the competition for a seat at *a specific* college is much tougher for today's students than it was for their parents. But it's not true that getting into any selective college is actually that much harder. Even top colleges accept higher numbers of students than they need because they know only between a third and a half of those accepted will say yes to their offer.

Of course, the marketing is designed to make students focus on a "dream" school and a "perfect fit." It's not about the similarities that colleges have—it's about the purported uniqueness of each. No one sends high school juniors a glossy brochure explaining that the top liberal arts colleges are pretty similar. Or a viewbook about engineering co-op programs that says here are a couple of good options for you. Who can blame students for focusing instead on individual brands? Remember that's what colleges are selling.

A national study of where students send their SAT scores found that students' choices cluster around type of college (public or private) and brand. The peer effects present in high schools amplify this trend and often push students farther from home. Once a few graduates from a high school go far away to college, students in subsequent classes follow, and with each graduating class the numbers leaving home grow until the concept of going away becomes the norm.

College-planning tools like Naviance reinforce these peer effects and help explain why so many students mistakenly think only a few dozen colleges are right for them. Naviance is an online service used in about 40 percent of U.S. high schools, giving it an outsize role in the college admissions process. Its most popular feature is the scattergram, where students can judge their chances of gaining acceptance to specific colleges through a graph of anonymous applicants with similar grades and test scores who previously applied from the same high school. A college is displayed only if the high school had at least five students—and in some cases, ten—apply there the previous year. Each applicant's decision (accepted, denied, or waitlisted) is illustrated with a unique color and symbol.

How much those scattergrams influence a student's college list is something Christine Mulhern, a doctoral candidate at Harvard's Kennedy School of Government, wanted to know. In 2019, she published a study that examined the college choices of students using Naviance in a school district with 4,000 graduates annually. On average, Mulhern wrote, students could access scattergrams for 47 different colleges and universities. She found that students were 20 percent more likely to apply to those colleges than schools without scattergrams. "Students prefer to apply to colleges at which they have some information about their admissibility," she wrote, "and where they are likely to be admitted."

Let's pause for a moment to explain what I mean throughout the book by a "selective" college. It mostly describes a set of around two hundred colleges and universities based on categories chosen by Barron's, which you can find in a popular annual guide called *Profiles of American Colleges*. It separates schools into selectivity categories from "very competitive plus" to "most competitive." In general, the two hundred "selective" schools accept fewer than half of the students who apply.

Over the last fifty years, half of American colleges and universities have become *less selective* in their admissions decisions, Stanford's Caroline Hoxby found, as the best prospective students applied to only the same small group of elite schools, ignoring hundreds of lesser-known schools. That's why the most selective institutions—representing only 20 percent of American colleges—account for about one-third of *all* applications submitted now.

The rising selectivity of those few schools grabs headlines every spring when admissions decisions are released, prompting an arms race among admissions offices to talk about just how difficult it was to get in. In 2019, Yale announced it was "impressed with and humbled by" the 2,178 students it accepted from a record high 36,843 applications—a 5.9 percent acceptance rate. Cornell received 49,118 applicants that same year, admitting 10.5 percent of them, "an extraordinarily gifted and accomplished group of students," according to the university's vice provost for enrollment.

The unending stream of superlatives led *New York Times* writer Frank Bruni to quip in a column that Stanford's acceptance rate had fallen to zero. "With no one admitted," he wrote, "Stanford is assured that no other school can match its desirability in the near future."

Joking aside, the plummeting acceptance rates at a small set of elite schools have had serious ripple effects, creating uncertainty in admissions offices further downstream. Whenever schools face volatility in enrollment—caused by demographic shifts or economic downturns—they turn up the spigot of name buys in the hopes of drawing additional applications. That in turn results in students applying to more schools to hedge their bets. As the number of applications skyrockets, colleges struggle to predict yield, the number of accepted students who enroll.

Wherever applications are growing, someone is planting the seeds of that growth. Rising application numbers appeal to alumni, prospective students, high school counselors, even Wall Street investors who buy bonds used to pay for campus buildings. They all see the rising numbers as a signal of popularity and quality in an industry without easy-to-understand metrics.

College admissions has always been a delicate balance between marketing and mission, and the impact of Bill Royall and his counterparts has pushed it further toward the side of commercialization in the last forty years. "Colleges are a business," Richard Whiteside, the former admissions dean at Tulane, told me before he died in 2019, "and admissions is its chief revenue source." While many people initially enter the admissions profession to serve the needs of students, they soon find out that selling the college is a necessity in an increasingly competitive industry. Admissions counselors are salespeople pitching a product to students, employed by colleges that need to meet a bottom line.

In 2013, a new generation of students started to arrive on college campuses. Gen Z, those students born in 1995 and beyond, have different expectations for college—most of all they want a job after graduation—and approach the search for the right fit in a very different way than their Millennial predecessors. Studies find that a third of today's students are "stealth applicants," meaning they have no contact with a college before applying. Instead of filling out a form at a high school visit, they "like," they "follow," or they "subscribe." Finding them requires a different marketing strategy for colleges once again.

The visitors arrive one after another, nearly every second. The first is Anonymous 5325015 from Toledo, Ohio. Another is Anonymous 9025345 from Sweet Home, Oregon. The third is a hit: David H. from La Porte, Indiana. He's visiting the freshman tuition web page.

From his office at the University of Toledo, William Pierce is watching these visitors arrive. The senior director of undergraduate admissions is not looking out his window at campus, but at a dashboard on his desktop computer. The feed (think Twitter or Facebook) is constantly scrolling with visitors to the university's website. They are tracked using their unique IP address.

The day I'm watching, most visitors are anonymous. Pierce digs deeper on one of them, looking at the "engagement summary" that reveals this person—or at least this particular IP address—has visited the university's website eight times over the last month, looking at thirty-two pages. Each click is a digital breadcrumb that follows the user through the website, compiling every movement as he advances. Every so often, a pop-up appears—a small box in the bottom right-hand corner of the screen or an image that covers most of the page. The goal is to collect some tidbit of information from this user. A name and email address are enough at first. Then perhaps another pop-up at another time will collect information on intended major or year in school. Once Pierce's system has a name, it's added to the university's customer relations management system, or CRM, which Toledo like most colleges uses to track prospective students and to serve them customized information. Sometimes the former anonymous user is already in the CRM system because the university had purchased the name and contact information through search. That's a precious commodity to people like Pierce because now he can customize what he sends to that prospective student based on his web behavior.

But that's not the only way Pierce uncovers his web visitors. Remember David H. from Indiana? He was revealed to the University of Toledo a different way. All those emails Toledo sends to would-be students from their name buys contain unique links. When David clicked on one, his data was connected to the back end of Pierce's system. Now the system could track the movements of students like David through the university's website and target them with personalized communications based on their interests. David had visited pages for the university's College of Business and Innovation a dozen times in recent weeks, even though on his SAT questionnaire he indicated he was interested in engineering. So now the university can mail him information about the business school without his ever asking. The university also knows he's from Indiana, so an announcement for an upcoming admissions information session near his home might pop up next time he visits the website.

Find it creepy? Maybe. But what the University of Toledo and most other schools are doing is no different than the invisible algorithms that Amazon, Zappos, Netflix, or virtually any other online retailer uses to offer you other things you might like based on your past selections. For colleges, this system is a lifeline in a digital age when students ignore traditional marketing from schools and apply to colleges without going to see them or attending a counselor's visit to a high school.

42

Toledo's software is designed by Capture Higher Ed. More than fifty colleges and universities use the Louisville, Kentucky–based company's system, including the University of Kansas, the University of Tennessee, and Colby College. In a recent year, the company tracked 20 million unique web visitors on its clients' sites. Most of that traffic is what is called "organic," meaning it's prospective students searching colleges' websites without being contacted by the schools. "Colleges have plenty of interested students, but they often don't know who they are," said Thom Golden, Capture's former vice president for data science. "This tool helps universities uncover those students." About 7 percent of users go on to complete interest forms that pop up on university websites served by Capture. Of those, 70 percent are organic visitors.

The primary goal of Capture's software is to turn an anonymous user into a known one, and then a prospective student and eventually an enrolled one. It also allows colleges to offer more one-on-one, personalized engagement with students rather than constantly showering them with general mailings. Today's students are accustomed to customization and instant communication. "In the past, if a student opened an email but then never inquired again we thought he wasn't interested," said Golden, who previously oversaw admissions recruitment at Vanderbilt University. "Now we can see through his website behavior that he actually is interested, it's just that the university didn't send him the right information, at the right time."

In 2014, Bill Royall turned sixty-eight years old. By then, his company's client list had grown to nearly four hundred schools. That year it collected $105 million in revenue from its admissions business. He was a mainstay at conferences for college enrollment officers—with his shock of white hair, well-tailored suits, round wire-frame glasses, and the company's signature red ampersand logo pin affixed to his lapel. Twice in the previous six years he had sold the company to private equity firms, remaining on as chairman of the board. Now he was ready for one last hurrah. The admissions marketing business was changing yet again. Just getting students in the door was not good enough for colleges anymore. With demographic shifts on the horizon, colleges also needed help keeping students year to year, getting them to graduation, and maintaining lifelong relationships with their alumni for fund-raising—the "student lifecycle" as it was called.

Other companies were already helping colleges manage these needs. One of them was the Advisory Board Company, which had made billions consulting in the health-care industry. In December 2014, the Advisory Board bought Royall & Company for $850 million. The colossal purchase price sent shock waves through college admissions offices everywhere even though they had helped feed the beast. After all, most college endowments aren't that large.

When I visited Bill Royall in Richmond, Virginia, we met in a mostly empty, stark-white office he still maintains in his former company's headquarters. The squat building on the outskirts of Richmond is now home to EAB, which the Advisory Board Company sold in 2017 for $1.55 billion to a private equity firm. The sale included Royall & Company. "It's the gift that keeps on giving," Royall joked to me.

He seemed riveted by his own story when he described it to me. I asked him how he felt about the ways the college search had turned into a seemingly never-ending process fueled by millions of pieces of mail and billions of dollars. He had no regrets for his role in creating the admissions monster. "Look, we've been able to contribute to access and opportunity and inclusion," he said. "We know of thousands of kids who go to college every year who wouldn't because they got recruited through us. When I look back on my legacy, to me that's the greatest contribution that our company made."

Bill Royall passed away in June 2020 of complications from amyotrophic lateral sclerosis, or ALS (often known as Lou Gehrig's disease). He was seventy-four. At the time, the COVID-19 pandemic was causing the widespread cancellation of admissions tests, the very source of all those search names. If fewer students end up taking the PSAT/SAT/ACT as more colleges adopt test-optional policies in the wake of the pandemic, the search business will undergo yet another transition as schools look for new ways of reaching teenagers.

The business of marketing colleges made Bill Royall a very rich man. As I waited for him and his wife, Pam, when I visited them in Richmond before his death, I flipped through a book in the reception area that profiled "the art of Royall & Company." Sculptures, paintings, and photographs hang everywhere around the three buildings that make up the office complex in Richmond, all collected by the Royalls over the years. In the preface to the book, the company's art director remarked that our perspective on art "changes as we learn more about its context." Quoting from John Steinbeck's *The Grapes of Wrath*, he wrote "we like what we know."* The same could be said for Royall's approach to selling colleges. He tried to widen the perspective of students, so that they might like more than what they knew.

Above all, Bill Royall made himself wealthy by realizing that all those teenagers (and their parents) were customers. When people told him not to send "window envelopes" because families might think it was a utility bill, he knew they were wrong. Teenagers had never received a bill in their life. They were thrilled to be sold to. For the first time, someone was reaching out directly to them, sending them mail, talking about changing their lives. That type of marketing altered the way parents and their children thought about going to college. For many of them being an American high school student now means swimming in a constant stream of messages about colleges, debating options all over the country, wading through stacks of mail, and getting tracked while you visit college websites. In the end, Royall didn't just expand the horizons for students, he also expanded our collective anxiety.

---

* This quote did not appear in *The Grapes of Wrath*. Wallace Stegner might have been the original source for this quote.

2

Defining Prestige

The Buyers and Sellers

On a crisp fall morning, a line of yellow school buses winds around the Baltimore Convention Center, as a throng of teenagers streams into the steel-and-glass complex. The students are arriving from high schools all around the region for what has been for generations a ritual of the teenage years: the college fair.

Before email and social media allowed colleges to connect with prospective students early and often, college fairs were a critical channel campuses used to fill the top of their recruitment funnel. Before the college rankings carved up schools into "tiers" and the rise of early decision admissions overhauled the conventional recruiting timeline, college fairs were important events that admissions officers circled on their calendars every fall.

Inside the dimly lit convention center, representatives from over three hundred colleges line up behind long rows of tables, with more than a dozen aisles stretching across the concrete floor. Each college has the same curtain backdrop with its name affixed on a tag. The only thing distinguishing each is the nylon flag draped over the front of their rectangular table and whatever cardboard signs, booklets, and swag they can fit on top.

College representatives wait patiently behind the tables for potential students to line up or show any sign of eye contact to help them initiate a conversation. "Did you get a viewbook?" a representative from New York's Le Moyne College asks those who pass by. "A pen? A dolphin?" he continues, holding up a magnet of the college's mascot, as many students, heads down in their mobile phones, just keep walking.

Anywhere you turn at this fair you feel like a customer navigating a shopping mall concourse. But it's not phone cases, sunglasses, or hair straighteners on sale. It's six-figure dreams about futures. And the shoppers have little sense of what they're buying. What's the difference between a liberal arts college and a research university? What are the requirements for a four-year degree? What does it mean to "major" in something?

Coming to this fair is like going to a car dealership and saying, "I heard I should get some type of automobile—maybe a pick-up truck or a fast roadster or a minivan. Is there even much difference? I just know it needs to have four wheels."

As I stood inside the Baltimore Convention Center, I realized I was witnessing the duality of modern admissions. Just as important as the students and colleges I could see in this hall were all the ones who weren't here. The savviest and the wealthiest—both the students and the schools—were absent, playing a different game, on a different field, all of which had started long before this last day of October.

Admissions isn't the rigid, easily defined process that applicants and their families widely assume it is. Colleges operate their admissions cycles in two different worlds, depending mostly on where they stand in the academic pecking order. Knowing how to navigate these distinct worlds makes you like an early explorer possessing a map of distant unknown lands.

The first thing to recognize is that colleges are either "buyers" or "sellers."

Sellers are the "haves" of admissions. They have something to sell that consumers want, typically a brand name that signals prestige in the job market and social circles. As a result, they are overwhelmed with applications, many from top students. Admissions officers at sellers see their role as the gatekeepers who allow suc-

48

cessful applicants into the inner sanctum for the opportunity to interact with other star students.

The buyers are the "have-nots" in terms of admissions—although they might provide a superior undergraduate education. They lack names that are instantly recognized when the scores of sports teams stream across the bottom of ESPN. Rather than select a class, their admissions officers must work hard to recruit students to fill classroom seats and beds in dorm rooms.

Whether a college is a buyer or seller matters to applicants for two reasons.

First, getting past the gatekeepers at the sellers is becoming increasingly difficult. If students have only sellers on their list, they risk getting rejected from every school they apply to. Second, sellers don't need to buy students with tuition discounts to fill their classrooms. They are prestigious enough that a large percentage of families are willing to pay full price. Most sellers offer financial assistance only to students who really need it or are truly exceptional. Yet many upper-middle-class families above the cutoff for need-based aid at a seller's school—which could range anywhere from $60,000 to upward of $200,000 with lots of caveats—think their financial reality is not what some formula says it is. They believe that every school offers a discount (they don't) or that every financial aid package is negotiable (it isn't). If your family can't easily write a $23,000 check for what the *average* in-state public college charged in 2020 or $51,000 for the *average* private school—and do that for four years—be sure to have a few buyers on your list where your chances for merit aid are better.

That said, you won't find a list anywhere that neatly divides the world of higher education into my two categories. Finding the buyers and sellers, particularly when it comes to figuring out what kind of discount you might get from a school, takes detective work. Even then, what you find is still a guess. Colleges are no more forthcoming about how they award financial aid than they are about how they select a class. That's because in the last thirty years the purpose of financial aid for the buyers (and even some

sellers) has shifted from helping low-income students afford tuition to maximizing a school's revenue.

To better understand what's happening, let's explain what we
mean by "financial aid." The common kind of aid is based on financial need. Parents disclose their income and assets on various forms
and aid is awarded through grants, loans, and work study.

Colleges also give out another kind of aid without regard to
how much parents earn. This is called merit aid, and it's usually
based on specific academic criteria, such as test scores and high
school grades, but not always. A lot of merit aid is simply bait
used to reel in accepted students—in some cases despite middling
grades in high school. Such offers usually come from the most desperate of buyers. The U.S. Education Department found that in
one year some 40 percent of full-time students at four-year colleges who had *less than* a B average and *scored under* a 1000 on the
SAT received "merit scholarships" from their institutions. We call
these "scholarships" and "merit aid." It's good marketing. If colleges referred to them as "coupons," parents and students might
feel a lot less excited. But that's really what they often are. That
$15,000 merit scholarship sounds nicer than "buy three years, get
your fourth free."

One way to think about the differences between buyers and
sellers is that the sellers—at the most basic level—don't have to cut
prices or massage the deals to get the lion's share of their students
to enroll. Instead, they have a sizeable percentage of students paying the full price. And when they make an admission offer, odds are
decent that students will say yes.

Sellers make up a fairly small number of four-year colleges and
universities, less than 10 percent. The vast majority of schools are
somewhere on the spectrum of buyers. On average, sellers admit
just 20 percent of applicants, while colleges as a whole admit two-
thirds. When sellers make an offer, nearly 45 percent of students
accept, compared with a quarter for buyers. And only 7 percent of
the financial aid sellers give out to students is a merit-based discount, compared with nearly one-third of aid at buyers.

I want to emphasize that none of this buyer-seller division is a reflection of the actual educational quality of the school. You can get a great education at a buyer. I went to one myself, built a satisfying career, and am now privileged to sit on the board of that same college.

Savvy students willing to look beyond the brand-name sellers can find great schools that are buyers. Compare, for example, two private science-focused universities 130 miles apart. Carnegie Mellon University, with a sticker price of $75,000 per year, accepts fewer than 20 percent of applicants and spends less than 7 percent of its financial aid on merit-based discounts. Carnegie Mellon is a seller. But just across the state line, in Ohio, Case Western Reserve, with a nearly identical sticker price, spends nearly 40 percent of its institutional aid budget on merit-based aid. Yet both schools attract top-tier students with average SAT scores that differ by less than 100 points.

The same distinctions exist between public research universities—even in the same state. The University of Virginia is a seller; the flagship admits just 26 percent of applicants and spends about 7 percent of its own aid dollars on merit scholarships. But in-state rival Virginia Tech is a buyer. Tech accepts around 65 percent of students who apply and spends 81 percent of its aid without regard to financial need. Yet the schools both have high graduation rates and ten years later, graduates earn nearly identical average salaries, according to the Education Department's College Scorecard.

All but a handful of the colleges at the Baltimore fair were buyers. Their admissions officers were like traveling salesmen who needed as many "leads" as possible to "convert" into a sale. Buyer institutions don't "craft" an incoming class the way sellers do. Buyers "make" their class by enticing students to apply, usually through an application process that is as simple as posting to Instagram. Then they enroll students by offering hefty discounts on their sticker price using what are euphemistically called merit scholarships. One of the schools at the fair, Susquehanna University in Pennsylvania, hit their enrollment target of 640 incoming students in 2019 only by offering discounts that averaged around 70 percent.

With that coupon, the typical freshman paid around $14,000 of Susquehanna's advertised $48,000 sticker price for tuition.

Not only do colleges occupy two different admissions worlds, so, too, do high school students. When teenagers and their families embark on the college search, they are largely empty vessels waiting to be filled with information. Over time, they separate into two worlds and follow different calendars as they hunt for a college. One group starts early as voracious consumers of information, reading guidebooks or regularly talking to counselors or others who can help them. They are what I call "drivers." The other world is occupied by "passengers" along for the ride. Some students are passengers by choice—myopic teenagers propelled by parents and counselors. Others might have the motivation to be drivers but they lack access to good advice either at school or at home.

The students I found at the Baltimore fair were mostly passengers. They were seniors but were just starting their college search at the end of October. At the very moment they were roaming the convention center floor unsure of what to do next, nearly three hundred thousand college applications from drivers around the country— early decision applications—were arriving at campuses through the Common Application. Those were submitted by seniors who don't show up at fall college fairs like the Baltimore one. They don't need to. They have essentially finished their search. That there was one set of seniors still in the midst of their search at the end of October and another basically finished illustrates the two worlds of admissions. There is no longer one single calendar. Thirty years ago, the fall marked the beginning of the college search process for nearly everyone. Today for many drivers it marks the end.

To better understand how students separate into drivers and passengers, I visited a high school that teaches an entire course for juniors focused on the college search. Granted, the school was far from representative. It was a private high school, the Friends School of Baltimore. The fact that the school even offers such a course, and that it's taught by one of the school's full-time college counselors, demonstrates the advantages that some teenagers start with in the application process. I know from writing about higher education for two decades that who goes to college depends almost entirely on how much his or her parents earn. I asked to observe students at Friends—the majority from privileged backgrounds and whose parents went to college—because I thought they'd be well informed. If they didn't understand the most basic aspects of college admissions, what would that say about everyone else?

On a Wednesday just after eight in the morning, I sat with fifteen high school juniors, who were listless in their first class of the day. "What makes a good college?" Darryl Tiggle asked, scribbling the question on the chalkboard, hoping to jolt the teenagers awake. The students called out answers to Tiggle's question as he wrote what they said on the board: low-admit rate, high SAT scores, average GPA, successful alumni, academics. On the last one, a boy slumped in a chair labored to define what he meant by "academics." Indeed, all the students struggled to define the term "quality." The conversation kept returning to whether a college is "known" as a quality school. In other words, its reputation.

Tiggle, an admissions officer at Tufts University before he came to Friends in 2009, asked the students to raise their hands if they thought reputation was an important indicator of quality. Half of the class did.

"How do you determine reputation?" he asked. There were blank stares. Despite an abundance of college rankings, government resources, and other consumer websites, the students were baffled.

"What about the rankings?" Tiggle asked. The students nodded their heads in near unison, but struggled to name any rankings they had seen recently. After what seemed like several minutes, a girl blurted out, "Isn't one named after a university?" ("Yes, the Princeton Review," Tiggle said).

As the class period wound down, Tiggle drew a line down the

board in front of him. He labeled one side "Universities" and the other side "Liberal Arts Colleges." He asked the students to name what they considered good schools for each column. Stanford, Yale, University of Chicago were first up in the university column; Colgate, Pitzer, Bowdoin went in the liberal arts column. As the students continued to shout out names, what struck me was that their list didn't exactly mirror the *U.S. News* rankings. But it still included mostly brand-name sellers.

"People knowing a college or not knowing them doesn't contribute to their goodness as much as you think," Tiggle told the students as the bell rang.

Tiggle first started offering the course six years ago, along with a summer program for parents, because "everyone is less sophisticated than we imagine when it comes to college," he said later. His goal is that by the time students present him with their initial list of colleges at the start of their senior year "we've watered it down" if the students have no shot at an Ivy League or selective liberal arts college, such as Williams, Amherst, or Middlebury.

The college list is an admissions task that students approach casually because they think of it as a document that evolves over time. For them, it's unlike other stress-inducing elements of the application process that have specific time pressures: the SAT, extracurricular activities, or the essay. But the list is not an exercise that should be left to teenage indifference. Sure, it changes during the year, but the first version is as important as the last. The types of colleges on the list (and their admissions priorities) impact many facets of the search farther down the road—whether you get accepted, of course, but, perhaps as important, how much financial aid you eventually get.

Both schools and students envision the college search as a funnel that narrows as it progresses. But the difference between the funnel for students and the one for colleges is how quickly the funnel narrows. While colleges have a wide funnel of prospective students at the top that tapers ever so slightly over the course of an admissions cycle, students get to the slender part of their funnel very quickly.

They start their search near the bottom of the funnel. The reasons for this are abundant and sometimes complex, but mostly revolve around our preconceived notions of quality that were on display in Tiggle's class and play out every year in the homes of high school students and in their counselors' offices.

A list that is top-heavy with ultra-selective schools, for instance, or fails to incorporate a mix of academic, social, and financial factors from the start will fail to produce a good fit in the end, no matter how it changes. The best antidote to students feeling disappointed in their college search is to approach the application process with an open mind and give themselves enough time to conduct a thorough search. After all, teenagers aren't just searching for a college. The best college searches are those that help applicants discover themselves on their way to becoming adults.

As Tiggle advised his students, just because you've never heard of a school doesn't mean it isn't good. By starting the search at the widest part of the funnel with enough time to narrow it, students and their families sometimes end up embracing an idea that was foreign to them when they started: that there is life beyond the elite, prestigious, brand-name schools.

When we buy a house, we have a specific set of needs—a certain number of bedrooms, an updated kitchen. We usually know the neighborhoods where we want to live, and, of course, we have a price range. When we go to a car dealer, we show up with a ton of information. We know the brands. We've read the consumer reports about performance and resale value.

College is different. It's an emotional decision, one economists refer to as an "experience good." We don't know what we're buying until after we experience it. Choosing the right college, the right major, or the right classes is difficult because we lack the tools to make bottom-line comparisons between options. As a result, the decision-making process is ill-informed, usually haphazard, and full of false starts.

Higher education is intertwined with prestige, a word that's been bandied about by students and parents for years when referring to the standing of colleges in a hierarchy. The irony is that the word was originally a derogatory term, defined as "illusion" and "conjuring tricks" in Latin and French. So maybe it's appropriate that no easy way exists to measure what's really behind the top brands in higher education.

These days when we talk about top colleges, we tend to label them as *elite* institutions. "Elite" was a word that barely registered on a Google Books Ngram search—which tracks the frequency with which words appear over a given amount of time—until 1940. Since then, however, it has spiked upward, surpassing the word "prestige" in the 1970s. An elite college now is almost exclusively defined by how hard it is to get into. It's like the rope line at a hot nightclub—it's about having the ticket to get in. Students are blinded by the labels. But why does it matter whether you get into the club if you hate the music playing inside?

Unlike in the corporate world where a company's prominence is evaluated in direct proportion to its earnings or stock price, colleges have no such clear standards. The result, as Malcolm Gladwell argued in the *New Yorker* in 2005, is that prestige in higher education is measured by the quality of students the admissions office admits, not by the education they receive. He compared elite colleges to modeling agencies. "You don't become beautiful by signing up with an agency," Gladwell wrote. "You get signed up by an agency because you're beautiful." In other words, Harvard admits kids who are smart or come from well-connected families and the university's job is to simply ensure it doesn't screw them up over the next four years.

When applicants overlook the mountains of published information about colleges, then prestige becomes a matter of perception. To spend any time in the pressure cooker of a prosperous suburban high school in the United States is to see how that perception is shaped by students and parents who view college as another luxury good. Just as driving a BMW or a Range Rover or carrying a

Louis Vuitton bag is a symbol of success, so too is an acceptance to an Ivy League school or any top-tier seller. In many communities, students and parents want a college to pass the "window-sticker test"—a college that's worthy of bragging about on the rear window of the family car.

High schools in the shadow of three major research universities turn the temperature on that pressure cooker even higher. In Chapel Hill, North Carolina, I met Nicole, a senior at one of the region's most competitive public high schools. Like Grace in San Francisco, Nicole is obsessed over going to a top college. I asked her why the name mattered so much to her. She started to tell me about her classmates, about how talk of luxury college brands permeates everything at school—the hallways, the classrooms, the athletic fields. A lot of the talk starts at home, she explained.

Among the 1,300 students at her school are a hefty number of teenagers whose parents are employed as professors, administrators, doctors, and researchers at nearby Duke, Carolina, and NC State. These hyper-accomplished parents view admission to the type of colleges where they work as offering the best promise of career success and economic stability in an increasingly competitive world. They want their kids to one day live in the kind of places where they grew up, and the path to a life in those neighborhoods— whether in Chapel Hill or any well-off metropolitan area—winds through the campus of a selective college.

It's in places like North Carolina's Research Triangle, which includes the college towns of Chapel Hill and Durham, plus the state capital of Raleigh, that a college's prestige is conferred through discussions that happen at coffee shops, dinner parties, and book clubs among parents who complain about how the admissions landscape at elite colleges has changed for their children. It used to be that kids who grew up in these neighborhoods had a somewhat easy path to a top college. Now it's a much more difficult path, although not as impossible as those conversations in coffee shops and dinner parties make it out to seem. Despite the lip-service that elite colleges give to seeking racial and socioeconomic diversity in their student bodies, they still largely enroll students in the top 10 percent of American incomes.

That said, fewer spots do remain for upper-middle-class (and often white) students with solid but not superb résumés. You can see it in the results of admissions season each year at elite high schools. Someone I know who went to a private boarding school in the Northeast told me that when he graduated thirty years ago, the school would send fifteen or so students to Princeton or Yale, while a college like Middlebury or Georgetown was considered a safety school. Today, it has flipped, and Princeton and Yale accept only two or three graduates. Or take the list that *Bethesda Magazine* publishes every year of college acceptances for graduates from the three top (and wealthiest) public high schools in the Maryland suburbs of Washington, D.C.: in 2018, more than 2,400 students applied to Ivy League schools and Stanford, and only 222 were accepted.

Whenever I write a story about college admissions for the *Washington Post* or the *Atlantic*, I inevitably get email messages like the one I received from a mother in the suburbs of Washington, D.C., in the fall of 2018. Her daughter graduated from high school the previous spring with a 4.6 GPA and scored a 1400 on the SAT (she even attached her daughter's transcript to the email). The girl applied to five schools, and was accepted to one: the University of Colorado, Boulder. "Even the counselors at the school were a bit surprised, despite the competitiveness of all these schools, that this was the outcome of her applications," the mother wrote. "Admittedly, I was a bit miffed too by my daughter's outcome of college acceptances. The University of Colorado has a lot to offer, but it is by no means a competitive school to get into."

Conversations among well-off parents about a college's prestige filter down to their children and shape their own viewpoints about college. Students are careful about what they share with classmates for fear the names of colleges they're considering will result in embarrassment, or worse, mockery. "You pick up the reputation of colleges from the people around you," Nicole told me. "You can see it in their facial expressions when you tell them where you're applying."

For these students, the marketing they get in bunches from Bill Royall's clients is now essentially worthless. It's all white noise. Their minds are molded by other influencers—their parents, their peers, social media, and the college rankings and guidebooks.

Nicole started working on her college list near the beginning of her junior year, writing comments about schools in a purple Moleskine notebook she carried with her. "As soon as I heard someone mention a college, I'd Google it," she said. Within seconds, the school's acceptance rate and notable alumni appeared giving her the first hint whether she had found a "name" college. Another click would reveal the school's *U.S. News* ranking. "If it's a school no one has ever heard of," Nicole said later, "there's no point including it." Schools like Muhlenberg College and even Indiana University, both of which her counselor recommended, never made her list as a result.

Tall with curly light-brown hair, Nicole speaks with a carefully modulated voice. She is a driver. In reality, though, like Grace in San Francisco and many other drivers, Nicole lives at times between both worlds. She's well informed but allows emotion—especially about prestige—to drive decisions. Or she ignores advice if it conflicts with her worldview. The early version of her college list, for instance, includes both the University of North Carolina at Chapel Hill and North Carolina State. But she's dead set against both, especially UNC. Too many kids from her high school go to those schools, she told me. Even though both universities enroll some 42,000 undergraduates between them, they would feel too much like high school to her. "I would rather go to a worse school than go to UNC," she said. "I wish it weren't so close to home. If UNC were in any other state, I'd love to go there."

By any measure, UNC is one of the nation's top public universities. It's selective—only 27 percent of applicants are accepted. In other words, it's just as good as—if not better than—any of the other universities Nicole was considering. And tuition for in-state students is less than $10,000 a year, a quarter of the tuition prices of the private colleges on her early list. Her stubbornness this early in the process seemed shortsighted, especially for a driver so interested in going to a prestigious university.

The search for Nicole began to turn real in February when she took the ACT for the first time. She scored a 31 (out of 36), the top 95 percentile nationally. That meant she was at the bottom of the top 5 percent of students nationwide. It's a score that most students would be ecstatic about. But the number disappointed Nicole because she didn't think it was good enough to attend a selective school. The following month, she took the SAT. She scored a combined 1490 (out of a possible 1600). Much better, though Nicole was nervous enough about the outcome that she decided against automatically sending the results to any college. She preferred taking the ACT. She felt it was better suited to her interest in math and her testing abilities, even though math counts for more on the SAT and no one really knows which test is "better" for students.

While students might favor one test over another, schools requiring standardized test scores for admissions remain agnostic. A generation ago, students took one or the other: the SAT was popular with students along the coasts, the ACT in the Midwest. Now many top-notch students take both, sometimes several times, and submit only their best scores. Colleges in the past wanted to see all scores. But in an effort to appeal to a generation who prefer to present a highly curated version of themselves in their application, most schools give students a choice about which scores they supply. It's just one way the drivers, who have the time and resources for test taking, shift the balance of the admissions process in their favor. Nicole and her mom wanted to alter that balance even further. Hoping to boost Nicole's ACT score, her mother signed her up for test-prep classes. She paid $600 for six sessions taught by a former high school teacher who tutored Nicole on the English section of the test, her chief weakness. The reality is that testing strategy might have been ill-advised for Nicole: sometimes it's just as useful, if not more useful, to work on your strengths since it's easier to improve on things you're good at.

The spring of her junior year Nicole and her classmates were pulled into the full force of the admissions maelstrom. Like more than half of her class, she wanted to apply early decision to some college. To do that, she couldn't wait until September to complete the test prep, take the ACT again, or visit campuses. There simply wouldn't be enough time before the November 1 early decision application deadline. While Nicole promptly started her search at the beginning of her junior year, applying early decision would shorten the other end of it, making eleventh grade, in effect, her senior year. Every date on her college-prep calendar would need to move up.

The rising popularity of early decision is the biggest contributing factor to the admissions calendar encroaching on the junior year in high schools like Nicole's, and in some cases, seeping into the sophomore year. In the early 1980s, 19 percent of students enrolled in the Princeton Review's SAT review course started before January of their junior year. Now, nearly two-thirds do.

The goal of securing a college spot by December of the senior year seems, at least on its surface, a prescription to reduce anxiety. After all, it eliminates the uncertainty of seniors waiting in the spring when they are competing against a bigger pool of applicants. But early decision also speeds up decision-making when students aren't quite ready for it. We know from neuroscientists and psychologists that the teenage brain is still maturing throughout high school—in fact, its structure and development continue into a person's twenties. Every month in high school is mentally like a year to adults. As a result, moving everything up, even by just a few months, to meet earlier deadlines curtails a student's performance, especially on the SAT and ACT.

By March it was time for Nicole and her mother to go on their first fact-finding mission. For months, they had been planning to visit colleges. Nicole's mom, who graduated from Rutgers, had hoped to show her a selection of schools to broaden her daughter's perspective. Indeed, if families have the time and money, early visits to colleges should focus on getting a feel for different types of campuses rather than on specific names. Often many of these visits can be done within a day's drive of home, even if the college isn't on a student's initial list. In North Carolina, for instance, Nicole and her mom could have visited a big public university (NC State or UNC), a small private liberal arts college (Davidson), and a regional college focused mostly on undergraduate teaching (Elon University). Again, the names weren't important at this stage. But Nicole had her mind set on a certain type of university. "She is dazzled by prestige," her mom told me, "and cold weather." Visits to other kinds of campuses would come later, Nicole thought.

So during spring break, Nicole and her mother visited five campuses: Northwestern, the University of Chicago, Columbia, Penn, and Princeton. All five of them are brand-name sellers that have the privilege of "selecting" a class. None of them was really "recruiting" Nicole. College visits during spring break are another example where the admissions calendar differs depending on a student's high school. Weeklong breaks in March and April are prevalent at private schools and well-off suburban public schools. But many public schools offer only a few days off in the spring, preventing students from making these road trips during the academic year, even if their parents could afford them. Nicole's mom likened the spring break trip to club sports teams, where parents travel long distances for games and stay in hotels all in an effort to develop their kids' talent.

A few weeks after Nicole returned home from the college visits, her latest ACT results arrived. She improved her score by three points to a 34. I asked her if the tutoring helped. "I'm not sure," she said. "It could be that the second time was easier because I knew what to expect."

Contrary to popular belief, test prep doesn't help students game the test. Few tricks to taking the SAT or the ACT exist. Test prep, if anything, helps students review content they might not know or have forgotten. Millions of students take some form of test-prep each year, everything from free courses offered by the College Board through a partnership with the Khan Academy to online and face-to-face classes with the Princeton Review and Kaplan that cost over $1,000 (some use private tutors who can cost $300 an hour or more). After years of maintaining that coaching doesn't help on the SAT, the College Board now says its "official" SAT practice course on the Khan Academy site can boost scores by as much as 115 points for twenty hours of work. A 2018 study by researchers at the ACT found that the only significant increase in test scores came from those test takers who reported working with a private tutor. Another compelling result: students' perception of their preparedness for the test impacted how they did. Students who reported *feeling* adequately prepared had higher scores than those students who didn't.

In May, Nicole sat for the SAT exam, again. The result: 1390, a drop of 100 points from March. "Thankfully no one will see those SAT scores," she said later. In the previous four months, Nicole had taken the ACT and the SAT four times. She sat for two SAT sub- *OMG* ject tests, in chemistry and math. She visited a handful of colleges. All this before she finished her junior year of high school. Her senior year was still another four months away, and she was already worn down by the college search.

Read almost any college guidebook or website offering college advice and it will often make the point early on that no two students want the same thing out of a school. The assumption is that the search is about finding the ever-elusive "fit"—that every student has both the time and the luxury of making a choice among many options. They don't. To put it in blunt terms: upper-middle-class and wealthy kids search for the perfect fit; poor and working-class kids usually don't have choices or don't go to college at all. While Nicole and Grace were nearing the end of their junior year with the major milestones of the college search essentially finished except for their applications, others in the nation's junior class that year were just getting started. One of them was Chris, a student I met at a small, rural high school in Pennsylvania, about an hour northwest of Allentown.

While Chris is physically imposing—a lineman on the football team, he's listed as six foot one and 220 pounds—he's also soft-spoken. He has deep-blue eyes and a heavy stubble for a teenager. Chris is a passenger, and not always by choice. For as long as he could remember, Chris had had his mind set on going to college. It was a chance to rewrite his family's history. His mom, an estimator for a construction company, earned a business degree at a community college when she was thirty-two. His dad died of complications from diabetes when Chris was in elementary school. For Chris, the search started, as it does for most students, when he took the PSAT as a sophomore in high school, in his case, though, because it was required. He scored 1160, in the top 89 percent nationally.

A few weeks later he started to get mail from some local colleges. He tossed the brochures and postcards without even looking at them. "I was a sophomore," he told me. "I didn't know why I was getting mail. I wasn't applying to college." Colleges say they market ever earlier partly to increase access for the rising number of low-income students like Chris who are graduating from high school, yet their message was lost on the exact kind of kid they claimed they wanted to reach. Chris also didn't have anyone to ask about his test scores or college. His high school was between counselors. His mom didn't know anything about the PSAT.

That was at his old school. Halfway through his junior year, Chris transferred high schools, his third transfer in three years. The first move was after his freshman year from a suburb of Allentown to a rural part of Pennsylvania in search of less expensive housing. At first, he enrolled at a Catholic school, but when that became too pricey for his mom, he moved to the local public school. When he arrived in the middle of his junior year, the moment when drivers have already started their search, no one in his class of a hundred students talked about what was next after graduation. Why would they? Their friends who had gone on to college didn't make it. They dropped out. They came back home and hung out with classmates who never went in the first place. For Chris's classmates, high school might really be the best it's going to be in terms of their education for the rest of their lives, which makes Chris's story more extraordinary.

When I first met Chris and his mom in Lehighton, it reminded me of what the small town where I grew up in Pennsylvania has become. The counties surrounding where Chris now lives were where anthracite coal, railroads, and steel mills were king in the first half of the twentieth century. But Lehighton, like my hometown and many other places around the country, largely missed the generation-long transition away from manufacturing and into an information-driven economy deeply entwined with the rest of the world. Lehighton is sparsely populated and mostly white. Only 16 percent of the county's population has a bachelor's degree. Sixty-four percent of the county voted for Donald Trump in 2016. We met at the Dunkin' Donuts high above the Lehigh River because it's one of the few places with the lights still on in a town of boarded-up businesses.

Chris told me when he arrived at his new high school he met with the school's lone counselor once, to sign up for his senior-year classes. He joined the football team. The coach was the first to ask him about college. Sure, Chris told the coach, he wanted to go. The coach asked Chris if he wanted to play football in college. Maybe, Chris said. That was the end of the conversation, the extent of college advising his junior year of high school.

Chris's mom encouraged him to sign up for the SAT in the spring of his junior year. That much she knew—if her son wanted to go to college, he had to take the SAT. Chris took the test in June. He scored a 680 on the reading and writing portion and a 630 on the math section, for a combined 1310. He knew the result was good. The average SAT score at his school is 935. Chris was, by far, the top boy in his class, and among the top three students overall. The school selected him for a two-week summer engineering camp at Lehigh University. It would be his first time on a college campus. He was eager to check out Lehigh. His teachers told him it was a good school. Most of all, he hoped the camp counselors would offer advice about the college search. He had so many questions, and his mental list started with a simple one: What should he do next? After a few days at Lehigh he realized that he wouldn't be getting an answer to that question, or any other. "The counselors didn't really explain anything about college," he said later. He left disappointed, and sour on Lehigh.

When he got back home, football practice filled his days, not the essay-writing workshops or the string of college visits common the summer before senior year in affluent communities. Near the end of July, his mom got a few days off work. Chris is a history buff, so she suggested they take a short vacation to the Civil War battlefields in Gettysburg, a two-hour car ride away. As his mom's gray Toyota Rav4 sped down Route 15, Chris caught a glimpse of a highway sign for Gettysburg College. At his old high school, a friend often wore a frayed sweatshirt from Gettysburg. Later on, Chris asked his mom if they could swing by campus. He half expected her to say no. They hadn't talked much about college since his SAT scores arrived but he knew that a campus 100 miles from home was like 1,000 miles to his mom—and a pricey private college at that. *It's too far and too expensive*, Chris could imagine her saying. Just as he did, his mom smiled and they headed over to campus.

It was sunny with a pale-blue sky, Chris recalled in telling me the story, the kind of summer day where campuses look just like they do in the viewbooks. Chris, his mom, and his thirteen-year-old sister strolled up and down the sidewalks that crisscrossed campus. They saw no sign of a tour. After about a half hour, he told his mom he liked what he saw. He was ready to go.

With just a few weeks left until the start of senior year, Chris's admissions calendar had already strayed from the one Nicole and Grace were following. It's as if the three rising seniors were traveling in different sections on an airplane. They will all arrive at their destination at the same time, but the experience of getting to college is completely different. Nicole and Grace were seated in first class. They got on early and had their own dedicated flight attendant in the form of their parents and counselors. Meanwhile, Chris boarded last and was vying for the attention of the overwhelmed flight attendants in the back of the plane.

That August, Nicole and her mom returned from another week-long vacation dedicated to college visits. Their itinerary took them from the University of Michigan to McGill in Canada, and finally to Middlebury, Dartmouth, the University of Vermont, Brown, and Northeastern in Boston. Anyone who has ever made the rounds of college visits knows that the small things can sometimes gain monumental attention with teenagers—a rainy day, a bad tour guide, lousy food in the dining hall. In Evanston, Illinois, after visiting Northwestern over spring break, Nicole and her mom perused a small boutique clothing shop on Davis Street. Nicole started to chat with one of the cashiers. She mentioned that they had just visited the University of Chicago the day before. *Where fun goes to die*, the cashier told her, repeating a version of the line made famous by Chicago students who mock the seriousness of the campus culture. "It was about the fifth time I heard that on the trip," Nicole said later. "If that's how people in Chicago perceived the place, it wasn't for me." Soon after, she crossed the University of Chicago off her list. Once again a driver was acting like a passenger, letting emotion drive the decision.

By the time Nicole and her mom arrived in Boston they were exhausted and almost skipped the visit to Northeastern. But the campus tour revived both of them. The university stressed its co-op program that placed students in real-world jobs while in college. It was in the North. It was in a city. It had almost everything Nicole wanted, except for the brand name. But like other students and parents on the tour who put the former commuter school on their itinerary, Nicole knew Northeastern's name was well known; it just wasn't Harvard. While Nicole and her mom didn't put it in my terms, Northeastern had moved from buyer to seller through a deliberate and strategic plan to attract well-prepared students just like Nicole.

Northeastern University lies at the epicenter of American higher education. Boston is where higher education was born in the colonial days, with the founding of Harvard College in 1636. Nearly four centuries later, Boston, as well as Massachusetts and the surrounding New England states, is home to the country's densest concentration of colleges.

But despite the rich location, Northeastern was struggling when Richard Freeland arrived as president in 1996. It had just eliminated 700 jobs, some 20 percent of its workforce. Admissions standards were modest. In the early 1990s, Northeastern accepted upward of 90 percent of applicants. The campus was a collection of utilitarian structures including several dorms, although most freshmen grew up nearby and commuted to campus. Its ace in the hole was the co-op program, which gave students a chance to combine work experience and academics simultaneously. But it, too, was, as Freeland once described it, "tired and mediocre."

At the time, urban schools like Northeastern weren't sought-after destinations for high school students as they are today. The 1992 race riots in Los Angeles that played out on television gave the impression that the areas around urban campuses weren't safe places. A year after the LA riots, the number of women in the incoming freshman class at the University of Southern California plunged to 40 percent. Penn was forced to encourage gentrification in the crime-plagued neighborhoods to the west of its Philadelphia campus in the early 1990s by paying for increased marketing, street cleaning, safety patrols, and bus service.

But as cities started to undergo a renaissance in the late 1990s, so did their college campuses. The leading edge of the Millennial generation began to enter college in 2000. This huge new band of students was looking for campus experiences different from those of their predecessors in places providing a mix of culture and job experience. Northeastern set out to ride the wave of urban popularity, and in the process, hoped to improve its own bottom line. Under Freeland's watch, Northeastern endowed professorships to attract better faculty and revamped its academic offerings to recruit higher quality students from a wider geographic area. It built more than a dozen new buildings, including a $1 billion complex of seven residence halls, as physical proof to visitors that it was on the rise.

Doing all that to raise your visibility and prestige is one thing. Making sure people know about it is another. For centuries, a college's cachet was based on its history and location. Reputation was an outgrowth of those institutions founded in the nation's early days. Think Harvard, William & Mary, and the University of North Carolina. Prominence was also bestowed regionally. When higher education was still mostly a local market, in-state flagships and nearby privates usually had a good reputation among high school students and their families who didn't know much about campuses a state or two away.

In the late 1970s and early 1980s, two developments shifted how prospective students and their parents now think about prestige. The first used the lure of financial aid to attract students by establishing a new administrative function on campuses: enrollment management.

When Jack Maguire took over as admissions dean at Boston College, he not only didn't understand why the school wasn't tracking prospects who reached out to his secretary for information, but the former physics professor also wondered why data wasn't driving decisions in how the college handed out financial aid. Until then, the various pieces of the admissions process operated separately. The admissions office didn't really talk to the financial aid office except to hand over files of admitted applicants. In 1976, Maguire, writing in Boston College's alumni magazine, coined the term "enrollment management" to describe the school's strategy for getting ahead of looming demographic and economic trends that threatened the survival of colleges and universities.

Enrollment management combined what had been until that point different roles on campuses including admissions, financial aid, and marketing. Those roles began to be combined under a new vice president, and most important, the office's approach was driven by data. In the early days, the data were simple, such as results of surveys about why accepted students didn't enroll. But over time, the data and the analysis increased in sophistication. In turn, the people who came to hold the top admissions jobs were guided less by their gut or concern for applicants. Instead, they were numbers-obsessed and focused on how they could achieve a list of goals given to them by their bosses—the presidents and trustees.

The second development was perfectly timed for this growing use of data in admissions: college rankings.

In 1983, *U.S. News & World Report* published its inaugural list of the top twenty-five universities and liberal arts colleges. The "ranking" was based on a survey the weekly magazine sent to hundreds of college presidents asking them to list what they considered the best schools. That first list bears little resemblance to the *U.S. News* rankings of today. It included only seventy-six national universities and liberal-arts colleges tucked away in the magazine and based entirely on the survey of presidents. The quantitative measures—numbers like class rank, SAT scores, graduation rates—came later. College presidents tried unsuccessfully to persuade the magazine's editors to halt further editions of the rankings. Stanford was ranked first in that inaugural edition, and its president called the rankings "a beauty contest, not a serious analysis of quality." Still, what the rankings did was establish a social order among colleges that was widely understood at the time, but rarely acknowledged.

By the 1990s, just as higher education was turning fully into a national and international market, *U.S. News* expanded its lists to rank more schools as well as added quantitative measures to bring a greater statistical feel to the exercise. Other publications, such as the *Princeton Review* and *Money* magazine, joined the fray with their own rankings. Soon the data-driven enrollment mavens at schools outside of the top 25 figured out they could manipulate the outcome of rankings by pulling various levers they controlled in admissions and financial aid.

While other college presidents criticized and distanced themselves from the rankings, Northeastern's CEO embraced them. "The rankings created a playing field that didn't exist before," Freeland told me when we met in Cambridge near Harvard's campus. Harvard's reputation was established centuries ago, he explained, well before Northeastern was founded in 1898. "Everyone thinks Harvard is great but no one knows why," he added. "How do you compete in that world?"

The rankings finally gave him and the Northeasterns of the world a fighting chance. To Freeland, the metrics that *U.S. News* used weren't unreasonable. They were measuring things that every student and parent wanted to know anyway. *How do my SAT scores and class rank measure up? What are my chances of graduating in four years? How many of my classes would have more than twenty students and be taught by a full-time professor?*

The statistical measures also provided a North Star for Freeland. Higher education is driven by tradition, and colleges are managed in part by their faculty. A university is like a large cargo ship. Turning it in another direction, and quickly, is difficult. A single goal would help keep everyone on campus on task, Freeland thought. He set a target and put it in the university's strategic plan for everyone to see: Northeastern would become a top 100 university during his presidency.

Freeland was unapologetic about setting a goal using a magazine ranking that most of his counterparts criticized publicly though many of them secretly wanted to move up, too. The problem was Northeastern was ranked 162. Its standing had barely budged in the years immediately before Freeland arrived from leading the Boston branch campus of the University of Massachusetts. The president put his troops to work to reverse-engineer the *U.S. News* rankings. He wanted to know exactly what Northeastern needed to do, and in what order, to move the needle. He wanted the secret sauce produced by an unassuming economist in Washington, D.C., who over the previous decade accidentally became one of the most powerful arbiters of quality in higher education.

Bob Morse was hired by *U.S. News & World Report* in 1976 for a job in its economic unit. The twenty-eight-year-old, University of Cincinnati–educated economist with a Michigan State MBA joined a small group of data geeks crunching government numbers and producing briefings that the magazine's writers used in articles about taxes and budgets. At the time, *U.S. News* was a distant third in a two-man newsweekly race between *Time* and *Newsweek*. Those rivals were headquartered in the publishing capital of New York and cast a wide shadow over Washington-based *U.S. News*. After years of struggling to maintain its relevance, the magazine was bought in 1984 by billionaire Mort Zuckerman, who went on a spending spree to upgrade the magazine's talent to compete with its larger rivals. Two years later, he poached Mel Elfin from *Newsweek* to help guide the magazine's editorial direction. The gruff former Washington bureau chief looked around the newsroom for ways *U.S. News* could differentiate itself from its larger competitors. Elfin immediately set his sights on the nascent college rankings.

Rather than bury a tiny list of colleges and universities in the weekly magazine, Elfin outlined an ambitious plan to publish a guidebook. It would include articles about the college search and the broader higher education industry to help parents and students better understand just exactly what they were buying. The guidebook, with the audacious name *America's Best Colleges*, would also incorporate an expanded list of ranked schools and a directory of colleges, and remain on the newsstand year-round to boost sales and the prominence of the rankings. Most of all, Elfin declared, the rankings required the appearance of scientific precision to gain the public's trust. He tapped Morse to evaluate what data could be used in combination with the reputational survey to create a new ranking formula.

In the late 1980s, the U.S. government wasn't collecting much data from the nation's colleges. It didn't even start tracking a basic statistic like graduation rates until the early 1990s. *U.S. News* enlisted an outside company, already gathering data for college guidebooks, to supply it with the numbers it needed to rank schools. By 1988, Morse had moved over to the rankings full-time and helped design a new methodology. The reputational survey that had made up the entire formula until then was reduced to 25 percent of a school's final grade. The rest would be calculated based on quantitative inputs: selectivity, test scores, high school class rank, share of full-time professors with doctorates, the endowment per student, and even the library budget per student. While college presidents denounced many of the measures *U.S. News* had chosen, Morse produced exactly the precision Elfin wanted.

To gain credibility with readers in those early days, it was critical that the magazine generate rankings that were both familiar and surprising. "When you're picking the most valuable player in baseball and a utility player hitting .220 comes up as the MVP, it's not right," Elfin once said.

As a result, the top three national universities in the rankings year after year were familiar names: Harvard, Yale, and Princeton. While the order of those three sometimes changed, readers recognized those Ivy League schools. Conventional wisdom already regarded those schools as among the best. They were familiar. At the same time, no one would buy a rankings guide if it only confirmed what they already thought were the best colleges. The list also needed surprises. And there were a few in the top 25 in those early days: Washington University, Rice, and Emory, all before they became well-established national brands. By choosing to emphasize academic measures at the beginning, Morse told me the magazine ensured the so-called face validity of the rankings. "We didn't choose the factors to have the Ivy League in the top ten," he said, "but they are the top performing schools in a lot of the indicators."

Even so, the magazine's criteria, which over the years has emphasized how much colleges spend on their faculty and students, work against public universities. In 1989, for example, 5 of the top 25 national universities were public. By 2019, only three were (UCLA, UC Berkeley, and the University of Michigan at Ann Arbor was barely in, tied for No. 25). Every college able to significantly improve its rank during that time was private.

Public universities—where 80 percent of American students attend college—remain scarce even in the top 50. When one scans the top list, it's puzzling to understand by any reasonable measure how world-renowned research universities such as the University of Washington, the University of California at San Diego, and the University of Wisconsin at Madison rank just above—or even lower than—private colleges such as Southern Methodist University, Tulane, and George Washington University.

The academic yardsticks *U.S. News* favored didn't just provide fodder to produce the rankings. They also signaled to students and parents what to emphasize when looking for a college—mostly the quality of incoming students rather than what undergraduates actually learned or what they did after graduation. Over decades, the rankings narrowed the view of seniors to focus on just a handful of schools. And in turn, the standards also sent a message to college leaders about what they should prioritize. By the late 1990s, college presidents and trustees were paying close attention to the rankings. None more than Richard Freeland at Northeastern.

For Northeastern to vault into the top 100, university officials determined they had to recruit higher-caliber students to boost the SAT scores and high school class rank of the incoming class. The hope then was that those students would stay enrolled to increase the university's retention and graduation rates. "It was very mathematical and very conscious," Freeland told *Boston Magazine* in 2014. "Every year we would sit around and say 'Okay, well here's where we are, here's where we think we might be able to do next year, where will that place us?'"

To attract better students, Northeastern needed to steal them from the grips of another, higher-ranked school. This would require a delicate dance of appealing to a new set of applicants while still attracting enough of the bread-and-butter students they always had enrolled in order to adequately fill a class. The process would take several years. As they enrolled more top students from the admissions pool they could reject more of the students they used to accept. Northeastern wasn't going to steal students from Harvard or MIT.

But it could start by taking a few who were considering Boston University and giving them a price break. Every year, it would entice a few more star students to enroll and reject an admission offer from a better school but one that wasn't offering as much money as Northeastern. Attracting those students had a ripple effect because they soon encouraged others from their high schools to apply.

Northeastern also started to move farther away from its home base in New England to recruit students. Again, it used the lure of merit aid to appeal to students, first from the mid-Atlantic and then the West Coast. Northeastern's admissions dean told Freeland that 15 percent of California high school students travel to Boston every year to go somewhere to college. They were already coming, so all Northeastern had to do was persuade them to choose it over Boston University, Boston College, or Tufts. "We were doing a ton of things to make the academic programs better and the campus more attractive," Freeland told me. "We'd get a kid [to enroll] from a high school that we never had before. Then the next year we'd have five [enroll]. The following year, fifteen. The students were our best marketers."

At the same time, the university signed up with the Common Application to boost application numbers. Because the number of applications increased but enrollment remained steady, Northeastern improved its selectivity almost overnight. "We did play other kinds of games," Freeland admitted. "You get credit for the number of classes you have under twenty [students], so we lowered our caps on a lot of our classes to nineteen just to be sure." By 2004, Northeastern had risen forty-two spots in the *U.S. News* rankings to number 120.

Freeland didn't think the university had much time to jump into the top 100. The tail end of the surge of Millennials would soon be graduating from high school. The number of eighteen-year-olds in the New England states was plummeting. The public colleges in Massachusetts were improving, offering a less-expensive option for students. "We had a sense of urgency," he told me. "I was convinced Northeastern wouldn't survive unless it got into the top tier of the rankings."

To move twenty more places, Freeland knew he needed to

tweak his strategy to hit the mark by 2008. The biggest barrier for Northeastern moving further, faster, remained the reputational survey, which still counted for 25 percent of the overall ranking. In many ways, the number was a lagging indicator. It might take years for college leaders to realize how much another school had improved. Freeland didn't have time to wait. Among Freeland's inner circle were several former political operatives who persuaded him to approach the *U.S. News* survey as a campaign. Together they estimated that between presidents, provosts, and admissions deans there were fewer than 750 people responsible for Northeastern's peer assessment. Freeland took the list of presidents. He sent them copies of the university's annual report. He mailed them full-page advertisements Northeastern placed in the *Chronicle of Higher Education* to tout its accomplishments. Each time Freeland included a personal note to be sure it got past a secretary. And when Freeland hit the road or went to a conference, he made a point of meeting as many college presidents as he could. "I knew their numbers, and if one of these places was more highly ranked than us, I'd make a point of dropping our numbers to make them realize we had better metrics than they had," he told me. "Knowing that I thought they couldn't give us a lower score."

Freeland retired as Northeastern's president in August 2006. The next day, while vacationing on Martha's Vineyard, he got a call from a former colleague. The newest edition of the rankings had been released. Northeastern had broken through the top 100. It was number 98.

And it didn't stop there. Now, more than twenty years after Freeland took office, the university has been transformed in both reality and perception. It kept climbing up the rankings, reaching number 44 in 2019, nearly tied with Boston University and Boston College. Northeastern accepted a record low of 18 percent of applicants in 2019, from a pool of more than 62,000. The median SAT score of the accepted students is now 1495. The Northeastern Nicole was applying to was radically different from that of just a generation earlier.

All the players instrumental in the birth of the *U.S. News* rankings in the 1980s are long gone from the organization, except for Bob Morse. I first met Morse during the summer of 1994, when I was an intern at *U.S. News*. Every day that summer, along with a half dozen other college interns, I stared at a monochrome computer monitor while entering numbers that colleges sent by fax (by then, the magazine had started to collect its own data). Years later, Morse lived a few houses from my family in Washington, D.C. Many mornings I'd pass him on his daily run, a ritual he tracked closely on his Timex Ironman watch.

At seventy-two, Morse is now the public face of the rankings. Yet he remains at heart a number-cruncher out of central casting: bespectacled, balding, almost always in a white button-down shirt. Although he speaks in a quiet, slow, monotone voice, people who follow the rankings flock to hear what he has to say.

On a Thursday near the end of May 2019, I sat in the back of a packed hotel ballroom in Denver as Morse described changes to the next edition of the rankings. His audience: institutional researchers on campuses. These were Morse's peeps, the college administrators responsible for giving *U.S. News* the numbers it needed to rank colleges. As he sipped from a can of Red Bull, Morse outlined how the rankings the year before had removed from its formula a college's acceptance rate—a number that schools often manipulated by boosting applicants to look more selective. In its place, *U.S. News* started to measure so-called social mobility—how well schools serve low-income students.

Even as the rankings evolve, they remain crucial to both the future of *U.S. News* and the elite schools ensconced in the top tier. The college rankings are a linchpin of the *U.S. News* brand, generating 29 million unique visitors to its website in 2019. The rankings are also essential to elite schools in maintaining their exclusive brands. Applicants pay attention to them. A growing number of college freshmen report each year that the rankings are an important, although not top, factor in their final decision, especially among those who go to a selective school. Indeed, when a top school drops in the rankings, it's forced to admit more students in subsequent years and is more generous with financial aid to make up for falling yield rates, according to a study for the National Bureau of Economic Research. Clearly students use the rankings to put some semblance of order to a chaotic process. But the rankings, in large part, also give prospective students a narrow lens on the college search: they don't look up and out beyond the top 10 or 20 or whatever.

In many ways, the rankings have become the tail that wags the dog in higher education. The race for prestige has produced winners among colleges, their presidents, and trustees, as well as their alumni who feel their degree is worth so much more now than the day they graduated. But many of those victories have come at a cost to applicants and society as a whole. Yes, before Bob Morse came calling asking for numbers about how many students graduate, how many alumni give, or how many professors are full-time, so much of what colleges did was hidden from consumers paying the bill. So Freeland is right that many of the *U.S. News* metrics made schools better for students.

Teenagers might like that their college lists include only top-ranked colleges, yet what they typically don't realize is that they're often the ones footing the bulk of the bill to build or maintain that prestige. A study of a major university ranked by *U.S. News* in the mid-30s found that it would have to increase its spending by $112 million per year to jump into the top 20, about $86,000 per student. During Freeland's tenure, Northeastern's tuition doubled to $29,000. Climbing the rankings required trade-offs, too. While the number of students from families making more than $200,000 at Northeastern grew from the single to double digits in percentage terms under Freeland's watch, he was almost embarrassed to tell me that the proportion of Pell Grant recipients—the poorest students at the university—dropped to 15 percent. That's at a school that once prided itself on educating the children of blue-collar Bostonians.

When Freeland and I met, we were in Cambridge, just outside the gates of Harvard. "The great irony of the *U.S. News* rankings is that the top 25 universities are not focused on undergraduate education," he said. "They care about research and graduate education." Prospective students are too often blinded by prestige and fail to take an inventory during their search about what they really want out of college. In the pursuit of sellers, they overlook their inherent flaws and ignore the benefits of buyers.

A few weeks later, I was in Hong Kong on business. It was near the end of another admissions cycle. As I hiked Victoria Peak, I overheard a small group of American women talking about the college search. I stopped to listen. One was a mother of a teenage girl who was on the wait list at Columbia. She was also accepted at Northeastern and had submitted a deposit to reserve a spot in the freshman class. Even if she got off the wait list at Columbia, her mother told her friends, it might be a tough choice to spurn Northeastern. The other women in the group seemed surprised. After all, Columbia was an Ivy League school, they said. The one mother then told her companions about Northeastern's co-op and said it would help her daughter's job prospects after college. They seemed impressed. They didn't know about the co-op, or much about Northeastern.

When I returned home, I called Freeland to tell him the story. Never in his wildest dreams did he imagine a bunch of American parents would mention Northeastern and Columbia in the same sentence, he told me. *And in Hong Kong, of all places.* "We arrived," he said. After two decades of work in reframing how prospective students perceived Northeastern, the university was firmly planted among the sellers in admissions.

PART TWO

WINTER:
Reading Season

3

Understanding Merit

Look at All the Bs

The first thing Mark Butt notices on the high school transcript is the variety of advanced classes. "Wow," he says, "this is a good curriculum."

It's the second week of November, and Mark, along with other admissions officers at Emory University, is sequestered in his office reviewing applications for the Class of 2023. They have just ten working days before Thanksgiving to read the nearly 1,800 applications that have arrived for the first round of early decision, one of three admissions cycles at Emory extending over the next five months.

On his desktop computer, Mark scrolls through the file of a boy from a private high school on the West Coast who wants to major in physics. He completed an honors calculus course as a junior as well as two college-level Advanced Placement classes—Chinese and physics. Now in the fall of his senior year, he is taking two of the more demanding AP Calculus and Physics courses offered in high school.

Like other selective colleges, Emory considers Advanced Placement and International Baccalaureate (IB) courses the most rigorous in a high school curriculum because they are assessed by national organizations. (Dual-enrollment courses offered by local colleges to high school students are seen by some admissions offices as less rigorous because they lack such oversight.) But it's not the AP courses on the transcript that catch Mark's attention.

He expects someone who wants to major in the natural sciences to load up on calculus and physics. In a sea of transcripts that look numbingly similar, two other lines stand out: painting and ceramics. He likes the mix of art and science.

Even so, it's not quite enough to automatically land this applicant in the admit bin. Though the transcript contains mostly As and A-minuses, it also has its share of Bs, a total of five over the four semesters spanning sophomore and junior years. Two of them are in easier honors math courses, a red flag for a physics major.

Mark glances at the test scores. They are important but not nearly as significant as students and parents think. Admissions officers use scores mostly as a check against the transcript. Do the test scores and grades line up? If not, a deeper look might reveal why, although grades and rigor always trump test scores. In this case, the applicant took the ACT twice, and scored a 34 both times. That put him in the top 1 percent of test takers nationally. Still, it might not be enough.

"What would he do at Emory?" Mark asks a colleague, Rebecca Kaplan, who is sitting across from him and sharing reading duties on this particular day. It's a question Mark asks frequently. He pictures the applicant as an Emory student: What classes would he take? What would he major in? What kind of campus community member might he be? Asking such questions sometimes reveals a different story than the highly sanitized version of themselves that applicants think admissions officers want to see.

As Mark speeds through the recommendations and Rebbecca scans the essays, both note the emphasis on art. "I'm reading him as undecided," Mark says, ignoring for the moment the major listed on the application. Although Emory doesn't admit students into specific majors, this applicant's eclectic taste in science and art could boost his chances later on when the admissions committee plows through the numerous applications of prospective physics majors who list pre-med as a second major. If that combination is a dime a dozen, someone with an interest in physics and art might provide a different perspective.

Mark taps on his desk as if he's playing the drums, and sighs, heavily. As a veteran of the Emory admissions process, he knows the caliber of the applications arriving in the coming weeks for regular decision. If this applicant is deferred until the spring round, he won't make it, Mark tells Rebbecca, a rookie reader who previously worked in the university's MBA admissions office.

"This is when it's hard, right?" she asks Mark.

It's not really a question. Rather Rebbecca seems to want a little reassurance that not every application requires such impossible choices. Mark smiles. He knows that many more tough deliberations await them in the months ahead. In the ambiguity of admissions at elite colleges and universities, only one thing is certain: the skills and talents schools are looking for are constantly in flux.

Whenever I sat inside committee meetings or read applications with admissions officers, I felt I was on a faraway planet, one very different from the one the science-fiction storybooks described. Admissions people have their own language. They read "files" instead of applications, they "pull up" applicants and "shape them down," and they have a dizzying array of acronyms: IC (intellectual curiosity), LTE (likelihood to enroll), HSI (high school index). They also have their own numbering system. They rate applicants from 1 to 5 or 1 to 9 or 1 to 10 with a formula that seems precise enough to land someone on the moon, but in reality is mostly amorphous. And they have their own office diet, made up of Diet Coke, mini chocolate bars, and homemade brownies.

As I take you inside this subculture, you'll come to understand, just as I did, the perspective of admissions officers. By the time an application reaches them, it has turned into a virtual "file." It has been filtered and massaged by pre-readers and machines that assemble its component parts into something that's easy to scan. The pieces a teenager toiled over for months, such as the essay, might receive one quick read. Meanwhile, parts of the file baked long before the applicant ever started the college search—the classes he took (or didn't take) sophomore or junior year, the activities he started to spend time on in middle school, the teachers he got to know—are what admissions officers really spend their time studying.

What they are looking for in the file is the entirety of a teenager's story. This detail is what I found most high school students miss in their rush to finish six or eight or ten applications in the fall of their senior year. To save time, they cut and paste from massive Google docs full of essays and short answers—taking a paragraph from their answer to Boston College's essay and using it for Emory or UCLA. They work on multiple applications at a time, instead of compiling them in sequence to better make the case of why they are the right fit for *that* college. In doing so, they abandon the cohesiveness of their own story, the one that is supposed to be at the foundation of "holistic" admissions.

Holistic admissions. If you've listened to an admissions officer give a presentation at a high school or gone on a college tour, you've probably heard the term. The concept of "holistic" admissions or "comprehensive" review (the terms are used interchangeably by schools) sounds reasonable. Grades and test scores might provide an incomplete portrait of an applicant, so why not look at the bigger picture?

But in practice, holistic admissions raises questions about fairness when admissions officers review tens of thousands of applications under the pressures of rigid deadlines. The more selective the institution, the murkier its process often is. Although it has the veneer of numerical precision, holistic admissions is pretty subjective. While colleges like the flexibility the process gives for a rough sorting of applicants, to a skeptical public, holistic admissions is confusing and secretive at best, and nefarious and illegal at worst.

That's why whenever I talk with high school students or their parents about college admissions, the questions they ask almost always begin with "how" and "why." *How* many Advanced Placement classes should we take? (I found it's common for parents to use "we" and "our" because they act as co-applicants in the process.) *How* do colleges weigh our SAT scores and grades? *How* should we spend the summer—volunteering at a homeless shelter or starting a business? *Why* didn't we get in, but a classmate did? *Why* do elite colleges care so much about athletes and legacies? Or, more pointedly, students ask why the groups they belong to don't matter to colleges.

The questions rarely have straightforward answers.

They keep coming, though, because applicants view applying to a selective college as a game with ambiguous rules (the *how*) and a final mystifying result (the *why*). In wanting to know the rules of this game, students and parents claim they want clarity and simplicity. They want a formula. *Why can't colleges just tell us the grades and test scores that will get my child admitted?* They want this transparency until they find out they don't have the right grades and test scores to get in. That's when they favor a process that considers the "whole person," one including what they think are *their* best attributes.

But how colleges define the worthiness of applicants tends to shift over time based on the institution's needs. At the most selective colleges—where spaces are few and demand high—the definition of merit has changed substantially over the last half century largely to preserve the social order and the interests of those in power. That means that for much of their history colleges focused on preserving the admission of white men.

What it takes to get into a top college is evolving once again, making it difficult for students and parents to keep up with the rules of the game. For one, schools are constantly tweaking their selection process based on data they're collecting about why undergraduates ultimately succeed on campus. Elite colleges are also trying to recruit more low-income students to reverse the perception that their campuses have turned into playgrounds for the wealthy. And selective schools are trying to avoid legal land mines as admissions policies come under increased scrutiny for bias by federal officials and the courts.

Spurned teenagers and their parents have come to realize the supposed "meritocracy" of the system is riddled with compromises and exceptions. But the term "meritocracy" was never meant to promote a supposed academic purity. Indeed, when British sociologist Michael Young coined the idea in 1958 he intended it pejoratively. His belief was that when the objective veneer of standardized testing and grades is stripped away, the advantages of a centuries-old class-based system remain.

Young's satirical term has been co-opted in the world of admissions by the very people he was mocking—students and parents who believe that grades and test scores alone should determine who is accepted amid rising application numbers and falling acceptance rates. When the Pew Research Center surveyed Americans in 2019 about eight admissions criteria colleges should consider, grades and test scores topped the list, by far, well above athletic ability, race, or first-generation and legacy status.

The reality is that by using only those two measures there are simply many more qualified applicants than there are spots at any selective school. Think about this: of the 26,000 domestic applicants for admission to the Class of 2019 at Harvard, 8,200 had perfect grade-point averages in high school, 3,500 had perfect SAT math scores, and 2,700 had perfect verbal scores. But Harvard had only about 1,700 spots to offer.

We act as if grades and test scores are an objective measure, like an applicant's height. But we rarely stop to talk about how every college uses a different ruler and every test prep company sells a stepladder. Those "objective" measures, the backbone of our supposed meritocratic admissions system, are often measuring something more like the size of a parent's bank account than the potential of an eighteen-year-old.

📖

Inside Emory's admissions office, Mark and Rebbecca remain undecided on the fate of the one West Coast applicant. Six minutes have passed since they opened the file, a slow pace compared to reading in regular decision.

To define merit in holistic admissions Emory uses a rating system. Almost every college that reads applications employs a system analogous to the one used in judging Olympic figure skaters—it gives an aura of precision to what is largely abstract. The only real difference between colleges is how many categories they assess and the numbering scale they use.

At Emory, applicants are rated in four areas: high school curriculum, extracurricular activities, recommendations, and intellectual curiosity, the last item a somewhat nebulous category determined by anything in the application from their essay to their activities. Each rating is on a scale of 1 to 5. To make sure there is consistency in how applications are read, Emory's admissions officers are given guidelines and go through several days of training each year on how to assign these numbers; less experienced readers are also paired with experienced admissions officers who understand what goes into a rating from years of reading hundreds of applications.

Mark and Rebbecca give this applicant a 4 rating for his rigorous curriculum; two 3s for his recommendations and intellectual curiosity; and just a 2 for extracurricular activities. He is co-chair of an academic club at school, but otherwise is what Mark describes as "light" when it comes to evidence of leadership.

Of the four categories, the rigor number is the most important, and at first blush seems the most objective because it's based on the assortment of college-level courses on a transcript. But it's still subjective: putting numbers to vague measures and doing a little math doesn't make those numbers objective. The rigor score is not a matter of simply adding college-level classes, however. It's also based on breadth across the major subjects—English, math, science, social studies, and foreign language—and what was available to an applicant at her high school. As a result, a student who takes seventeen Advanced Placement courses could end up receiving the same rigor score as a student who takes five if that's all his high school offered.

Mark types a few notes in the file. "Definitely a kind, gentle, thoughtful and deep thinker," he writes. I'll hear similar glowing descriptions of applicants over the coming months at Emory and elsewhere. But being a good person is not good enough at top colleges that reject thousands of capable kids each year. Mark labels the applicant a "low admit." It's a term that signifies he is an easy target to move to the deny pile later on (that's exactly where he'll end up).

Mark is one of the most senior admissions officers at Emory. His official title is director of undergraduate selection, which essentially means he's charged with making applications move through the process smoothly, and on time. That last part has been a difficult task in recent years, as Emory's application numbers have risen. With them, so, too, have the qualifications of applicants, making it harder to get in.

Still, at top colleges everywhere good students continue to make the cut, without any special "hook" to gain acceptance. For example, there is the boy that Mark and Rebbecca consider early on with a 1460 SAT score whose grades have been on an upward trend since sophomore year. He has taken two years of AP Calculus, "which is great," Mark notes, along with a year of AP Chinese ("Love the dualism" Mark adds). The applicant wanted to take a more rigorous course-load his senior year, but the counselor notes in his recommendation that he advised against it so the student could also enjoy his extracurricular activities. Those include the football team and the botany club, which he founded. "That's a quirky combination, but cool," Mark says. The pair agree that he's an acceptance.

Emory's lush campus, with seven thousand undergraduates, is nestled in the affluent suburbs of Atlanta. *U.S. News* consistently ranks the institution around number twenty among national universities. The prominence of its medical school and hospital combined with the longstanding reputation of its liberal arts majors has made it a popular destination for undergraduates in recent years.

After taking nearly two centuries to surpass the twenty thousand application mark in 2015, it took Emory just four years to top thirty thousand in 2019. The surge in applications taxed the admissions staff, who typically spent their winter months in solitude reading files from their geographic territories and writing long summaries. So Emory, like dozens of other selective schools with rapidly rising numbers of applications, started to pair readers and divvy up the review of individual applications in order to move faster.

In the paired-reading approach, Mark is known as the "pilot." He focuses on the academic side of the application. He assesses the transcript, looking for the rigor of courses and grades, checks the test scores, reviews the recommendations, and takes notes. Rebbecca weighs the student side of the application. On her laptop, she examines essays, extracurricular activities, alumni interviews, and other sections of the application. On many files, Mark asks Rebbecca what the applicant's parents do for a living to add context to what the student has accomplished.

Right now, they are reading the applications for one high school on the West Coast. Mark manages recruiting in the western region and knows many of the schools that send bundles of applications to Emory. Reviewing all the applicants within a "school group" saves precious time because he's explaining the school's curriculum only once. If Mark is unfamiliar with a school, he'll dig through the "school profile" that accompanies transcripts and describes the curricular offerings.

The school profile is one piece of the file that applicants probably never see or even know exists but is critical to their prospects because it gives a snapshot of their high school. It's the all-important context for the applicant. It's also another way that high schools vary widely. The profile is part information, part promotion. In scanning dozens of these profiles, I found that some are nothing more than slapped-together Word documents. But others—usually from private schools or top public schools where counselors know their importance—are slick advertisement-like reports that include tons of details, including a list of colleges where recent graduates have enrolled. The not-so-subtle message is that this high school *must be good* because they sent students to Harvard, Stanford, and Yale, etc.

In their reading, Mark and Rebbecca don't try to pit two students from the same high school against each other head-to-head. Reviewing all the files from a specific school at the same time helps them understand what is possible, so they can better interpret what a single applicant has achieved, although it often makes comparisons unavoidable. And while teenagers might think their credentials are first-rate based on the narrow view of their one high school, few actually are outstanding once they reach the wider pool of applications from around the world. When admissions officers read applications, they find elements to both praise and fault. Their job is to balance the two in making a decision, often in minutes.

A few applications later, Mark reaches a file tagged as an athletic recruit. Emory competes in Division III, a group of mostly small colleges that prohibit athletic scholarships. But the university's coaches still recruit athletes to fill squads in eighteen sports. As at most Division III schools, Emory's coaches talk frequently with admissions officers when recruiting prospective athletes to ensure they have the academic qualifications to get in. Mark remembers this student in the recruiting process, particularly his high school grades.

"Look at all the Bs," he says. In his junior year, the applicant, who is white, had mostly Bs and B-pluses on his transcript. He took the SAT once and scored a 1490. "He can definitely do the work here," Mark says. "I don't love him, but the team does." Consider that the applicant received the same numerical ratings, just in different categories, as the previous student who was ultimately rejected. (This applicant scored higher on extracurricular activities than the other one but lower on intellectual curiosity.) The only difference in the end is that this student had a hook—he was an athlete the coach wanted. He got in.

It used to be that admission to a selective college, at least the best public universities, *was* based on a set of clear standards that were simple to understand. To get into the University of California's most well-known and competitive campuses at Berkeley and Los Angeles in the 1950s, for instance, all you had to do was complete a set of high school courses in history, English, mathematics, and science "with marks that will make an average of grade B." In total, the admissions standards listed in the undergraduate catalog at the time took up a little more than five hundred words, less than a page.

Compare that to today. The "Freshmen Requirements" at Berkeley alone spreads across seven web pages and includes over 2,500 words. And while the minimum requirements for state residents are remarkably similar to the 1950s—still a B average but in a broader set of courses—they come with this warning: "Satisfying the minimum requirements is often not enough to be competitive for selection." Indeed, UC Berkeley and UCLA tell prospective students they review applications using a holistic process that looks at both academic and non-academic factors "using a broad concept of merit" across six factors all of "which carry no pre-assigned weights."

Whether colleges use a broad concept of merit or a narrow one, we still struggle to define what we mean when we say admissions should be based on merit. Ask thirty students, parents, high school counselors, and college admissions officers for a definition of "merit" and you'll get thirty different answers.

What's more, parents especially tend to conflate "merit" with "achievement." I can't tell you how often I've heard parents say how "hard" their child worked to score a 90 on an algebra test, finish an English literature paper, or win the 800-meter dash in track. Parents mistake achievement, often associated with one specific and fixed event in the past, with merit. That's why colleges typically weigh the score on the four-hour SAT (achievement) less than the grades earned over four years of high school (merit).

Watching the reviews of applications and listening to admissions officers' description of merit over eight months, I came to understand the term defines a mind-set they look for in an applicant, rather than a specific attribute. They're looking for signs an applicant refuses to acknowledge a ceiling on her ability and keeps persevering at tasks. That's why they scan transcripts for rigorous courses in a variety of subjects, appreciate when students collect a recommendation from a teacher outside of their major area (a pre-med student with a recommendation from an English teacher, for instance), and look for students who have committed to an activity for an extended period of time and seek out a leadership position.

What I didn't appreciate until I witnessed the admissions process firsthand is how individual merit is weighed against an entire class of undergraduates. When it comes to the selection process, teenagers and parents have the same blind spot I did. An applicant might display merit on his or her own, but how does that student fit into the larger class? It's like the puzzle piece that at first looks like it belongs in the box, but when you try to fit it in you discover it's part of a different puzzle. "Elite colleges are there to create a set of people who are going to be productive together and in concert with each other," Harry Brighouse, a philosophy professor at the University of Wisconsin at Madison, told me. The question, he said, is how an applicant's "behavior will mesh with the skills and knowledge of others."

But let's not kid ourselves about the level of precision in crafting a class at an elite college. In reality, the schools are not choosing a class as much as they are sending out invitations to join a class. Not every student will RSVP yes to those invitations (some 350 students turn down even an invite from Harvard in any given year). At most selective colleges, only one-third to half of applicants accept an offer—and admissions deans don't really know *which one-third or half* despite sophisticated models that tell them whether they'll hit their enrollment target. In the end, it's unclear if an incoming class would be that much different if admissions officers worried less about shaping a class in making their decisions. The simple fact is a sizeable piece of any freshman class at a top-ranked college is eerily similar to that of any other highly selective school.

Like a professor quizzing her students, Robin Hennes presses
soon-to-be admissions readers at the University of Washington on
how they scored an applicant on academic merit. "How many of
you gave a three?" asks Robin, the assistant director of admissions.
Ten hands shoot up. "A four?" Another eight hands go up. "A five?"
Three more hands go up, although somewhat tentatively.

This is the second day of training for newly hired admissions
readers at the University of Washington in Seattle. The thirty part-
time readers in the room are mostly graduate students at UW, as it's
known (or informally, U-Dub). The would-be readers are reviewing a dozen practice applications—their homework from the night
before—with two seasoned admissions officers. For the next two
hours, the group evaluates the applications from last year's admissions pool to ensure decisions between readers are relatively consistent with each other—as much as that's possible when analyzing
so much information open to so much interpretation.

Despite what the public might think, full-time admissions professionals at big public universities don't read most of the applications submitted each fall. There are simply too many of them. UW
received 46,000 applications for the Class of 2023, and it has seventeen full-time admissions officers. So the bulk of the reading task at
UW falls to an army of part-time readers. Graduate students who
are readers receive a full-tuition waiver and a stipend for the quarter of about $6,000. Other part-timers are mostly retirees looking
for a short-term gig. They earn $25 an hour.

In return, the readers are expected to review seven applications
an hour, 125 a week, and 1,000 applications over the course of the
two-and-half-month reading period. That's about eight minutes,
on average, per applicant. Unlike the admissions calendars of top
private colleges, which typically have several application cycles,
UW has only one deadline in the middle of November.

The goal in reviewing different types of students and scenarios in the training sessions—and later on in a regular cadence of

"norming meetings" for everyone during reading season—is to prevent any single reader from making an outlier decision. "There is no right answer," Robin told me later. "There's no science to it, and that's the problem. It's why we get so many split scores among readers."

The application under discussion is from a Washington resident. At UW, applications receive three scores from readers on a 1 to 9 scale (9 being highest): academics, personal, plus an overall number. The overall score mirrors one of the other two—most of the time the academic score—but not always.

Welcome to the ambiguities of holistic admissions. Here's how confusing and nonstandard all of this can be. Emory uses four categories and a scale of 1 to 5. At Washington, it's three separate scores and the scale is 1 to 9. Even though many colleges have adopted the Common Application and standardized the ingredients, once the files get into their offices most institutions have cooked up their own special recipes for reviewing them.

At UW, the applicant being reviewed has a 3.69 GPA and 1020 on the SAT, a solid student but below the mid-range of grades and test scores for those typically accepted at UW. The applicant earned mostly As and Bs until her junior year of high school, when her grades dropped significantly—a D in math and two Cs in Spanish and biology. That raises concerns with Robin, as does the student's weak senior-year schedule. It includes two IB courses, but one is in film. "It's probably an enjoyable class, but not what I'd bring to the senior year," Robin said. "We put an emphasis on senior year rigor because it's the last chance to prepare for college."

In this case, a committee of admissions readers "normed" this applicant a 4 on academics, or what Robin referred to as a "strong 4." About half of the readers-in-training hit the mark; most others were very close.

A further look through the applicant's file turns up a likely reason for the grade slippage: a moving story about being hospitalized her junior year for severe depression and thoughts of suicide. That critical piece of information doesn't change the academic score, however. Instead it's counted toward the personal score, which takes into consideration "significant personal adversity," according to UW's admissions handbook. "If you tear up at the essay, it shouldn't impact your assessment of academics," Robin said. How colleges handle disclosures in applications about mental-health challenges is all over the map. They can't discriminate against the applicants, so many flag such applications for further review to be sure the college has the necessary resources for students to stay enrolled and graduate. That's why high school counselors generally advise students against writing about their mental-health history unless it's specifically framed to explain inconsistencies in grades or as a story about emerging stronger from a struggle.

For UW's personal score, applicants are graded on a curve. They all start with a 3, a number assigned to the "typical" high school experience. From there, a point is added for exceptional extracurricular activities. Perhaps the applicant is captain of a sports team, was selected for all-state orchestra, chosen as an Eagle Scout, or earned a black belt in karate. But much like the "personal" score in rating schemes at every other university with holistic admissions, the number at UW is largely subjective. It gives readers wide discretion to potentially boost applicants who have faced obstacles or to mitigate for poor test scores and grades.

Because UW is banned by state law from considering an applicant's race and ethnicity in admissions, the personal score allows creativity in improving racial diversity by using criteria that are often alternatives to race—students' socioeconomic profiles and the hardships they have overcome. For Washington applicants, the personal score is mostly about ticking off points on the way to 9. First-generation college students receive a point. So do low-income applicants, as well as those who note in their application that they participated in the university's array of college-prep programs, which are mostly aimed at underrepresented students. Check off all three? That's three additional points on the personal score.

"It feels weird to be ticking off points," said Dave Sundine, an associate director of admissions, "but it's us trying to acknowledge these backgrounds."

The personal rating again splits the scoring of the readers-in-training. Most would-be readers give the applicant a 7, but a few assign a 6 or an 8. Veteran admissions officers awarded the applicant an 8. But how much that personal score helps an applicant in the end is unclear. It's the overall score that determines who is ultimately admitted and that number often mirrors the academic rating, not the personal rating.

Yet in the vagaries of holistic admission, even that's not a hard and fast rule. Normally, an academic rating of 4 and a personal rating of 8 will result in an overall score of 4. But in the case of our applicant, admissions readers awarded an overall score of 8 and required the applicant enroll in the university's Equal Opportunity Program, which provides academic advising and other support services to undergraduates. Some two hundred freshmen arrive at UW each year through that program.

The tensions inherent in college admissions require such trade-offs by a school's gatekeepers. Sitting in these training sessions gave me a sense of the types of compromises that public universities, in particular, need to make in the selection process. UW, founded in 1861, is the state's premier university, its public flagship. Ranked in the top 25 among public universities nationwide by *U.S. News*, UW is well known for its programs in science and medicine, and being in Seattle and in the shadow of Microsoft and Amazon, for computer science and engineering. It's also one of the most beautiful college campuses in the country—laid out by the Olmsted Brothers with an alignment that frames Mount Rainier in the distance.

Among undergraduates, public flagships like UW tend to draw applicants with a wider range of academic abilities than many top private universities because of their well-known brands, big-time sports, and in-state tuition prices that residents feel, rightly or wrongly, make the campus the *only* higher education option available to them. Public flagships across the country enroll some 2.6 million students, 11 percent of all students enrolled in higher education. Like private colleges that have become more competitive, public flagships are now turning away applicants who would have been accepted in the past.

At private colleges one tension in the admissions office is often between full-pay and low-income applicants; at publics it's between in-state and out-of-state. UW and other public flagships have sought out-of-state and international students in the last decade because they typically pay higher tuition, offsetting the erosion in state funding for higher education. As recently as 2004, UW received 64 percent of its budget from the state; in 2019 the state's share was 36 percent. To make up the difference, UW started recruiting overseas. The number of international students in the freshman class ballooned from just thirty-one in 2008 to more than 1,100 a decade later.

Like in many other states with top-ranked flagships, in-state students are drawn to the prospect of earning a prestigious degree at a substantial discount. Those from upper-middle-class and wealthy households who qualify for little or no financial aid at private colleges often find tuition at their state flagship is a relative bargain. Their share of the undergraduate population has increased slightly at flagships across the country. At UW, nearly one-third of students come from families in the top 10 percent of incomes nationally, crowding out students from the poorest households in the state.

Partly in an effort to enroll greater numbers of low-income students, selective colleges have significantly broadened what admissions officers count in the personal rating. When schools started assessing personal factors more widely in admissions in the early 1980s, that rating was largely limited to extracurricular activities, community service, and artistic or athletic talent. Now the personal rating has morphed into a catch-all category. At UW, in addition to leadership and community service, it includes—and now I'm quoting from the admissions handbook given to readers—overcoming a significant educational disadvantage, tenacity, insight, originality, concern for others, or coming from a high school that has sent few students to UW.

But even contextual information ultimately has the potential to benefit wealthier students because they are prepped to talk about things like "cultural awareness," another plus factor for UW's personal rating. Consider two applications reviewed during training. One was from a well-off student from a top high school in Washington who wrote an essay about understanding cultural differences as a child when she lived in Indonesia. Her personal score? 5. Now consider an immigrant applicant who had one activity listed: working in her family's restaurant. Did helping her family require her to forgo activities? Did anyone at her low-performing high school tell her to boast about making sacrifices? Who knows. Her personal score? 3.

When students apply to college, they submit an application full of grades, test scores, essays, recommendations, and activities—an account of all their accomplishments thus far in life. The irony of college admissions is that the decision whether to admit someone is based on the future, not the past. It ultimately hinges on a judgment about the potential of that teenager over the next four years on a college campus, not what they've done the previous four years in high school.

The use of numerical ratings in holistic admissions makes it seem that admissions officers are like actuaries at a bank assessing someone's credit score, income, and debt obligations to approve a loan. But unlike bank underwriters, who work with specific guidelines, admissions officers are more akin to Wall Street brokers predicting future performance of a stock based on past results.

"The whole process is about finding potential," John Latting, Emory's admissions dean, told his staff as they gathered for the first day of training and the beginning of the all-important task of assembling the Class of 2023. "It's about asking what kind of contribution can this person make to our community?"

After a fall season of almost nonstop travel pitching the university to prospective students, the admissions counselors at Emory and most other colleges returned home in late October to the solitary and sedentary life of evaluating applications. The admissions staff at Emory is much larger than that at UW, numbering nearly sixty people, including part-timers and counselors at Oxford College, a two-year liberal arts college embedded within the university. It's a group closer in size to an NFL football team than the smaller and intimate squad it was even a decade ago when Emory received 15,000 fewer applications.

As an icebreaker, John asked his staff to introduce themselves with the name of their high school. The point of the exercise, he tells them later, is to remind them of the vast array of high schools, but also who they were at eighteen. "That's who you're reading," John said.

Just as there is no admission "system," there is no single approach to "reading" applications. There are about as many routes to picking a class as there are streets in a big city. One study by the College Board found colleges rely on seven primary paths to selecting a class, but even among those, there are variations on the approaches.

Selective private colleges tend to have multiple readers review an application (either paired or on their own) and then some portion of those applications goes to a selection committee made up of full-time admissions officers. How much colleges rely on committees to make decisions on applicants differs greatly. Some schools might have all their early applications go to the entire committee, while others usually compile a selected number of files that could benefit from further discussion. At big selective publics, individual readers and their supervisors hold most of the power over an applicant's fate—committees are almost unheard of on those campuses given the size of their applicant pools and time limits.

At Emory, Scott Allen has been reading applications from New York City teenagers for twenty years. On a Wednesday in November, he's holed up in his office reviewing early decision applications with Chris Pace, another admissions officer. From a list of applicants, Scott calls out an identification number and the pair pulls up their first read of the day. The application Scott is looking at has been transformed into a set of tabs on the left side of the screen, one for each significant piece of the file, such as the Common Application, transcripts, and recommendations. The opening page is full of key statistics on the applicant, boiled down to the most important numbers like those on the back of a baseball card.

Every pilot, the primary reader in the paired approach, has a specific way of running these sessions, and Scott is no different. He prefers to read in silence at first before engaging his co-pilot in dissecting the application. Scott peers at his computer monitor, its blue glow shining on his round face and reflecting off his wire-frame rectangular glasses. After two minutes, he turns to Chris.

"A lot of activities were shorter commitments during the week," noted Chris. "Nothing long-term."

Admissions officers look for devotion to an activity or hobby for a prolonged period of time rather than "sign-up clubs" to fill in the blank spaces on the application. Not only does sustained involvement give students an opportunity to become leaders, but it shows a passion for something. The pair agrees on a 2 rating for extracurricular.

Sometimes, one reader wants to assign a 2 and another a 3, and they end up compromising without much discussion because other applications are waiting. Almost no applicant gets all 5s, and there is no specific combination of numbers that automatically generates an acceptance offer. "You can get a zero in a category and still get in," an admissions officer says during the training.

Scott scrolls through the recommendations of the would-be biology major. The applicant is a student at a public school in New York City, where counselors carry large caseloads, which means less time for each student. The result is a fairly routine, almost form letter. The teacher recommendations provide greater information. The transcripts and test scores are remarkably similar to what they've seen so far in other files—a 3.7 GPA, 1370 on the SAT, five Advanced Placement courses. After a few more minutes, they agree it's a "low admit." One of the applicant's parents went to Emory, so the teenager will get another look when a committee reviews legacy applications closer to decision time (she won't make it in).

Scott and Chris quickly get into a groove, moving through each file in under ten minutes in their first few hours of reading. Each applicant has a unique numerical code, but after a while many of the other numbers and key identifiers that accompany the applications begin to look the same. Everyone wants to major in biology, psychology, or business. They all scored a 1390 on the SAT and have a 3.7 GPA—a number that's been deflated from high school standards through a recalculation by Emory. So again, the readers look for something that's different.

A few files later, Scott pulls up another biology applicant: 1340 on the SAT, 3.81 GPA, three Advanced Placement courses, only one grade lower than an A since ninth grade. But this umpteenth science applicant arrives with a glowing recommendation from an English teacher who compliments the applicant's combination of interests. She has also shadowed a doctor during school breaks along with internships that were "oriented around medicine," Chris said. In the short summary, Scott writes, "recs report energy." She will be an almost certain admit.

The applicants on Scott's docket are listed in order by something called the Latting Index (named after the admissions dean). Like many selective colleges, Emory recalculates grade-point averages for applicants. The new GPA ignores freshman-year grades—ninth grade is a transition year and a long time ago, according to Emory officials—and disregards marks for physical education, lunch, driver's education, study hall, and other noncore classes. (All the GPAs for Emory applicants listed throughout this book are the recalculated ones.)

The Latting Index is calculated using a formula that folds the revised GPA into an applicant's best test score to produce a number on an 8-point scale. The number is not a cutoff for admission. Rather the number is a rough average used to quickly eyeball academic credentials and sort applicants within high schools or regions. Because most scores fall between a 3 and 4, differences between applicants are found in the first or second decimal place—yet another example of how the process offers the appearance of precision when it is largely qualitative.

"Use your judgment and be consistent," is a mantra echoed frequently during the Emory training. It's repeated so often the first day of training that whenever someone says, "use your judgment," the rest of the room joins in a chant, "and be consistent."

Teenagers spend months, even years, crafting a college application—and then, as I witnessed, it might get reviewed in just eight minutes. Here's the secret: that might still be fairer than the old way.

Traditionally, at least two admissions officers read applications on their own and then wrote summaries for the admissions dean or for a presentation to the selection committee. The time needed to read an application would vary between fifteen to thirty minutes depending on its complexity and the experience of the admissions officers.

But that traditional system began to collapse under the weight of ballooning application volume at dozens of schools. In 2013, admissions officers at Penn invented the paired approach. It's called Committee Based Evaluation, or CBE for short. About fifty other schools adopted the idea, with little fanfare.

Then in January 2018, a front-page article in the *Wall Street Journal* headlined "Some Elite Colleges Review an Application in 8 Minutes (or Less)" exposed the paired-reading approach being used to deal with the masses of applicants. It generated hundreds of comments and social media posts, many of them negative, from college counselors, parents, and teenagers who wondered if eight minutes was enough to give them a fair evaluation. (Don't fret, applicants: eight minutes is a very rough, back-of-the-envelope calculation. There is no official average.)

While the approach has its fair share of detractors even among admissions deans, schools like Emory maintain its benefits outweigh any downsides. They say it trains new readers by pairing rookies with veterans and reduces bias because it forces readers to defend their evaluation with a partner. Still, it's hardly one system, even within a single admissions office. When I was spending time at Emory, I sat with readers who reviewed simultaneously on their own in silence and then discussed applications while others talked through the application from the second they opened the file.

Adhering to consistent standards over many months of reading season is a Sisyphean task for admissions officers given the tensions inherent in their jobs. For one, they are human beings, not machines programmed to make decisions. They each bring their own bias to the table and they learn as the process unfolds, especially readers new to the job. They work with incomplete and imperfect information provided by applicants and high schools. They review an ever-increasing number of files under immense time pressures and sometimes with different colleagues. And they struggle with the same human frailties as any of us—they get distracted, tired, hungry, and sick. It's not that their choices are arbitrary, but their reasoning for those choices is sometimes unclear.

Second, every applicant isn't judged by the same yardstick despite what the public might think happens or wants to happen in the name of fairness. Admissions standards aren't applied *consistently* because they are applied *in context*. Admissions officers judge applicants' achievements based on the opportunities they were given. What courses did they take from the classes available to them? How many students in their high school go to college? What might a college expect from them once they get to campus?

Does this put an extra onus on applicants who go to the best public and private high schools and have grown up being ferried by their college-educated parents to violin lessons and club volleyball games? You bet it does. They are expected to take an array of advanced classes. It's assumed they have earned good grades and received high test scores. For them, these things are simply a given if they're applying to a selective college. It's their starting line in the admissions process. The starting line is different for an applicant who holds down a part-time job to support parents who didn't go to college or attends a high school that offers few advanced courses and sends only a small number of graduates to college.

At the same time, some parts of the application count more than others depending on what the college prioritizes and the particular moment in the selection process. Grades might carry a greater weight, for instance, during the initial "rough" sort of applicants in the winter, while personal qualities take priority during the "finer" sort right before admissions decisions are released. Applications considered during early decision usually receive a more forgiving and leisurely read than those reviewed during the rush of regular decision.

This is why admissions deans have been described as a "walking bundle of contradictions." While wide-eyed teenagers see deans as all-powerful gatekeepers, they have supervisors—presidents and trustees who are always putting demands on them, not all of which are in the best interests of applicants. College admissions is a constant balancing act, to please the bosses, as well as other constituents—faculty, coaches, alumni, donors, and at public universities, politicians.

Like most deans, John Latting never planned a career in college admissions. He grew up in working-class Martinez, California, where few teenagers traveled very far to college, mostly because the state had two massive, well-known public university systems in UC and Cal State. "I thought you had to pick one," Latting told me. He looked at UC Berkeley and Cal Poly, and applied to Berkeley and Stanford ("It was across the bridge," he said). Both schools accepted him. He chose Stanford.

Latting recalled his Stanford acceptance letter included a short personal note from the dean of admissions at the time, Fred Hargadon. Hargadon was a legend among undergraduates at Stanford, Latting discovered when he arrived on campus in the fall of 1983. Known simply as "Dean Fred," he had instant-recall from the applications of undergraduates he met. He drove a convertible with a license plate that read simply, ADMITS. A year later, when Hargadon departed Palo Alto for the College Board, the *New York Times* called him the "dean of deans."

His presence on campus made an impression on a young John Latting, who hadn't realized admissions could be a career. "Everyone knew what he represented," Latting said of Hargadon. "He had special insight into not who would be the best students case-by-case, but what's the best class." A few years later when Latting was starting to think about life after graduation, one of Hargadon's sons, Latting's teammate on the Stanford rowing team, suggested a job in admissions. Unlike many admissions officers who were introduced to the profession as a tour guide or in a work-study job, Latting never worked in admissions as an undergraduate. In 1987, the year he graduated with a philosophy degree, Stanford had five openings in its admissions office. He started the following fall.

An entry-level job in admissions has always been either the start of a career or a quick stop after college for young adults trying to figure out what's next. For Latting, it was intended to be the quick stop. He enrolled in graduate school at Berkeley to prepare for what he thought would be his forever career: a college professor. But halfway through his doctorate, he realized that scholarly life was too solitary. What interested him were the social forces that collided to reveal the teenagers whose applications he'd read in the Stanford admissions office. When his soon-to-be wife got a teaching job at Caltech, he followed her and landed a job in the admissions office there.

Later, after a stint running the admissions operation at Johns Hopkins University, he moved to Emory in 2011. Then as now, elite colleges and universities were under increasing pressure to enroll more low-income and first-generation students. Latting felt he could contribute more to those efforts at Emory than at Johns Hopkins. Since he arrived, the share of Emory undergraduates from the bottom half of the income distribution has risen to 22 percent, from 13 percent (meanwhile, Hopkins's rate is 19 percent).

Latting is tall and lanky, with the body of a former college rower. He is dressed for the first day of a new admissions season in a blue V-neck sweater and brown corduroys. He is soft-spoken and talks with the halting style of the professor he wanted to be. In many ways, he conveys a counterbalance to the sales-driven, marketing approach that permeates admissions offices in the modern era.

But don't be mistaken by his low-key approach. As with admissions deans everywhere, Latting pays attention to numbers and he makes compromises—this many low-income students but that many legacies or this average SAT score but that much diversity. In the months ahead, his staff will manage a similar give and take, often in minutes. Don't make too much of an applicant's numbers, Latting tells his staff, but don't ignore them either in holistic review.

Then Latting showed the admissions staff a PowerPoint slide displaying the top factors that most predict freshman grades at Emory. The top one, by far, is the recalculated GPA, followed by the rigor of the high school curriculum. Much lower on the list were SAT and ACT scores and AP test scores.

"Don't waive off the numbers," Latting reminded them, "under the name of holistic review." It sounded like another contradiction in a job full of them.

Figuring out the rules to the game of selective admissions is a relentless pursuit in economically privileged communities among parents who want their kids to go to what they define as the best colleges. They don't necessarily see higher education as a public good designed to benefit society as a whole but one that should serve their own specific ambitions and goals. This tension between the societal and individual benefits of higher education is why the subject of race and class often comes up in conversation about who gets in and why.

Since affirmative action policies emerged in the 1960s, colleges have aimed to enroll diverse classes of students to improve the learning experience for everyone. I usually tell well-off parents worried about the admissions prospects of their children that they'll be fine almost anywhere they go to college. Presumably they have the safety net of a solid education behind them and the social and professional connections of their parents. Yet the questions about how to get into a top school go on because too many parents consider that higher education only has benefits if their child gets accepted to his dream school.

Today, holistic admissions is nearly ubiquitous among selective schools because the process gives admissions officers wide discretion to admit the class they want. The irony is that holistic admissions was born in the early 1900s out of a desire to exclude students—not broaden the class.

Before World War I, elite universities admitted students based largely on their score on an entrance exam and enrolled mostly upper-class white Protestant students from boarding schools. After the war, the nascent "high school movement" in the United States accelerated, turning secondary schools into a nationwide system for mass education that better prepared students for college. In 1910, only 9 percent of American youths earned a high school diploma; by 1935, 40 percent did.

Better educated high school students, however, presented a problem for Ivy League colleges: Jewish students excelled on admissions tests and were being admitted in numbers that made parents and alumni of the New England patrician class uncomfortable. As Jerome Karabel chronicled in his 2005 book, *The Chosen*, the colleges first developed the elements of today's holistic admissions in a secretive and deeply offensive effort to keep out Jewish students. The schools requested letters of recommendation and began to consider extracurricular activities, as well as the geographic location of applicants (in order to expand their footprint outside of New York City, home of large clusters of Jewish students). This is when legacy status became a significant plus in admissions because there were so few Jewish alumni. The goal was to avoid selecting students on academic merit alone.

Even as late as the 1960s, the vestiges of this anti-Jewish system remained, with the Ivy League favoring "personality" and "character" in admissions decisions. Yale asked students to include pictures with their application, measured the height of its freshmen, and, until 1965, asked alumni interviewers to list the physical characteristics of prospective students they met. But the civil rights movement of the late 1960s forced the schools to rethink their definition of merit yet again, and with it, their admissions criteria. University leaders knew they'd have a hard time justifying a bias for prep school applicants over public school students and wealthy white Protestants over Jewish and black students (although legacies were left untouched). Rather than having holistic admissions be a cover to exclude students, colleges could now use it to expand access not only to Jewish undergraduates, but also to women and particularly black students through affirmative action policies.

Throughout the 1970s, debates over the admissions policies at highly selective schools erupted on a regular basis. Professors expected intellectually motivated students in their classrooms and pushed for a process focused on academic prowess. Alumni worried about growing numbers of minority students and led uprisings to ensure generous legacy preferences were preserved. A top alumni fund-raiser for Yale wrote to the president of the university, which was facing deficits at the time, wondering "how the Yale Alumni Fund will be doing 15, 20, and 25 years from now"—a not-so-veiled threat that preferences for alumni children should remain.

In the decades that followed, the role race ultimately came to play in admissions was decided in places far from college campuses—in the courts and at the ballot box. Three times since 1978, the U.S. Supreme Court has heard cases about race-based admissions policies, and each time it has ruled that colleges may consider race or ethnicity as one of many factors in accepting students. Frustrated by their losses in the courts, opponents of affirmative action appealed directly to voters in the states. In the last twenty years, six states passed measures to ban affirmative action in educational settings, while two others did so through executive orders and legislation.

The chipping away at race-conscious admissions has put higher education on the defensive for nearly five decades. In the early years, colleges employed a moral argument—race-based policies are necessary to make up for past discrimination. But in recent decades, they hit harder on the idea of educational diversity—that without students from different backgrounds the education of everyone suffers. Giving students the opportunity to learn from peers is a major benefit of a college education, one that will be even more important to students once they graduate and enter a diverse workforce. That's why Fortune 500 CEOs largely back race-conscious admissions policies as an economic necessity.

But for the nation's top colleges, fighting to preserve race-based admissions isn't simply about taking a principled stand. Their own self-interest also motivates them: they don't want to lose the ability to choose a freshman class however they like. Any future court decision that strikes down affirmative action could also put limits on holistic admissions. That likely would force schools, for the first time in more than a century, to move to a more transparent set of academic measures in admitting students. It's why top colleges are worried about yet another lawsuit aimed at eliminating race-based admissions policies, this one involving Harvard.

Unlike the past admissions cases argued in front of the Supreme Court, the suit against Harvard brings a new wrinkle. The plaintiffs in previous cases who alleged a student of color took their spot at a college were white. This time, opponents of race-based admissions shrewdly chose a different set of plaintiffs whom affirmative action was once seen to help: Asian Americans. And rather than file the suit on behalf of one aggrieved student, who in previous cases often became the subject of attacks in the media, the case against Harvard was brought by a membership organization created just for the occasion, Students for Fair Admissions (SFFA).

On elite college campuses, Asian Americans are seen as the "new Jews," with grades and test scores that substantially surpass those of many white applicants. One influential study in 2009 by two Princeton sociologists found that a hypothetical Asian American student needed to score 140 more points on the SAT than a white applicant and 450 more points than a black student to have an equal chance of admission to an elite school.

In the suit against Harvard, the SFFA alleged that Harvard engaged in "racial balancing," attempting to build each incoming class with a specific racial breakdown under the guise of holistic admissions. In recent years, that has resulted in freshman classes that are about half white, 20 percent Asian American, 15 percent black, and 12 percent Latino. An internal Harvard study estimated that admission based solely on academic credentials would cause Asian American students to make up about 43 percent of the class and send the enrollment of Latino and black students plunging. Harvard officials denied they strived for a certain level of diversity. They admitted—like most selective colleges do—that they consider race, but only as a "plus factor" once an applicant is seen to possess other desirable attributes to get over the bar for admission.

At issue in the case is exactly how Harvard deploys its version of holistic admissions. Application readers at the university assign scores in four categories—academic achievement, extracurricular activities, personal qualities, and athletic abilities—plus an overall score that takes all factors into account. Once again, it's the personal category, the catch-all of categories in any holistic admissions scheme, that is in dispute. At Harvard, the personal category includes everything from essays to alumni interviews. The plaintiffs concluded in their analysis of Harvard admissions data over four cycles that Asian American applicants have higher academic and extracurricular scores than any other racial group at the university, but they have the lowest score on the personal rating. SFFA attributed the disparity to long-held stereotypes that Asian American students are one-dimensional applicants focused mostly on academics.

The Harvard lawsuit went to trial in Federal District Court in October 2018. Just as the two-week trial in Boston was wrapping up, Grace, the Asian American senior from San Francisco, was finalizing her application for early decision at Dartmouth. When I talked with her soon afterward, she was second-guessing herself, going over all the things she wrote in her head and wondering if she had explained herself well enough or highlighted the right set of activities.

"Every time I think about it, my stomach drops and I keep thinking of scenarios good and bad that could happen," she wrote in her journal. "But know I can't do anything about it."

In mid-December, she received a reply from Dartmouth. A decision on her application was deferred until the regular decision round. It wasn't entirely a rejection, but close to it. Grace knew the competition for seats would be tougher in the spring when she'd be up against a huge number of applicants.

I asked her if she had followed the Harvard admissions trial and whether she thought being Asian American had worked against her at Dartmouth. She said friends talked about the case and how the standards for college admissions were set higher for Asian Americans. That's why she spent time in her application emphasizing her passion for the environment in her activities and main essay. She wanted an admissions reader to *see her personality*.

In her essay, she had written how she was appointed to a seat on a government commission, which "taught me not only about how to write resolutions and contact supervisors, but also to gain a holistic understanding of problems and to evaluate all options and possible solutions." She had hoped that the essay would show the admissions office that her activities were not simply checkmarks on the application, but in the end it wasn't enough. "Who knows what any of these schools are looking for exactly," Grace told me in December.

Affirmative action is just another way that holistic admissions have helped colleges create a black box that only they can see inside.

Before reporting this book, I knew that admissions was a hard job. Robin Hennes showed me just how hard.

Late on a Friday afternoon, before I left Seattle on a red-eye flight back east, I found the assistant director of admissions in her University of Washington office. The hallways on the third floor of

Schmitz Hall, a 1970s brutalist building that houses UW's admissions operation, were a virtual ghost town. It seemed everyone else had left for the weekend, except for Hennes. This was weeks after training for the part-time readers had ended, and the team was now in the depths of reading season. Hennes was staying late to catch up.

"I've read 7,200 files so far," she told me. As someone who reviews more applications than anyone else on the staff, she is both a no-nonsense pragmatist who doesn't linger over sob stories, but also an idealist who talks often about the important mission of admissions to promote social mobility.

I asked her if there was an easier way to select the freshman class at UW. Giving applications a thorough review using an evaluation process designed to handle a fraction of the numbers is a challenge not only at the Seattle campus, but selective public universities everywhere. Across the country, major public universities have been inundated by applications in the past decade. The fifty state flagships received 1.3 million applications in 2016, up 79 percent compared with a decade earlier.

Hennes explained to me that UW had already changed how it evaluates applicants twice in the last two decades in response to shifting legal and political realities. Twenty years ago, the university used a mechanized approach. It followed a formula that combined high school grades and test scores on a 100-point index. Students knew what it took to get in before they even submitted their application. The university didn't require essays or even an extensive list of extracurricular activities.

Because minority students who scored below the cutoff on the index were given extra consideration for admission, the index was shelved after voters in Washington State approved a ban on affirmative action in 1998. A new admissions system was created. It still relied heavily on a numerically driven approach to admit part of the class and a fuller review for the remainder of the pool, which considered an applicant's socioeconomic status as an alternative to affirmative action.

The hybrid process was found to be too confusing, however, and led to the development of the current system and reading every application. That seemed like a reasonable demand when the process was developed in 2006. At the time, the university received 16,000 applications, and two-thirds were admitted. By 2018, the university was juggling more than 46,000 applications, while admitting fewer than half.

"No matter how you review applications," Hennes said, "it's not going to seem fair if your child is denied admission."

What UW looks for in applicants is likely to change yet again, and soon. As entry to the university becomes increasingly competitive among state residents, faculty have asked if holistic admissions adequately takes into account disadvantaged students who might lack the credentials of their wealthier peers. There is talk on campus of rebalancing the personal and academic factors, so that the personal rating drives more of the overall score.

Hennes is unlikely to see that change. After more than thirty-five years on the job, she plans to retire soon. Raised in Seattle, she went to the University of California at Santa Cruz in the late 1970s, and then returned home a few years later to take extra courses at UW to become a teacher. To make ends meet, she performed odd jobs, including painting houses. One day, her mother, who worked at UW's business school, received a call from the admissions office asking if she had any leftover applicants from a job she had just filled. The admissions office was looking for counselors. "My mom said, 'Oh, I should tell my daughter about your job,'" Hennes recalled. She applied and was hired a few weeks later.

When Hennes started at UW in 1984, the admissions office didn't select a class as much as it processed one. Admissions was an automated system with specific cutoffs for grades and test scores, a clear line between those who got in and those who didn't. Then, in the last two decades, as public colleges expanded their recruiting footprint to capture more out-of-state students and their bigger tuition checks, they were forced to adopt the recruiting practices of their private counterparts. A jump in applications followed, made up of a very competitive applicant pool without a commensurate increase in the size of the incoming freshman class. That situation required the adoption of holistic admissions, which in itself made the lives of the admissions staff more complicated.

What I came to realize is that legal challenges and political debates have turned admissions deans into Rube Goldbergs, forced to build increasingly intricate systems to take into account ever more factors. They may wish for an easier and less convoluted selection process, but the contraption they have designed has too many overlapping and incompatible parts to work efficiently. The mechanism may ultimately serve the interests of their institutions, but a convenient by-product is a vague process that keeps applicants in the dark.

4

Playing the Odds

Early Decision

The weekend before Halloween, Nicole huddles with her mother in their North Carolina home weighing her options for early decision. Applications for ED, as early decision is widely known, are due at most colleges November 1. That's just five days away. Nicole is still debating what to do: where to place her single, binding bet or whether to submit an ED application at all, asking almost anyone who will listen for advice. Right now, she's leaning toward the University of Pennsylvania. An independent counselor her mom hired, however, thinks she has a better shot at Dartmouth given her grades and test scores.

In the living room of their 1990s stone-veneer house, Nicole, wearing an oversized Penn sweatshirt, and her mom go back and forth for nearly an hour over the merits of the two schools. Both are Ivy League schools so it's like arguing over who is wealthier, Bill Gates or Warren Buffett. Nicole's mom and dad both have MBAs. Nicole wants to get a jumpstart on business courses, with a major as an undergraduate. But the reality she faces is that the route into Penn is much more difficult through its business school, the world-famous Wharton School.

Nicole has put off finishing her Dartmouth application, and she knows that if she ends up moving in that direction, plenty of work awaits her in the next few days. "Don't forget," Nicole says, still trying to persuade her mom, "the acceptance rate for ED at Penn is something like 22 percent compared to 8 percent for regular."

For months, Nicole's mom has questioned her daughter's interest in applying ED. And now just before the deadline, she still does. She knows getting accepted ED eliminates any possibility of comparing financial aid offers from multiple colleges. A few days earlier, Nicole had received a letter from Tulane University inviting her to be a "priority consideration applicant," an offer that came with the possibility of a partial scholarship of up to $32,000 per year. At the very least, Nicole's mom thinks she could shop that letter around to other schools if her daughter is accepted to the New Orleans school.

What's more, she wonders if Nicole is really in love with Penn or is seduced by the name brand. "I heard you say you loved a college other than Penn when you left that college," her mom says, drawing out the word *loved* for emphasis.

"No, *you* liked other schools more than you liked Penn," Nicole interrupts, with a tight smile. Without saying the name, they both know they're talking about the final stop on their summer tour— Northeastern University. Nicole's mom likes Northeastern's co-op program and how it could help her daughter land the all-important job after graduation. For Nicole, Northeastern's brand is good, but not quite good enough to put it at the very top of her list, at least in October. "I just spent the last seven years of my life focusing solely on getting into the best college that I possibly can."

As the conversation drags on, both mother and daughter seem to want to get back to the Kansas City Chiefs football game they've been ignoring for the last half hour. "You've worked hard," Nicole's mom says as they turn back to the game, "and it would be worth it to see what your options are."

Nicole is not alone among seniors analyzing ED numbers in the final hours before making a pick. In the middle of October, as I interviewed three dozen seniors, most told me they would apply early decision, *they just didn't know where.*

ED is one of the many rules of the admissions game that has changed over the years, giving students little choice but to respond with their own shift in strategy. Seniors—and we're really only talking about the drivers who are in the know—now treat ED as a cold-blooded calculation in the admissions game.

The transformation of admissions to the data-driven world of enrollment management has furthered the idea that getting into a top college is a game rigged by colleges, one with many rules to master. As in any game, the players in admissions are constantly trying to outmaneuver their opponents. They carefully weigh every move. They constantly plot to gain even a tiny advantage. Both colleges and applicants are players in the game, although schools are more like the everyday stars who always seem to play offense while students are the scrubs left to flounder on defense.

In this game, few moves are as consequential as early decision. Indeed, few things have contributed as much to the insanity of the admissions process. It's the origin of the compressed calendar students now must follow in their college search. It's the source of the growing divide between the buyers and sellers among colleges, as well as the one between drivers and passengers among students. It's been called a "racket" that "penalizes nearly everyone" by a former editor of *U.S. News & World Report*, the same organization that produces the rankings early decision is partly designed to game. And it has even come under scrutiny by the U.S. Department of Justice.

Early decision and early action (or EA) cause so much hand wringing because they are most popular among the colleges that are sellers and the high schools with many drivers. After all, no one is rushing to get into a school that accepts most of its applicants anyway. Selective colleges make up the majority of the 450 schools that offer ED and EA. To give you a sense of how pervasive it is, only nine of the top 65 *U.S. News* national universities and liberal arts colleges *don't offer* ED as an option. Not only that, the more selective the college, the larger the number of early applicants they receive. Most come from private and suburban public high schools where students are usually familiar with early admission programs.

Early decision is a mechanism that from its start, and through several iterations since, has been fashioned to assist colleges in managing their application pools in uncertain times.

Harvard, Yale, and Princeton wrote the original rules with an arrangement they called the "ABC" system. Applicants from feeder schools—mostly private boarding schools—received a preliminary assessment and were awarded a rating of A, B, or C. An A was a clear admit; B meant admission was uncertain, and C was a likely deny. Admissions deans at other elite colleges looked on with both envy and worry. "It seems to me the practice is going to become more prevalent," the admissions director at Williams College wrote in a 1955 report. "The problem will be not to let it go too far."

But go too far it did. By the end of the decade, ED, as we conceive of it today, was adopted by the Seven Sisters colleges (Barnard, Bryn Mawr, Mount Holyoke, Radcliffe, Smith, Vassar, and Wellesley), and others followed in the 1960s, pressured by students who didn't want to wait until the spring for a decision. In 1965, close to 60 percent of Amherst's incoming class came in through early decision. In the early 1970s, Harvard, Yale, and Princeton eliminated the ABC system and replaced it with something they called "early evaluation," a precursor to today's "early action."

Find all those terms confusing? Let's stop for a moment to walk through the rules about early admissions—at least the official, written instructions developed in 2005 by the professional association representing college admissions officers.

First, it's important to take a deep breath and recognize that the vast majority of applicants to college—95 percent in any given year—don't roll the ED dice. They apply regular decision. Regular decision allows students to apply to as many schools as they want, anytime up until January of their senior year (and in a few cases even later). Colleges review applications and send a decision by the end of March. Some schools respond soon after they get applications in a process called "rolling admissions." Either way, students have until May 1 to commit to a school. The process essentially takes up a student's entire senior year of high school.

Early decision pushes the admissions process backward to

the junior year of high school because students must choose one college and make a binding commitment—by the beginning of November—just a few months into their senior year. Colleges release those admission decisions in the middle of December. If a student is accepted, the college search is over. The applicant is obliged to go to the ED school (although there are ways to get out of the commitment).

Students deferred or rejected in the ED round are left with about two weeks during the busy holiday season to apply somewhere else for regular decision or to rush an application to meet yet another early deadline, called ED2. Some schools offer that second early decision round, with deadlines perfectly timed to come *after* top-ranked colleges send out their ED1 decisions. Their unspoken goal is to win a few more binding commitments from emotional teenagers at a vulnerable moment by turning them to their preferred second choice.

Finally, there is early action, or EA. It's similar to ED in that students apply early and hear back in December or January. But the key difference is that students are not required to attend if accepted and they have until May 1 to make their decision. Some schools with EA, including Harvard, Princeton, Stanford, and Yale, further restrict students from submitting applications to other private colleges during their early rounds.

After reading those rules, you're probably wondering why colleges have built what seems like yet another Rube Goldberg machine to manage early decision. Simply put, ED is one more way for schools to gain an advantage in admissions. Although schools sell ED as an insurance card that both sides can play in the game, the spoils largely go to the colleges.

In 2016, Tulane University hired Satyajit Dattagupta to oversee the university's enrollment operation, a decade after the New Orleans school was forced to shut down for an entire semester in the wake of Hurricane Katrina.

By the time Dattagupta arrived at Tulane, the university was more popular than ever—at least as measured by applications. The numbers were soaring, allowing the university to become more selective. But Tulane's yield rate lagged behind competitors. Only 23 percent of students accepted to Tulane ended up enrolling, compared to 32 percent at New York University and 34 percent at the University of Southern California.

Admissions is often described as a mix of art and science. Dattagupta, who was in his early thirties at the time, was part of a new generation of enrollment leaders tipping the balance toward science. The old lions of admissions were retiring. Many of them were drawn to the profession for idealistic purposes. They came with degrees in history, English, philosophy, and psychology. They wanted to counsel teenagers and craft a class of undergraduates with potential.

Dattagupta traveled a different path to the admissions office at Tulane. He had a bachelor's degree in computer science and an MBA. As an undergraduate at Southwest Minnesota State he worked for the university's technology office, not its admissions office. He did, however, help build an enrollment management system for the university. That's what got him hooked on the science of enrollment.

Around the time Dattagupta finished his MBA in 2007, admissions was following every other industry into a data revolution. The admissions office, traditionally managed by experience and gut instinct, was now driven by spreadsheets and dashboards operated by leaders who grew up in the era of *Moneyball*. That was the name given by author Michael Lewis in his 2003 book to the phenomenon of baseball teams managing players by analyzing statistics to make decisions. Now the same thing was happening in admissions with increasingly sophisticated models to build each incoming class. This sea of numbers told admissions officers who was most interested in the school, who would enroll if accepted, and even how much financial aid it would take to attract them.

When Dattagupta started to dig into Tulane's numbers, the

yield rate also worried him. Tulane had already decided to offer ED and a more flexible EA option the year he arrived. Those programs would help boost yield by forcing a portion of accepted students to make a binding commitment, but it wouldn't be enough. To really move the needle, Tulane needed to stretch the bounds of early decision and get inside the minds of prospective students to understand how interested they truly were in coming to New Orleans.

Tulane piles on the early deadlines with three rounds: EA, ED1, and ED2. Why so many options? Because Tulane is a backup school for many highly qualified applicants. When students are admitted to more than one school, they need to make a choice. Tulane often loses in that head-to-head battle, especially when paired with a higher-ranked school. Although schools like to tout super-high application numbers or super-low admit rates as a sign of their popularity, it's the yield rate that provides a better signal of how desirable a school is to students. After all, teenagers can apply to ten colleges, be accepted everywhere, but can enroll at only one school.

Running two binding ED rounds gives Tulane a lever to improve its yield. But that process doesn't make it much different from other selective schools with two ED cycles. Where the university really tests the boundaries of early admissions is in the interplay between early action and early decision.

Let me explain. During my interviews with high school counselors and independent admissions consultants, when I asked about the colleges that push the norms of binding early plans, few schools were mentioned as often as Tulane. That got me curious. I posted a question on College Confidential, an online admissions forum, in the Tulane thread asking applicants about their early admissions experience at Tulane. In the following days, I received more than three dozen email messages, mostly from parents.

One of them was from a mother in Florida whose daughter, Hannah, had applied EA to Tulane in early November. Just *a week later*, she received an email from the university with an offer to switch the application to ED2. "Getting admitted as an ED II applicant means your college search is over!" said the email, which the applicant's mother shared with me (she was copied on the message as well). While Tulane was Hannah's first choice, she wanted to hear from other schools where she applied, her mother told me. She refused to change to ED2.

Perhaps Tulane was Hannah's first choice. But when she didn't switch, Tulane's admissions office assumed the university wasn't at the top of her list. In December, Hannah was deferred to regular decision, despite her strong credentials: ten Advanced Placement courses, a 4.5 GPA, and a 1420 on the SAT. After the deferral arrived, Hannah started to receive a flurry of follow-up emails, again suggesting a shift to ED2. This time, the emails included a subtle hint. *If Tulane is your first choice school, you may want to consider switching to Early Decision II.* That was followed by a less subtle hint: a big box labeled "Switch Your Application." What was left unsaid was that a switch might demonstrate the applicant's interest in the school and perhaps boost her chances of being accepted.

Then Hannah's mother noted the timing of the message—it arrived Friday, December 22, the day when many high schools across the country started their long winter break and when applicants were the most anxious about admissions. "They timed it when there's no one to turn to for guidance or information," Hannah's mother told me. "Not her counselors at school. Not the admissions reps at Tulane." The whole episode soured Hannah on Tulane. In March, she withdrew her application before receiving a final decision. She was eventually accepted at New York University and enrolled there.

For schools such as Tulane with ever-growing application pools but with too many accepted students turning down an offer, early admissions is the strongest indication of what's called "demonstrated interest"—the willingness of the applicant to actually enroll. "Demonstrated interest" is one of those jargony terms describing what has become an important metric to colleges. Measuring it helps protect their yield rate as they wade through rising numbers of inquiries and applications. Their reasoning goes something like this: Why admit applicants who are often on the bubble—and risk looking less selective—if they're planning to go elsewhere anyway?

Demonstrated interest is yet another way that colleges hold the upper hand in the admissions game and attempt to manipulate their yield rate, although applicants are quickly figuring out how to solve this part of the puzzle. About one in five schools say demonstrated interest is of "considerable importance" in their admissions decisions, according to an annual survey by the National Association for College Admission Counseling. That's about the same weight they give to counselor recommendations and essays, and *even more* consideration than given to teacher recommendations, class rank, and extracurricular activities.

Schools measure demonstrated interest in a variety of ways beyond early admissions applications. How many of their emails did you open and how quickly? Do you follow them on social media? Did you show up when an admissions representative visited your high school? Have you taken a campus tour? Or they ask a supplemental question on the Common Application about why you want to attend the school. Dattagupta told me the response to that essay on Tulane's application is most important for him in measuring an applicant's interest. "We can easily detect students who copy and paste the 'about us' section from our website," he said.

There's evidence that *the better* the student, the more demonstrated interest might matter to his admissions decision—especially at buyers like Tulane that are just below the very top of the pecking order.

In 2017, a group of economists published a study looking at two years of contacts that a highly selective university made with more than twelve thousand applicants. They found that applicants who visited campus increased their chances of getting accepted by 30 percent compared with those who went only to off-campus events (although those who went to off-campus events also got an admissions boost over those without any contact). The most interesting finding was that students with the *highest* SAT scores were really helped by visiting campus. That suggests colleges which track demonstrated interest are reluctant to admit smart students who don't engage in the admissions process for fear of being used as a safety school.

If a school tracks demonstrated interest—which many reveal in their Common Data Set questionnaire found via an Internet search—applicants can dupe the very techniques colleges use to follow them. Attend a visit by a college's representative to your high school and be sure to check in. Sign on to the school's website and look at it routinely.

The mother of a Massachusetts teenager told me she opened every single one of her son's email messages from Tulane while he was away at summer camp before his senior year of high school. Tulane was his second choice after Emory, and she wanted to do everything to improve his chances. He applied EA to Tulane and ED to Emory in the fall of 2018. He was accepted to both campuses. He enrolled at Emory.

Although Tulane lost that one student to Emory, the university's laser-focus on demonstrated interest has paid off overall. The emails encouraging students to switch their application to binding early decision, for instance, yielded 625 additional early decision applications in the first year of the program. Ninety-five were accepted and enrolled. Dattagupta acknowledged to a reporter for the *Wall Street Journal* that he heard complaints about the emails, but the nudge worked as intended. That's what matters to his bosses.

"We all want to serve the students," Dattagupta said, "but at the end of the day I'm the dean of admissions and I have a responsibility to my institution." And on that measure, Dattagupta posted a big win for Tulane in 2019. That fall, more than one-third of the 1,800 students Tulane accepted ended up enrolling. After years of trying, the university had finally surpassed the 30 percent mark on yield.

In a seminal article on early admissions in the *Atlantic* in 2001, James Fallows, the former editor of *U.S. News*, explained how ED has evolved since the 1950s, outlining what he described as "three ages" of early decision. The first age was the founding years in the 1950s and 1960s. The second age arrived in the 1980s. It was designed to fill beds during the lean Generation X years. The third age that followed occurred because the surge of Millennials arriving on campuses allowed colleges to worry less about filling beds and focus more on using ED to game the rankings. As schools tried to move up the rankings—and turn into sellers instead of buyers— the easiest levers to pull were those controlling selectivity and yield.

Here's how it worked: Before the Common App and filing applications online really took off, applicant pools were still relatively modest compared to today's numbers. Say a college received 12,000 applications a year and needed an incoming class with 2,000 students. A yield rate around the typical 33 percent would require the school to send out acceptances to 6,000 students. That gave the college an acceptance rate of 50 percent, which at the time was okay, but definitely left them out of the sellers in higher education.

Adding early decision could quickly improve both yield and selectivity of a would-be seller in the eyes of the public and *U.S. News*. That's because schools blend their rates from all their admissions cycles. So say a school received the same number of overall applications, but accepted and *automatically enrolled* 500 out of 1,000 applicants in ED and the remaining 1,500 through the regular decision. Now yield suddenly increases because one-fourth of the class promised to come if they were enrolled, and selectivity climbs as well because the remaining 11,000 applicants—remember, the same applicants that were there without ED—are now fighting for fewer spots. That's one way some schools, including Penn, Vanderbilt, and Northwestern, steadily moved up the rankings beginning in the late 1990s.

I found in reporting this book that a fourth age of ED has since emerged, arriving in 2008. There's no good time for the stock market to crash or a housing bubble to pop, but for colleges the onset of the Great Recession couldn't have come at a worse moment in the admissions calendar—in the fall of 2008, just as high school seniors were finalizing applications. The collapse of the housing market, in particular, raised fears in admissions offices everywhere because officials knew that tuition bills in the previous decade were largely subsidized by home equity loans. If parents of high school seniors could no longer use the house as a bank, college leaders worried their enrollments would tank.

Colleges needed to act quickly, and the first tool they reached for was ED. As a hedge against an economy that was souring fast, selective colleges increased the number of students accepted in their binding early rounds. They didn't want to take a chance that they'd struggle to fill seats in the spring.

Schools that traditionally filled maybe a quarter to one-third of their classes through ED boosted that proportion to upward of half in the fall of 2008. When the economy rebounded, however, the sellers didn't return to their old ways. I reviewed 2018 admissions data for 64 schools as reported through the Common Data Set. I found that among the top 62 schools on the *U.S. News* list of national universities and liberal arts colleges, there were 50 schools in which early decision admits made up at least one-third of the total enrolled class and 19 in which they made up at least half.

Most schools don't widely advertise their early admissions statistics. When they do, they often tell families the *percentage* of a class accepted in the first round because it sounds better than giving them the raw numbers (those figures can be found in each college's Common Data Set form). Vanderbilt, for instance, filled 53 percent of its incoming class through ED for the fall of 2018. To students and parents hearing that statistic on a campus tour, it emphasized that the university still has roughly half the spots to parcel out in the regular round. But what Vanderbilt didn't talk about as much is that its regular round would bring in upward of thirty thousand applications. The number of seats left to fill in the freshman class by then—just 750.

In the days right before and after Halloween 2018, the Common Application forwarded more than 55,000 early decision applications to its member colleges, one-quarter of all early applications filed by students during the ED period. One of those was Nicole's.

On Monday, October 29, Nicole and her mom draft a recommendation letter for the supervisor from her summer volunteer work. The supervisor makes some edits and signs it later that day. The letter is a last-minute addition. The next day, Nicole hits Submit on her early decision application—to Penn's Arts and Sciences school. In one final attempt to get ahead in the game, Nicole decides the odds are better if she tries to enter Penn by an alternative route to the ultra-competitive Wharton School.

That same fall, the *Washington Post* declared in a front-page headline that "early applications surge at prestigious colleges." While the growth in early-round applications to schools overall is slowing down, it's not doing so among the sellers. In the fall of 2018, early application totals jumped 42 percent at NYU, 39 percent at Rice, 21 percent at Brown, 19 percent at Duke, and 17 percent at Notre Dame.

The rich colleges are getting richer because seniors are willing to apply ED if they perceive the regular pool at one of their top-choice schools is just too competitive. Sure, there are plenty of early applicants ready to make a binding commitment to their dream school. But the seniors I met in reporting this book and the high school counselors I interviewed said that's not the case for the majority of ED applicants. It's a choice they are forced to make just two months into their senior year. They really don't know where to apply ED, which is why many seniors find themselves still weighing their decision only days before the deadline.

When they do place that single bet, research by Harvard's Kennedy School has found one in three students selects what they perceive as the "pragmatic" option rather than the "ideal" college. What's more, scholars of game theory have found the "time creep" that tends to come in a competitive selection process—when everyone is trying to get a jump start—increases the chance of a mismatch because students are making decisions without all the information they need.

Clearly, colleges are the winners in this round of the admissions game. Yes, ED provides certainty for students. But the practice largely benefits colleges because early applicants never find out whether they would have been accepted to another top-choice school or if a different college might have offered more financial aid. (To their credit, some ED schools, including Emory and Davidson, meet full need for those accepted early, so the packages might not be that much different elsewhere unless the student applies to a buyer that could give piles of merit aid.)

Every year a whole new crop of applicants applies ED—most of them to sellers—blinded by the long-standing and popular perception that going early offers a better chance of getting in than regular decision does. There are two basic reasons this belief persists, especially among the drivers in the admissions process.

First, the admissions statistics selective colleges love to promote don't lie, although they may exaggerate the advantage. Among the schools that offer early admissions, the average acceptance rate for ED is more than 10 percentage points higher than for a regular admit, a gap that has only widened since 2011. That's the average, however, in the survey by the National Association of College Admission Counseling, and it's likely skewed by less-selective institutions.

At the sellers, the gap between early and regular is actually narrowing as more students apply early and the size of the freshman class remains unchanged. For example, when selecting the class that entered in the fall of 2019, Duke admitted 18 percent of the students who applied early and 6 percent of applicants in regular decision. Just a year earlier, that spread was 21 percent for early and 6 percent for regular.

To give you a sense of how much more competitive ED has become, when James Fallows wrote his *Atlantic* cover story on early admissions in 2001, he noted the most extreme difference in admissions rates between an early and regular admit was at Columbia. For the Class of 2004, Columbia accepted 40 percent of its ED applicants and 14 percent of its regulars, a gap of 26 percentage points. Nearly 20 years later, for the Class of 2023, as the numbers applying in both categories have skyrocketed, Columbia accepted only 15 percent of earlies and 4 percent of regulars, a gap of only 11 percentage points.

The second reason applicants widely believe that ED is an easier route is because researchers tell us so. The most comprehensive study on ED came in 2003 by Christopher Avery of Harvard's Kennedy School of Government and two colleagues. They analyzed more than five hundred thousand applications from the admissions offices of fourteen selective colleges in the *U.S. News* top 20. What grabbed all the media headlines and stuck in the minds of prospective applicants was this: applying ED increases your chance of getting accepted by 28 percent. The researchers found that applying early was essentially equivalent to scoring 100 more points on the SAT.

A 100-point advantage might not sound like much. But scan the list of top universities in the *U.S. News* rankings. Look down the column of SAT/ACT scores, which in the rankings measure the middle half of scores of accepted students (meaning a quarter of accepted students score above and a quarter below). What you'll quickly notice is how even a 100-point swing upward on the SAT can put an applicant in the middle of the pack at a whole set of higher ranked schools. Holistic admissions, of course, measures much more than test scores, but 100 points could mean the difference being admitted to Rice instead of Boston University, for instance.

To Nicole and other seniors I met who applied ED, calculating their chances of getting in was always on their mind. A few weeks after she applied to Penn, Nicole told me she expected to be deferred to regular decision. I asked her why. "Our school has a bad relationship with Penn," she told me. The previous year, Penn accepted only one senior from her high school out of thirty-six who applied, and that student ended up going elsewhere.

Sometimes a high school that traditionally sends a bundle of applicants to a college gets "zeroed out," meaning no one gets accepted. It's usually meant as a message to counselors to send better applicants the following year. But I never heard of a college punishing a high school if an accepted student didn't enroll (unless it was an ED student who backed out of a binding agreement).

I wondered if Nicole's counselor had told her that to prepare her for a rejection. Even drivers in the admission process are sometimes misinformed. *I hear that . . .* was the beginning of many conversations I had with applicants and their parents. What they heard wasn't usually from an admissions officer at a college, but something they read in a message forum on College Confidential, Reddit, or Facebook.

Such outlets, and the Internet in general, were supposed to democratize the college search by evening the playing field between applicants and schools. But often all they did was amplify the misinformation. When I waded into the forums myself I felt I was reading hotel reviews on TripAdvisor. There were so many contradictions. Some advice was just plain wrong. Even when applicants or their parents heard something directly from an admissions officer they assumed it applied to every school where they were applying.

On the evening of December 13, when Penn was scheduled to release its early decisions, Nicole was at a game at a nearby high school. Her mom and younger sister came to meet her. After the game ended, Nicole slipped into an empty hallway with her phone cuddled into her shaking hand. She signed on to the Penn admissions portal. Unlike the old days, there would be no anxious waiting for the thick envelope.

The tears started almost as soon as she saw the words "with genuine regret." It was a denial.

"There's no scenario where they see me attending," she told me when I talked to her soon afterward. "Everything I envisioned about going to college was about going to Penn." Sitting talking to me, Nicole contemplated her remaining options. But she also started to replay the last several weeks to me. "Now I'm questioning all my decisions."

She wasn't the only one. A Texas senior I followed through the process was denied by Duke during its early decision round. The rejection upended the college list she had been working on for years. When we talked in December—in the midst of the holidays and fresh from the Duke rejection—she was busily working on applications for several schools to meet January deadlines: Rice, Yale, Brown, UNC–Chapel Hill, University of Rochester, and William & Mary. The thing about all of them is that they weren't even *on* her list when we first met just two months earlier. "I was a lot more hopeful," she paused, "at the beginning of this year."

Unless you really know where you want to go to college and don't care about financial aid, applying early takes your attention away from seeing the forest of the college search for the one tree of ED. You get so focused on the ED school in October, maybe even earlier. Many ED applicants don't do anything else on their college search in November and early December while they wait. All the students I followed in the fall of 2018 who applied ED were confident they'd get in. Perhaps they had never faced disappointment other times in their lives. But then they didn't get in, and panic ensued, as with the applicant from Texas (who got into UNC–Chapel Hill in January, where she eventually ended up).

Another piece of advice: if you apply ED and it doesn't work out, don't restart your college search. It's worth a checkup on your overall list but applying to even a handful of additional schools at a stressful time of year will only add to your anxiety. And be sure to have other applications ready to go in early December in case ED doesn't work out.

How could these seniors be so wrong about their chances? Maybe it was that their ED choice was ultimately an unrealistic one. Maybe their counselors and parents weren't honest with them. But maybe there was another explanation. Maybe the numbers about early admissions that they analyzed didn't reveal the whole story. Maybe they overestimated their chances of getting in. Maybe how seniors needed to approach their early options was shifting.

Or maybe the new era of early admissions that emerged from the depths of the Great Recession had changed the process more than anyone thought.

When I first started researching the admissions process, I read the official rules of the game for early decision outlined earlier in this chapter. Then I met high school counselors and independent consultants hired by parents and heard about the unofficial rules they communicated to applicants—mostly that ED is an easier path for getting in, especially for students who don't need to worry about financial aid.

But it was only later on, when I spent time inside admissions offices, that I came to understand that ED has a whole set of other rules, some written but many not. It reminded me of trying to explain a baseball game to my two elementary school daughters. The game has basic rules—balls, strikes, and outs. But then there is something that happens in every game—a force play or an infield fly, for instance—that requires further explanation to really appreciate what's happening on the field.

That is how I came to interpret the game of admissions over the course of the nearly two years I was embedded in this world. Just when I thought I understood the game, I ran across yet another set of more complex rules. Much as no single admissions system exists, there are few absolutes when it comes to early decision, either. Different schools play by their own sets of rules depending on their needs.

Here's the thing to recognize about early admissions: because of its binding commitment, one ED admit equals three or four admits in regular decision. That's because basically every early admit enrolls but only one out of three regular admits might end up as part of the freshman class. As a result, admissions deans approach the ED pool like an NFL general manager approaches the player draft: fill critical needs in the early rounds. Those needs differ by school, however, so applicants can't anticipate what might strengthen their early application. Some schools want full-pay students in early decision. Others need underrepresented students. And others want well-prepared men to balance against a large number of admitted women.

There is what the college wants in its early admissions pool and then there is the reality of who is actually applying early. Early decision pools at all but the upper echelon of sellers are skewed by geography, income, and even gender.

Let's take a look at the early decision pool of a typical highly selective private college in the Northeast to get a sense of who is applying and the impact it ultimately has on who gets in and at which point.

Suppose a college has a national reach and draws applications from all fifty states during an ordinary year. For ED, however, the college receives the bulk of its applications from students in the East and Midwest. Early decision is popular with seniors in those states because more nearby colleges offer ED as an option than those in the South and West, and as a result applicants are more familiar with it.

A closer look at the ED pool for this private college turns up another geographic oddity: it's missing a lot of seniors from California and North Carolina who overwhelm the college with applications for regular decision. That's because those students are also considering the top-ranked public universities in their states, including UC Berkeley, UNC–Chapel Hill, and UCLA. In California, students can't even apply to any of the UC schools until November 1. Chapel Hill offers early action but students don't hear back until the end of January.

Geographic diversity is important to this private college in all rounds, but where you live might matter more so in early decision. All else being equal, the ED applicants from states that send few applicants will have an edge in the early round, especially if admissions officers expect the normal run of applications from those low-sender states in regular decision.

Let's suppose this private college is also balancing its gender ratio. As in higher education overall, women outnumber men in the applicant pool and on campus. So, qualified female applicants start at a disadvantage during every round of admissions at this school and at most colleges. But during early decision—before this college has a full picture of their incoming class—women hold the most leverage and their best chance of getting in. One study of ED at a highly selective college found that women were slightly less likely than men to be accepted in early admissions, *but 16 percentage points less likely during regular decision.*

Suppose, finally, this private college is "need-aware" in admissions. That means that like the vast majority of private schools it factors in a student's ability to pay in who it admits. We'll fully explore financial aid in a later chapter, but admissions officers at this school spend the week before ED decisions are released moving applicants in and out of the admit pile based on their financial needs. Their goal is to fill 45 percent of the overall incoming class with ED applicants, but do it by spending only 35 percent of the total financial aid budget.

That's possible to achieve at this school and many other colleges with an ED round because the early pool skews to wealthier applicants. Students from upper-middle-class and wealthy families are willing to trade the ability to compare financial aid offers for an increased chance of getting in. Among seniors who score the highest on the SAT/ACT and apply ED, one in three come from families earning more than $250,000, compared to one in five from families with incomes under $50,000.

At this point, you can see that our fictional Northeast college has shaped a substantial chunk of its freshman class from an ED pool with all sorts of idiosyncrasies. Above all, though, this college has locked in as many students that can pay full freight, or close to it, who will subsidize needier students arriving in regular decision. Even at Emory—which doesn't take an applicant's ability to pay into account and promises to meet the full financial need for all admitted students—ED students have *half* the financial need of those accepted in regular decision.

There's a widespread perception that applying ED puts students at a disadvantage for financial aid. That may be the case at schools with limited resources because they know accepted students are committed to coming, so the college could short them on financial aid. But like everything else in the admissions game there is no hard and fast rule. At least one study on ED found just the opposite—that financial aid is more generous for early decision students because schools sometimes run out of money for regular decision admits.

These trade-offs that happen in admissions offices during early decision aren't reflected in the official acceptance rates. Those rates are the ones that lure seniors into thinking their chances are better by applying early. But many of the seats available in the early rounds are essentially off-limits to most students. Indeed, what has perhaps changed the most in this "fourth era" of early decision is how the process is used as a vehicle to fulfill certain demands put on admissions offices—by two groups in particular.

The first group are national programs that recruit many low-income and first-generation students to top colleges. Two of the largest and most well-known are QuestBridge and the Posse Foundation. Both nonprofit organizations work differently, but in essence they are talent scouts for colleges. Both also require substantial commitments from their partner colleges. One is that the schools must provide four-year scholarships covering tuition, room, and board to students selected through the programs (schools also pay QuestBridge a finder's fee of $3,500 for each student placed). The other is that students selected for the programs are accepted during early admissions.

The second, and far larger, group putting pressure on admissions offices is intercollegiate athletics. Nearly all recruited athletes at elite schools now receive their spot in the incoming class through early admissions. The rise of youth travel teams and high school students who specialize in a single sport year-round has made the recruiting process much more competitive. College coaches want to get a jump-start on their competition. Even in Division III, college coaches start identifying potential recruits in their sophomore year. Not surprisingly, coaches like early decision because it locks in their key recruits. But even admissions deans favor this approach because they're not pressured to admit five tight ends for the football team at regular decision in order to yield one for a coach.

The more schools can fill their critical needs in the early rounds, the more flexibility they have in regular decision.

It's not that the students accepted in ED are exceptional in the grand scheme of a college's entire admissions pool. But they are sure bets. Top schools will take a gamble on an ED applicant only when they believe regular decision won't yield a stronger candidate. (So if you're an early applicant, show why a school should take a chance on you, especially if your grades, curriculum, and test scores might be sub-par by the college's standards.)

For admissions deans, coming out of their ED rounds with a lion's share of full-pays, low-income students, and athletes is like winning the trifecta, especially if they can do so while maintaining the academic profile of incoming students and without overspending on financial aid. It's yet another round of the admissions game where a college's victory is bittersweet for applicants.

"Early decision serves the needs of colleges and universities a hell of a lot more than it serves students," said Chris Gruber, Davidson College's admissions dean. "In this pressure-ridden role, having early commitments is a relief." It was a rare confession by an admissions dean about the realities of the job, at least publicly. Perhaps it's because Chris had just felt the sting of the process in his own house: a few days earlier, a school deferred his daughter's early-action application to regular decision.

I was sitting with Chris a few minutes before nine a.m. during the first week of December in 2018. The admissions committee was about to convene for its fifth day to pass judgment on applications for the first round of early decision.

In the tedious machinery of the modern admissions office, a meeting of the full admissions committee is a bit of theater. Admissions officers are called on to present applications they have read, recall details about a particular high school in an instant, and defend their take on an applicant under intense questioning from colleagues. The back-and-forth between admissions officers moves at a breathless pace, and the discussion about any applicant typically culminates in a dramatic up or down vote.

Not all schools rely on a committee to make admissions decisions. Davidson has this luxury because it receives a manageable number of early applications—525 for ED1 in the fall of 2018. One of the advantages of applying early is not that applicants might get an easier review per se, but those on the bubble seem to get a more in-depth one than those who arrive in the much busier regular round. At the same time, some students aren't ready to apply early to college. Changeability is a critical aspect of adolescence. Don't rush an application for early decision just because you think your chances of getting in are better. For many students who really don't know where they want to go—but apply ED for the admissions advantage—doing so ends up being a distraction from the college search.

On the Friday that I'm at Davidson, the group of sixteen admissions officers gather around a long conference table on the first floor of the admissions office, a small white brick house on the edge of campus. The wooden blinds on the windows are shut, darkening the room—either to ensure the secrecy of the committee's work or to keep the group focused on the task at hand with a major snowstorm forecast for a few days from now that could end up derailing their schedule.

Admissions officers at Davidson still read applications the old-fashioned way—on their own, not in teams of two. Each reader typically reviews anywhere from 350 to 450 applications in a year, most from the geographic regions they oversee.

The rating system Davidson uses for its "academic index" is calculated on a 10-point scale. Once again, the admissions officers follow a cryptic recipe wrapped in what is supposed to look like a mathematical formula. The index is made up of six components: high school grades, rigor of classes, the academic caliber of the high school, recommendations, written materials from the applicant, and a final category that gives admissions officers some leeway to tweak the number based on a variety of factors in the application, including test scores.

Just after nine, the committee gets to work. Kortni Campbell, the senior associate dean of admissions, presents one of the first applicants—a boy from a New York City high school. His rating falls short of a 7 on the academic index, which means that if this group decides to move him forward his application is automatically sent to a separate faculty committee for final approval. But Kortni is on the fence anyway, so it's not clear he'll even get that far.

A committee member notes that the school is "markedly weaker." It offers few Advanced Placement classes. The applicant posted two Cs in required classes early on in high school, but he improved to a solid set of Bs with the exception of a C-plus in chemistry junior year.

A committee member asks about the chemistry grade. "Is that regular chemistry?"

"Yes," Kortni replies. She notes that one encouraging sign is that his highest grades are in the toughest classes.

"I wish he had more depth, but it is what it is," says another committee member.

Kortni admits she has concerns, which is why she wanted to discuss this applicant with the larger group. This is where applying early could provide a lift for a weaker applicant, especially when the regional admissions officer is intimately familiar with a student or a high school and has time to argue the case in the more measured pace of the ED committee. As the debate advances, Kortni seems to become more convinced this applicant is a good fit. She carefully builds her argument, a skill she honed in her previous career as a nonprofit lobbyist.

What stands out in his application, she says, is that the applicant participated in Davidson's July Experience. That one fact seems to really turn the group in his favor. The three-week summer program is for high school juniors and seniors who take two courses with faculty members while living on campus. About eighty students participate each year, and like similar pre-college programs that are increasingly popular on campuses nationwide, it allows both sides to get to know each other better. It also provides a steady pipeline of applications from students who typically yield at higher rates if they're accepted. For admissions deans, the programs provide both demonstrated interest and insurance the applicant can do college-level work.

"Is the Why D about his JE experience?" someone asks, using shorthand for the "Why Davidson?" essay question and the "July Experience"—just some of the language full of jargon, acronyms, and plenty of numbers that I'll hear throughout the day.

Kortni nods with an easy warm smile. The July Experience is "how he feels connected to this place," Kortni tells the committee. She talks with a firm but calming voice that befits the yoga teacher she is in her free time. She adds that the applicant wrote in his essay about how taking classes with Davidson faculty members made him realize "he needs to raise his game."

After seven minutes of discussion, Chris, the admissions dean who is leading the committee's proceedings, has heard enough. "Do we want to advocate by way of the faculty admission committee?" he asks. There are no objections. His fate will be left up to a small group of faculty (the student is eventually accepted and enrolls).

Over the course of the next three hours before they break for lunch, the committee members debate more than fifty applications.

One is an applicant with several relatives who, over two generations, went to Davidson. His legacy status garners him a closer look by the committee even though he's sitting just above a low 7 on the academic index—a ranking that for most applicants on this day gets them quickly moved to the defer or deny pile. This senior is "deep" in his class of five hundred seniors, notes the admissions officer presenting the application. Although many high schools have eliminated class rank as an official measure—less than half of applications to selective colleges arrive with a class rank—Davidson still estimates one even if it's not provided. It's a way to assess the risk of a prospective student: Davidson is more likely to take a chance on students farther down the ladder in a rigorous high school than those just below the top at a run-of-the-mill school. But what really gives the committee pause on this candidate is a senior-year grade—a D in an elective. The group agrees to defer to regular decision when they'll have a fuller set of grades.

Many of the discussions on this late fall morning center on what applicants have done lately with their grades and in which courses. Six of the ten points on Davidson's academic index come from those two components alone, putting students with top grades in tough classes well on their way to getting in.

Because of Davidson's mid-November early decision, admissions officers sometimes start reviewing applications without any senior-level grades in hand. In the past week, however, first quarter grades started to arrive, rounding out the picture for many applicants. One senior who a week ago seemed on her way to getting accepted is pulled back because of a C in the first quarter of calculus. "I'd like to say 'yes,'" says one of the admissions officers, "but I'm worried." In a game that's always in flux, one wrong move can end the contest for the applicant.

The committee is looking for grades that are either consistently good throughout high school or on a steady rise from the start. What concerns them is a downward trend or one that is "spiky," which Mike Mansuy, an admissions officer, the second reader on this applicant, uses to describe this candidate. Even so, he recommends an admit because she is the oldest of five siblings and works part-time. "She has significant family responsibility," he tells the group, offering up context for the grades.

Another admissions officer at the table asks how many hours she works. "She says thirty hours a week," Mike answers as he quickly glances at the application on the laptop in front of him. "That's a lot of hours in the senior year," the other counselor says. "I'm skeptical she's working that much." The senior gives the barest of details about her job selling snow cones, however, so the committee is left to wonder. If she had included more information about her job that could have been the one tiny detail that turned the conversation in a different direction. Instead, the girl is deferred until regular decision.

A deferral is not as easily handed out to another applicant a few files later from a high school that Kortni notes "we do a lot of business with." The student scored a solid 1340 on the SAT, but her transcript is filled with Bs. This is an example of where it doesn't pay to apply ED to a college that may be a stretch, especially if it's a popular destination for applications from your high school.

The academic caliber and composition of the admissions pool at highly selective colleges—both early and regular decision—rarely fluctuates from year to year. Admissions officers have a sense of what's coming and early decision sets the bar for what the class will eventually look like. So a school is unlikely to take a chance on an applicant unless its priorities have shifted (it wants more students from the Southwest, for instance) or admissions officers are concerned some other issue out of its control might impact the makeup of the applicant pool (protests on campus, for example). This is where a tool like Naviance can help you to determine if your single ED bet should be placed at a college that's less popular with your classmates and one that's less of a stretch academically.

In this case, the girl is outright rejected because the group knows she won't be able to compete with the applicants who come from this high school for regular decision.

In a sea of sameness that becomes the committee's deliberations after several hours, it's once again a small element in a file that turns the group's opinion. Someone briefs the committee on another case and tells his colleagues he was leaning toward a deny or deferral halfway through the review. The applicant's rigor score was a 1.5 out of 2. She scored a 32 on the ACT. The admissions officer says he felt the student "didn't check off all the boxes" on academics because she focused on other things.

Then the reader turned to the essay. "That's when I got interested," he says. And so does the rest of the committee. Several sit up in their chairs to hear better. Others turn away from whatever is distracting them on their laptops. Their attention is clearly focused in hour three of deliberations.

For those who review applications, personal statements often sound numbingly similar. And at first this one does, too. The applicant writes about her passion for wildlife preservation. But for this girl it's more than a passing interest, as the admissions officer tells the committee: she is a certified mahout. A few of his colleagues around the table raise their eyebrows—either they want to hear more or they're unfamiliar with the term. The admission officer explains the applicant trained to become a caretaker for elephants in Thailand, bathing and feeding them and returning them to their habitat.

"Did her privilege give her the chance to do that?" someone asks. The committee member wants to be sure his colleagues are not easily swayed by a glamorous tale.

As a debate goes on, I'm thinking back to the applicant who had to work to help her family. She probably only dreams of going overseas, let alone to Thailand to care for elephants. But after a few minutes, the committee seems satisfied the girl is well aware of the advantages she had growing up, and perhaps more important, has shown some empathy toward others. When the vote is called, all hands go up to support admission.

This may be a game, but watching these decisions at Davidson— just as I did in my visits to other colleges—made me realize there are few strict rules. Decisions aren't arbitrary or random, of course, but they're also not formulaic. How can they be when a story about an elephant might make the difference?

5

Finding an Edge

Athletes and Legacies

On the morning of March 12, 2019, I was driving across the Chain Bridge that connects Washington, D.C., to Northern Virginia to interview a high school senior when my phone started buzzing incessantly with news alerts and text messages. In Boston, federal prosecutors were announcing the indictments of dozens of wealthy, well-connected parents, including famous actors, lawyers, financiers, and corporate executives—all accused of paying bribes to get their children into Yale, Stanford, and other big-name universities.

After spending nearly a year inside competitive high schools, I already knew the lengths some parents would go to get their children into top colleges. But as a friend texted me excerpts from the indictments, each one more shocking than the last, I soon discovered that this scheme was different.

It went well beyond the everyday "back doors" into colleges that cynical applicants and their parents largely assumed were common practice in admissions offices. They already thought the game was rigged against those who had no choice but to come in through the front door. They thought that a hefty donation or a well-placed connection could get a mediocre applicant in anywhere through one of those back doors.

Even the federal prosecutor gave a nod to that in his press conference announcing the indictments. "We're not talking about donating a building so that a school's more likely to take your son or daughter," Andrew Lelling said. "We're talking about deception and fraud."

What came to be known as Operation Varsity Blues was outright cheating, stunning in both its audacity and sprawling scale. It was all orchestrated by the alleged fixer at the center of the scandal, Rick Singer, who advertised himself as a legitimate college admissions counselor.

The parents of "Yale Applicant 1," as she was identified in federal court documents, paid $1.2 million to have her designated as a star soccer recruit to the Ivy League school even though she didn't play the sport. Actress Felicity Huffman allegedly paid $15,000 for a complicit proctor to correct her daughter's answers on the SAT, giving her a score of 1420, a 400-point boost over her PSAT score. And my favorite: parents who paid $200,000 and photoshopped their daughter rowing to secure a spot on the University of Southern California's crew team.

By that afternoon, reporters and television producers were calling me to ask how the actions of a few rogue coaches and SAT proctors could go totally undetected in admissions offices. I thought back to the previous week when I sat with admissions officers at Emory who were trying to shave a thousand admits from the class over the course of just a few days. Then I realized how quickly the last five months had gone by and the tens of thousands of applications the three schools I followed had reviewed in that time.

Did I see anything suspicious as I was reviewing applications?

None of the three schools I followed was named in the investigation. While applications readers would sometimes raise questions about absent pieces of information or other inconsistencies, the issues were usually minor: unfamiliar acronyms, missing scores for AP tests, or a recommendation that mentioned a school club not listed elsewhere in the file.

Even in those cases, the readers usually didn't have time to search the Internet for additional information, so they moved on, assuming, perhaps, that these were oversights and nothing more. I discovered that applicants could increase their chances of grabbing the attention of an overburdened admissions reader if they provided key details about everything the student wanted them to know, right down to descriptions of high school clubs and the specific duties of a summer job even though there was no way to know if those details were always accurate.

Admissions counselors are not hired to be detectives. The high volume of applications and small number of staff leave the process vulnerable to embellishment or outright lying, especially at selective colleges.

The Varsity Blues scheme worked because Rick Singer found what he called "a side door" into universities. I spent most of the last chapter explaining the complicated written, and unwritten, rules of admissions. But a set of hidden rules to this game also exists that only certain players get the chance to access. Singer exploited this deeper set of rules by navigating the complexities of what admissions officers call "tips" or "hooks"—the criteria they use to give any sort of preferential treatment to an applicant.

The idea that any student gets a leg up is at the root of nearly every question about the fairness of the admissions process. Among the advantages given to any one group, the hook based on race and ethnicity is probably the most debated one. It's the hook, along with that given to first-generation students, that well-heeled parents complain about privately with friends as the unfair edge that prevented their son or daughter from getting into an elite school.

Yet they rarely mention the unfairness of two other hooks that are uniquely American, far more prevalent, and perpetuate a culture of privilege and entitlement among students at selective colleges: legacies and athletics. Perhaps parents don't say anything because those thumbs on the scale largely benefit wealthy and white students.

It's important to pass along a reality check here regarding college athletics. When you think of intercollegiate athletics you probably envision the two sports that dominate the cable channels and the sports pages: football and basketball. And when you imagine the players, you probably picture squads filled with black athletes. You wouldn't be wrong in that impression: a significant proportion of players on those college teams—45 percent in basketball and 40 percent in football—are African American. The natural assumption: black students get the benefit of athletic preferences.

However, when you step back to think about all the teams that most colleges field, the locker rooms are, in fact, dominated by white, wealthier students. According to the National Collegiate Athletic Association, 61 percent of student athletes in 2018 were white (compared with 52 percent of undergraduates overall). The most popular sports on campuses by participation numbers skew white: 60 percent of the men and women's track teams; 66 percent of the soccer teams; and 85 percent of lacrosse teams.

At selective colleges, white athletes make up even larger proportions of athletic squads: 65 percent in the Ivy League overall and 79 percent at top liberal arts colleges such as Williams, Middlebury, and Wesleyan. Nearly half the recruited athletes at Harvard come from families making $250,000 or more (compared with one-third of the class as a whole). That's why white parents, in particular, who worry their kids will be squeezed out in the admissions game, see playing sports as the best way to break into a top college.

In many ways, Varsity Blues was an egregious case of something that has been going on in private high schools and suburban public schools in a more widespread, and legal, way for years. What Rick Singer understood was that college athletics is so much more than the University of Michigan football team playing in front of 107,000 screaming fans in the "The Big House" or the March Madness basketball tournament that brings a halt to workplaces in the spring. Indeed, Singer recognized that the majority of college athletes play in relative obscurity on teams few spectators ever go to see. They're those sports you rarely think about except during the Olympics, ones like water polo, squash, and sailing—all of whose participants are heavily white. Singer also knew that because colleges needed to fill the rosters of all these sports, his ploy was an easy way to get past the admissions gatekeepers.

While Singer's scheme focused on teams that compete in Division I, colleges everywhere face pressure to sustain an athletics program across an array of sports. The average Division I university fields teams in nineteen sports and is allowed to award athletic scholarships; in Division III, schools aren't allowed to offer sports scholarships, but the needs are nearly as high: eighteen sports. Without the cooperation of admissions officers, coaches can't supply their teams with players.

To be sure, athletes aren't the only applicants with special talents given a boost in admissions. So too are musicians, artists, and debaters. But the preferential treatment given to athletes is far more systematic and prevalent than that for any other talented applicant. When it comes to getting into a selective school, you're much better off taking up water polo, fencing, rowing, or some other niche sport than playing the tuba in the band or the lead in the school musical. College sports not only exert a gravitational pull unlike any other extracurricular activity—including music and the arts—they create a huge quantifiable need to fill positions each year. Most schools have many more athletic teams than orchestras or debate teams. What's more, even a small Division III school with two dozen sports might have upward of seventy coaches and assistants on staff whose off-season job is to shepherd their recruits through the application process. The music or theater departments on campus might have people who relay their preferences about incoming students to the admissions office, but their numbers are not nearly as large as those who make up the athletics staff.

Because athletics is now known as an increasingly popular door into a top school, it's one reason why parents in affluent communities are rushing to get their kids—as early as elementary school—on youth travel teams. They see athletics as *the* ticket—and maybe a free one—to college.

In almost any well-off suburb, you can see parents piling their children and duffel bags full of cleats, hockey sticks, and swim gear into the back of the family minivan. Their destination? Daily practice for a club team or some far-flung town for a tournament.

Perhaps the only thing that has rivaled the changes in college admissions over the last three decades for U.S. families is the massive transformation of youth sports. This generation-long transition has turned locally run neighborhood teams and school squads into a network of quasi-professional private clubs with six-figure budgets and frequent interstate travel.

This new reality for young athletes is almost exclusively a symptom of rising college costs: parents shell out thousands of dollars a year and skip family vacations hoping, praying that their son's slider or daughter's drop kick will one day pay off with a full ride at a college somewhere.

Here's the problem with that strategy: the odds are impossibly long for anyone to land an athletics scholarship. Nearly 8 million kids played high school sports in 2019. But only 495,000 of them ended up competing in college, and many fewer—just 150,000 or about 2 percent of those who participated in high school—received scholarships, according to the National Collegiate Athletic Association. If you're expecting a *financial* return on the investment in your kid's sports, you're better off putting your money into a plain-vanilla savings account.

When you watch television on a Saturday in the fall, you probably think every college athlete gets an all-expenses paid scholarship to play. Far from it. A very small percentage of athletes lands that kind of deal. Most of your neighbors, in fact, who tell you that their child earned a "sports scholarship" actually received something worth less than a very used car. The "full-ride" athletic scholarship is largely a myth perpetuated by coaches in youth leagues and passed around by parents on the sidelines.

Only six sports in Division I—football, men's and women's basketball, women's gymnastics, women's tennis, and women's volleyball—award scholarships that cover the entire cost of every athlete's education. Otherwise, colleges are limited in how they give out money in dozens of other sports. Take Division I lacrosse, as an example. Schools are allowed to give the equivalent of a dozen scholarships for men and women. Most college teams have about thirty-three female and forty-four male players. Or take swimming as another example. A college team has about sixty swimmers, but can give out only the equivalent of two dozen scholarships in total.

Because college sports on almost every campus lose money—at least directly—what happens is that the best athletes get most of the money, and the rest of the team gets the leftovers. It's not uncommon for recruited athletes to receive little more than a few hundred dollars to cover books. Also, to save money, schools don't always give out their full allotment of scholarships. In a recent year, George Mason University awarded only one-third of the dozen softball scholarships allowed. The same year, the University of Cincinnati awarded the equivalent of 2.26 scholarships to its men's track team, one-sixth of its total to a team with forty men on its roster. Schools are playing the odds: they know that competitive students who played a sport their whole life often want to be on a Division I team no matter what—so why give them a lot of money if they don't need to.

Often, it's only when the reality of paying for college comes into full view in the waning days of high school that parents grasp that the athletic scholarship a club team's coach mentioned when their kid was ten was a fantasy. Then parents realize the return on their investment in sports was no better than the discount tuition coupons colleges hand out to nearly everyone, whether they're athletes or not.

But playing a sport *can* pay off in the admissions game. Athletics can assist applicants in a different way, one likely to prove far more valuable than a meager scholarship: access to an elite school that otherwise might be off-limits academically.

One morning while visiting a high school, I met Jack, a senior lacrosse player who when he listed his athletic honors for me—from team captain to all-conference squad—I assumed was about to commit to a Division I school. Instead, Jack told me he wanted to go to an elite college in the much-lower-profile Division III.

"Admissions is just so competitive at this moment," he told me. "I thought 'Is there any way I can make this process a little easier?'"

Sports would be the ticket to make the admissions process easier for him and thousands of other athletes like him. If drivers and passengers in the college search follow different timelines, athletes adopt yet another schedule—one that moves the search process up even earlier to the first two years of high school. At a time when many freshmen and sophomores are still finding their bearings in high school, athletes are already thinking about college. Jack started working on his college list when he was fifteen so he could reach out to coaches. As I spoke with him, I thought about the science of the teenage brain, its changeability, and how the athletic recruiting process distorts the high school experience for applicants who want to play in college.

While most high school athletes bask in the fanfare that comes when they commit to a Division I program, Jack knew he wasn't quite good enough to be recruited by an elite school in the top NCAA division. If he wanted to pursue a Division I school, he told me, his best option would turn out to be one in the middle of the pack in lacrosse at a school with mediocre academics and very little scholarship money to give out. That's why he wanted to aim for a top-tier academic institution, even if it meant playing in Division III. While he'd give up a chance at the money, a degree from an elite school, he thought, would be much better in the long run.

In March of his sophomore year Jack joined Hudl, an online recruiting site where he uploaded video highlights from his games for college coaches to easily view. That spring, when his classmates were just beginning to think about college, he had already started to narrow his list: Penn, Bates, Middlebury, Amherst, along with a few others. He was under a time crunch to pick three or four schools to visit over the summer and early fall for their "prospect days," where players display their talents in person and on their own dime.

For athletes, getting into a selective school is a matching game played with coaches rather than a lottery played with the admissions office. Athletes and coaches must first find each other and be a good match. Once that happens, the coach becomes the applicant's guide and advocate, assisting him through the admissions process.

How colleges recruit athletes varies widely by school. In general, coaches start looking at athletes a year or two before their applications are submitted to the admissions office. (The NCAA has strict rules on when coaches can first reach out to recruits, but athletes are allowed to initiate conversations with coaches at any time.)

Just like students fall in and out of love with colleges during the search process, so do coaches with potential recruits. A piece of advice for athletes in the recruiting funnel: always ask coaches about where you stand both academically and athletically. Because coaches are balancing multiple recruits, they often are vague about your place on the team, your chances of getting in, and how much aid they can offer. "Coaches are always shuffling around recruits," Jack told me. "They have different needs and wants at different times in the year. So, it's often about being in the right place at the right time."

When Jack went to the camp for prospects that Amherst put on, the coaches didn't seem interested. But a few months later, one of the coaches saw him play at a national tournament. "I had one of the best games ever," he told me. "That one game and suddenly I was back on Amherst's radar."

Halfway through Jack's junior year, Amherst and several other schools reached out asking for his transcript and test scores. When Jack visited Amherst that summer, the coach told him that his grades were good enough to get in as a recruited athlete. The issue was his SAT score. It was a 1250. That score put him in the bottom quarter of Amherst's incoming class. The average score of an Amherst freshman was around a 1460. In August before his senior year, he took the SAT again and pushed his score above a 1300.

When he didn't hear back from Amherst by the middle of September, he thought they had lost interest, and he started his early decision application to Penn. But at the end of September, he got a call from Amherst: the coach would endorse his application. Two and a half months later, a binding early decision acceptance arrived from Amherst.

Amherst is an elite, small New England college in Western Massachusetts. It annually competes with Williams College for the top spot in the *U.S. News* rankings among liberal arts colleges. But the other thing you should know about Amherst is that it likes to brag about how it is home to "the oldest athletics program in the nation." It cares about athletics, a lot.

Yes, so do other schools that tend to grab the sports headlines every week—Penn State, Alabama, Ohio State, and the list goes on. But the difference between those schools and Amherst is that while sports permeate the culture at a place like Ohio State, athletes themselves don't overwhelm the student body of some 47,000 undergraduates. Because Amherst and other top liberal arts colleges are so small—Amherst's enrollment is just shy of 1,900—athletes take up a significant portion of the incoming class and the campus.

In the fall of 2018, Amherst enrolled 676 athletes over its four classes of undergraduates, thirty-six *more* athletes than the University of Alabama overall. That's the same Alabama where the football team reached the College Football Playoff four consecutive times since 2016. Amherst has 200 *more* athletes than Northwestern University, a member of the Big Ten power conference. Because Amherst's student body is tiny, athletes tend to stick out more than they would at an Alabama or a Northwestern. At Amherst, athletes make up about 36 percent of its undergraduate population compared with just 2 percent at Alabama and 6 percent at Northwestern. I know it can sound crazy to say Amherst and Alabama have the same number of athletes. But think about it this way: both have baseball teams with thirty-five players, and women's soccer with twenty-five athletes, and men's basketball with sixteen players. So while Alabama has lecture halls that can hold nearly the entire Amherst student body, the university only needs so many first basemen.

Because they field dozens of sports with attention paid to making sure each roster is full, selective colleges like Amherst or Harvard find themselves with fewer spots for nonathletes, especially as the volume and quality of these applicants increase. On campuses where the competition to get in is stiff and seats severely limited, admissions *is* often turned into a zero-sum game because of athletics.

Let me explain. Many selective schools reserve a specific number of "slots" in admissions for athletes to hold them a place, so they don't get crowded out by higher achieving nonathletes. Georgetown allocates about 158 slots out of 1,600 in its first-year class to coaches in twenty-two sports. Bucknell holds 170 slots out of about 970 seats in the class. The University of Virginia earmarks 180 slots out of 3,700 spaces in the class.

A slot is a virtual lock on admissions for an athlete, although schools don't guarantee slots for specific applicants. Admissions officers still pre-read the applications of highly rated athletes to see if they're in the ballpark academically. A plug from a coach or athletic official can provide a strong hook for applicants whose academic accomplishments otherwise might not ensure admission. Rick Singer used the slot system to his advantage. He knew coaches in minor sports didn't always use every one of their spots in a particular year because key positions were already filled on their roster. Meanwhile, overburdened admissions officers wouldn't have time to evaluate the athletic prowess of recruits, or even check that they played the sport. They trust the coach's evaluation as long as the applicant is close enough academically.

Here is how the slot system plays out on a campus like Amherst. The college reserves sixty-seven admissions slots in each incoming class for what it calls "athletic factor" athletes, where the "athletic prowess weighs heavily in the admission decision," according to a 2017 report produced by a committee of Amherst professors, graduates, and students. Fourteen of these slots are allocated to the football team alone.

At Amherst, another 60 to 90 admissions spots go to "coded" athletes with top academic qualifications, but who the report noted are "admitted at a much higher rate than the general admission rate" for nonathletes with similar qualifications. In all, that means Amherst dedicates somewhere around 157 admissions spots to athletes a year—when the *total* incoming class is only about 490 students.

By making room for so many athletes, Amherst makes it so much harder for everyone else to get in. It rejects nearly 9,000 students from a pool of 10,000 applications. Like most elite colleges, Amherst is trying to become more racially and socioeconomically diverse. But its athletic teams are largely white and wealthy. Three-quarters of Amherst athletes are white; just 6 percent of male athletes and 2 percent of female athletes are from low-income backgrounds. Compare that to the rest of Amherst's student body: a little more than half are students of color and nearly a third are low income.

So, to achieve the diversity it wants, Amherst's admissions office needs to accept an abundance of minority and low-income students among nonathletes in its applicant pool. This stark division along race and class lines in admissions is another explanation for why white upper-middle-class parents, in particular, see athletics as the only viable pathway into elite colleges for their children. Youth sports participation by top-earning families (those making over $100,000) continues to grow, while it shrinks for everyone else. To further their admissions edge, more of those teenagers are taking up sports that historically haven't filled the high school sports pages of the local newspaper but ones where selective colleges field a team. The fastest growing high school sports for boys are fencing, volleyball, and lacrosse; for girls, it's lacrosse, fencing, and rifle.

Sports are an integral part of American collegiate life. I'm a college sports fan. Members of my family have been college athletes, and two of them coach at a Division III school. I have met many college athletes and coaches in my two decades of reporting. Whether athletes should get a substantial preference in admissions is not a question about their talent or dedication to their sport or academics. Rather, it's a question whether *one* type of extracurricular activity should trump every other activity when it comes to admissions decisions.

One could argue that at Division I schools, athletes contribute to the bottom line in revenue-producing sports that attract screaming crowds and television exposure. Those athletes are often the very best in the country at what they play. But that's not the case at Division III. Many athletic teams at elite colleges are no different than any other student club, yet in the admissions process they are given an extreme advantage.

When Bill Bowen, a former president of Princeton University, joined a group of researchers in studying the admissions records of nineteen highly selective colleges in the early 2000s, he found no hook was stronger in assisting the prospect of an applicant than athletics. The study revealed that minority and legacy applicants got a thumb on the scale, while athletes received a whole fist. If the average applicant had a 40 percent chance of admission to one of the schools based solely on test scores and other variables, that student's probability for getting in skyrocketed to 70 percent if he was an athlete. In other words, an athlete was about 30 percentage points more likely to be admitted than a nonathlete with the same academic record.

Before he died in 2016, Bowen produced some of the most significant research on the role that race, class, and athletics play in the admissions process. In 2001, Bowen co-wrote a book with James Shulman called *The Game of Life: College Sports and Education Values*, which reviewed the admissions records of 90,000 students at thirty selective schools over four decades. The schools included Yale, Princeton, and Williams, as well as Duke, Michigan, and UNC–Chapel Hill. Bowen and Shulman reported that recruited athletes were less representative of the rest of the incoming class. Not only were they largely white and wealthy, but they also clustered in certain majors (economics, political science, and history) and were in the bottom third of their classes. Once on campus, athletes consistently underperformed their counterparts in the classroom and were less involved in student life outside of sports.

But, like a lot of what I've learned in college admissions, nothing is quite as simple as it seems at first. A few weeks after I read *The Game of Life*, I heard a presentation by an athletic director at a Division III college that is a buyer. What she said about the athletes on her college's twenty-five teams was almost completely the opposite of what I had just read: they were more engaged and more likely to graduate than the average student on campus. Then I read a report written by a former colleague who is now a professor at the University of Georgia about sports at small, less-selective colleges, and it started to make sense.

The report found that hundreds of small colleges—many of the buyers in my earlier analysis—have increased their investment in athletics since the 1990s as a way to recruit students they might not otherwise get. Small colleges have added football to attract more men. Colleges in the South have added field hockey to attract more applicants from the North, where the sport is more popular. And schools have added lacrosse and crew to bring in more affluent students.

While the senior I met who got into Amherst used his athletic abilities to get a leg up in admissions, other high school athletes end up trading down academically to continue playing in college. All those students playing club sports in well-off American suburbs might not have the grades to get into Amherst and Yale, but they are highly sought after by schools farther down the food chain who like their grades and their ability to pay—and have a roster spot to fill. If you're a parent who just spent the previous decade underwriting your child's athletic dreams, make sure they are choosing a college because it's a good academic and social fit, not just because they want to continue playing a sport. Remember, as the NCAA's ads remind us: most college athletes go pro in something other than sports.

The outsize role athletics plays in admission is a relic from a previous era in higher education when sports defined the character of a man. Another leftover from that time is an admissions hook discussed in Chapter 3: legacies. The preference given to the sons and daughters of alumni is nearly ubiquitous in elite higher education. Few schools, however, like to talk about legacy admissions or publicize acceptance rates for the children of alumni.

That's one reason Harvard fought so hard to keep certain documents under seal in the discrimination lawsuit filed by Asian American applicants. But the judge didn't buy Harvard's argument that its admissions ingredients were like the formula for Coke, and, as a result, the secret about legacy admissions at Harvard was revealed.

Between 2009 and 2015, the acceptance rate for legacies at Harvard was 34 percent. That compared to a 6 percent acceptance rate for everyone else during the same period. In any given year, legacies make up around one-third of Harvard's freshman class.

Legacy status doesn't just help in the admissions process, but also in the college search. Selective colleges offer special on-campus programs for alumni who are going through the college search with their children. One mother who went to a two-day program at Wesleyan University with her husband and daughter described it as a "boot camp" for getting into a top school. Admissions officers conducted mock interviews and directed workshops where students and parents reviewed sample applicants and represented the admissions committee. Students also attended undergraduate classes on campus. The boot camp, the mother told me, "both generated excitement about Wesleyan but also prepared us for disappointment about how hard it is to get in."

Colleges defend legacy admissions on two fronts. First, they say legacies are just as academically qualified as non-legacies. But two studies have shown that's not true, including one by Bill Bowen, the former president at Princeton, which still considers parental ties in admissions. He found in reviewing entering classes over three decades that applicants who were the sons and daughters of alumni had a nearly 25 percent higher chance of getting accepted than a non-legacy with the same SAT score.

The other reason colleges say they consider legacy status is to engender goodwill with alumni, particularly when it comes to asking for money. Again, the research tells a different story. A study conducted for the book *Affirmative Action for the Rich* found that at seven universities that dropped legacy preferences between 1998 and 2008, there was "no short-term measurable reduction in alumni giving as a result."

To give you a sense of the advantage given to legacies and athletics at an elite college it is helpful to consider a document from the treasure trove released before the Harvard admissions case went to trial.

In the Class of 2019, Harvard tagged 1,378 applicants special circumstances. Those included athletes, legacies, and the "Dean's Interest List," a confidential group of applicants mostly related to top donors. Their acceptance rate was 41 percent. That compared to a 4.2 percent acceptance rate for everyone else.

Think about it this way: Harvard sent out only 1,781 acceptances to the 30,000 domestic students who applied for the Class of 2019. One-third of them, 567 to be exact, went to students with special circumstances.

That's exactly the type of surefire admission offer that Rick Singer's clients were looking for. "What made it very attractive to so many families is I created a guarantee," Singer said in his plea hearing soon after indictments were handed down in the Varsity Blues case. Singer created that guarantee through his side door at a much lower price point than a multi-million-dollar donation made to the university that might have helped an applicant through the back door.

Parents seem to think that giving gobs of money in exchange for an admission offer is widespread in higher education, although deans deny the practice is as prevalent as the public is led to believe. In the wake of the Varsity Blues scandal the *New York Times* reported that an "entry-level" gift for admissions is $10 million or more, a figure that several admissions deans dispute. The deans told me they track the admissions decisions of many VIP applicants of interest to university fund-raisers, trustees, and the president, but spots aren't sold to the highest bidder. "We deny plenty of students that the development office would have preferred we admit," one dean told me.

Still, there is evidence money influences admissions decisions at selective universities. Officials at the University of Southern California traded emails about how much money applicants' families could donate, according to documents filed in the Varsity Blues case. Applicants were described with notes such as "given 2 million already," "1 mil pledge," "previously donated $25k to Heritage Hall," and "father is surgeon." Northwestern's president admitted to the student newspaper in 2019 that he reviews more than five hundred admissions applications every year including legacy applicants and students whose family members have donated to the university.

Daniel Golden, in his 2006 book about the influence of money in admissions offices called *The Price of Admission*, uncovered perhaps the most famous case of preference for a big-money donor: Jared Kushner, the son-in-law of President Donald Trump and a senior White House advisor. Kushner's father donated $2.5 million to Harvard in 1998, and also met with the university's president. Soon afterward, Jared was accepted on what administrators at his high school described as a less-than-stellar academic record.

📖

Soon after the Varsity Blues scandal broke in March 2019, I reached out to Nicole in North Carolina. It was a few days before colleges would start releasing their acceptances for regular decision. This was the odd lull in the admissions calendar for seniors. They sprint through the fall, just to wait out the winter, only to rush again in April to make their final decision. It was yet another advantage that colleges have in the game. Nicole and her mom were holding multiple dates in April for campus visits. They just didn't know where.

Nicole looked restless. The hopeful certainty of the fall had turned into the actual reality of the spring. She realized she was lucky in that she already had three offers in hand from UNC–Chapel Hill, NC State, and Northeastern. But she was still holding out hope that her ticket would be punched by Dartmouth.

I asked her what she thought about Varsity Blues. She told me when she first heard the news, she looked to see if any of the schools she applied to were caught up in the scandal. None were.

"I would've been furious if one of those slots could have gone to me," she told me. I thought the scandal would have persuaded Nicole and the other seniors I was following that the game needed a whole new set of rules, one that leveled the playing field for them.

But unfortunately the scandal just reaffirmed Nicole's belief—and that of many parents I talked with—that going to a brand-name school mattered. There were people willing to risk going to jail to get their kids into a top school. Nicole and other high-achieving strivers were still willing to play the game by the rules colleges had set—provided, of course, they won in the end.

6

Comparing Grades

High School Matters

The United States is home to some 25,000 public and private high schools. The variety is staggering. Small rural schools with fifty seniors, no Advanced Placement classes, and a focus on sending students to community college. Rich suburban schools with thousands of students, dozens of sport teams, and expensive cars in the parking lot with college stickers. Private and charter schools. Catholic schools. Boarding schools. Public schools that spend $15,000 per student; and others in the same state that spend $6,000.

During my time inside admissions offices I quickly discovered that the unit being evaluated was less often the *applicant* than the applicant's *high school*.

Colleges, in essence, are recruiting and evaluating high schools, not students. Admissions officers target certain high schools for fall visits to court prospective students. They know some high schools so well they can easily recall a counselor's name. Before admissions decisions are sent to students, most selective colleges sort their applicant pool by high school. The high schools that traditionally send the most applicants receive another look to see how the admits, denials, and wait list offers are distributed throughout the senior class. That's when many top colleges conduct a round of "counselor calls" to give advance notice to certain "feeder" high schools before decisions are sent to their students.

The college–high school relationship is pivotal because counselors are brokers who advise teenagers on their college list and can steer them toward a college (or discourage them from applying). History shows that applicants tend to travel in clumps from their high schools: campuses receive applications from several thousand high schools, not tens of thousands. When Human Capital Research, an admissions consulting firm, analyzed 130,000 applications to a brand-name college over the span of a decade, it found that just 18 percent of high schools were responsible for 75 percent of applications and 79 percent of admitted students.

For would-be applicants, the high school context in which you're ultimately judged presents a Catch-22. You're helped by applying to colleges that know your high school and counselors, but hindered if you don't stack up well against classmates who are also applying. Yet if you apply to colleges that are less popular among your classmates, admissions officers often aren't familiar with your high school. If a college really wants you, they'll look past that, but for some applicants the lack of familiarity can be a disadvantage. It's another contradiction in a business full of them, so you and your counselor should use both the application and outreach to colleges to tell them everything you can about your high school.

One question I get frequently from applicants and their parents is how colleges compare students from different high schools. The simple answer is they don't—at least not in explicit side-by-side comparisons. What they try to do is measure an applicant's academic and personal achievements based on what courses are available at their specific high school. But yet, as they review hundreds of files over many months, admissions officers can't help making comparisons between high schools and taking that into account as they build a class. You see it when they agonize over accepting even above-average students from less-rigorous high schools. A key metric Davidson uses to judge the quality of a high school is the proportion of students who go to college. That number determines how "deep" admissions officers want to go into a school's senior class to admit students—the more students who go to college from that high school, the more willing they are to take a chance in accepting students ranked lower in the class.

The best hope for applicants is that the admissions officer reading their file knows something about their high school from yearly visits. Admissions officers are assigned regions of the country and travel mostly during the fall to recruit prospective students. They don't visit every high school in that region, just the ones that send lots of applicants every year or the ones they wish would send more.

If an admissions officer from a school on your list does visit your high school, remember that person may be the reader of your application, so make time for the visit. Attendance at these sessions also helps colleges track demonstrated interest. A high school counselor in Colorado told me that one of her students had applied early action to Tulane but was absent from school the day a representative from the university visited. Tulane deferred him. When the counselor called Tulane, she was told the student didn't seem very interested. She sent a screen shot of his perfect attendance except for that one day. A few weeks later he was accepted.

Applicants interested in a selective college that doesn't visit their high school might find it more difficult to get accepted. That's the dilemma facing Chris, the senior from Pennsylvania. After his impromptu visit to Gettysburg College over summer vacation, he put the liberal arts college at the top of his list.

In mid-September of his senior year, Chris was scheduled for the obligatory meeting with his school counselor to talk about his plans after graduation. He was reluctant to go. "The counselor wasn't much help when I was getting ready for the SAT," he told me later.

On the morning of the meeting, Chris walks into the suite of administrative offices at his school, a run-down beige cinder-block box from the early 1970s. Unlike prosperous public schools with sizeable college counseling offices teeming with guidebooks and college brochures, Chris's counselor is tucked away in a cramped office. It's a subtle message to these students that counseling at this school is less about what's next and more about the social and emotional problems in their lives right now.

While Chris waits, he scans the list of colleges visiting the school that fall. Seventeen colleges are on the list. Most of them are schools close by. Gettysburg isn't on the list. Nor is any other selective college.

Few colleges in general visit high schools like Chris's. It is rural. It is poor. It is small (about 100 students in the senior class). And only 30 percent of the previous year's class went directly on to college. It's just not worth the time or money for a college to send someone. In the fall of his senior year, Chris was more likely to see a military recruiter than a college representative roaming the hallways.

Suburban high schools welcome as many college representatives in a *day* as visit Chris's school in September and October. Even though colleges say they want to find diamonds in the rough with Chris's scholastic record—a 1310 on the SAT and A average—they rarely do because they either don't look hard enough or they can't come to terms with lowering the institution's SAT average. If Chris were in a different high school—a suburban, affluent, competitive school—he would have an entirely difference experience. Dozens of representatives from colleges would have come to visit, counselors would have pushed a wider range of colleges earlier in his high school career, and he'd have five selective colleges on his list, not one. It's just one example of how the high school sometimes matters more than the applicant.

But Chris's path to college is about to change.

After a few minutes of waiting, the counselor greeting Chris is not the one near retirement and largely indifferent to his college plans. This time he is met by a woman who looks like she could be in high school herself. She introduces herself as Michelle Bailey, a 2017 graduate of Franklin & Marshall College in Lancaster, Pennsylvania. She explains she has been assigned to Chris's school for the next two years as part of the National College Advising Corps, a national nonprofit that places hundreds of college advisors in underserved schools to supplement full-time counselors.

"Ms. Bailey took one look at my grades and SAT scores," Chris recalled, "and told me there were a lot more colleges out there than the ones coming to the school in the fall."

Low-key and quick to smile, Michelle had spent the previous year on a Fulbright scholarship teaching English at a rural elementary school in Taiwan. But she was drawn back to the U.S. by the National College Advising Corps. Five years earlier, one of the program's advisors had helped Michelle get to F&M. She grew up not too far away in Central Pennsylvania and went to a high school much like the one where she finds herself now working. In Chris, she sees someone similar to herself in high school: a high-achiever but one lacking direction in the college search.

Michelle thumbs through Chris's transcript. His senior-year schedule is tough, at least for this high school. Chris is taking four AP courses: American history, literature, chemistry, and computer science. That is *every* AP course the school offers. Think of the two other seniors you met in earlier chapters: Grace and Nicole. Grace's school in San Francisco offers twenty-seven Advanced Placement courses. Nicole's in North Carolina has twenty-nine (and two other high schools in her *same* district offer more than thirty).

The number of AP courses, indeed the entire curriculum available to Chris, is out of his control. What happens in a high school classroom day to day is determined by individual schools at the local level. Because schools are also locally funded through property taxes, the strength of the curriculum is usually a proxy for wealth. As the former MIT admissions director B. Alden Thresher wrote in his book about admissions, "most of the real screening" for selective colleges is "rooted in the home and school environment of children from infancy on."

When Chris left the meeting with Michelle, Gettysburg was still at the top of his list. On Michelle's suggestion, he added another elite liberal arts school to his list: Lafayette College, thirty miles from home in Easton, Pennsylvania. Chris knows his grades and SAT score make him a competitive applicant to both schools. Football might also help. Now the question is how admissions officers will judge his high school academic experience at a small, under-resourced high school in comparison to applicants from top suburban high schools.

An applicant's high school is the foundation of two of the most important criteria in admissions: grades and depth and breadth of courses. For those colleges that require the ACT/SAT, the test score provides a third critical metric. That score is also tied to the high school since test results are closely correlated with family income, and so, too, with school boundaries.

Even in holistic review, those three measures provide admissions officers with the tools for a "rough sorting" of applications—to separate competitive applicants from the not-so-competitive right off the bat. Selective colleges favor grades and test scores because thousands of statistical studies over several decades indicate they predict a student's first-year grades, and in some cases, grade-point average throughout college.

But the metrics also present problems. For one thing, there is no common high school curriculum, even within states. For another, there isn't a standardized grading scale.

Advanced Placement and International Baccalaureate courses are one way top colleges measure the quality of a high school. AP Calculus, in particular, has become the strongest signal of preparedness for an elite college. Eight in 10 college students who completed AP Calculus did so because they thought it would look good on their college application. In 2019, 67 percent of freshmen at Harvard reported they took AP Calculus in high school, and another 30 percent took some kind of calculus class. That's *all* first-year students at Harvard, no matter their major. But consider this: only half of American high schools offer a calculus course. The vast differences between what high schools offer put selective colleges in a bind. How do they balance their desire to have a diverse and excellent student body against what courses were available to applicants?

Grading itself in high schools is equally convoluted. Some use a 10-point increment on a 100-point scale. Others use a 7-point one.

At many the 5.0 has become the new 4.0. Points are added to GPAs for any combination of honors, AP, or dual-enrollment courses. Schools have multiple valedictorians as well as students with all As and a few Bs who rank below the top tenth. And then there are a handful of private schools, like Saint Ann's in Brooklyn, that don't even give grades but instead write full-page reports for each student.

At the same time, grades everywhere have steadily risen since Generation X—the parents of today's college applicants—left high school. About half of American teenagers now graduate high school with an A average, compared with fewer than 40 percent in 1998, according to a report by researchers at the College Board. Other studies have reached similar conclusions, all using different sets of high school grades. When students apply to college, the degree to which their grades might have been inflated is often unclear to someone reading the application. And the high school profiles that are supposed to provide a guide to admissions officers aren't much help: many omit the range of grades for the senior class.

When the GPAs of applicants are all in the A range, it's difficult for admissions officers to make distinctions among students. That's when test scores offer another measure for interpreting grades and differentiating between applicants. But test scores present their own set of problems. Students tend to score higher the more often they take the test, and in the case of the SAT, over 50 percent of test-takers sit for the exam several times. A study by three economists of 10 million–plus SAT takers between 2006 and 2014 found that those who retook the test lifted their score by nearly 50 points.

Sitting for the test multiple times also helps the applicant's so-called superscore, the number that combines the highest verbal and math score, no matter the test date. Roughly 8 out of 10 colleges use the superscore in admissions. The study found an applicant's superscore increased by 88 points, on average, because of multiple takes.

So, taking the SAT early and often *could improve* the chances of getting into a top college (more on that in a minute). But who retakes the test varies greatly. Higher-income students—from families making over $100,000—tend to sit for the test multiple times, as do girls, white students, and Asian American teenagers. Perhaps the most interesting finding from this study was that students who scored just below a round-number threshold were more likely to retake the test. Students who got a 1380 instead of a 1400, for instance, believe that 20-point gap could make the difference between getting in or not to their dream college.

The question for students is whether sitting again and again for the SAT or ACT will turn out to make the difference for them. The answer? It depends. Exactly how colleges use test scores in their decisions is often shrouded behind the cloak of holistic admissions, and even more difficult to figure out after colleges adopted test-optional policies in the pandemic.

One survey of admissions officers by their national association found that an improvement of 20 points on the math section of the SAT or 10 points on the verbal section can significantly improve a student's likelihood of admission, especially for students with high scores applying to selective schools. Knowing that might make you want to do everything you can to improve your test score, even by a little.

But another study found that the greatest variation in SAT scores among accepted students happens at the extremes in terms of selectivity—at uber-selective schools and the least selective schools. What that means is that top colleges accept students with a perfect 1600 as well as plenty of applicants closer to an 1100, a score which might be the norm at less selective schools.

The admissions officers I observed and those I talked with at other schools often use test scores as a counterbalance in their decision-making—almost as a confirmation of the grades and high school curriculum. Test scores are seen as only a snapshot in time in comparison to the four years displayed on a high school transcript. It's those high school grades and course rigor, research shows, that measure more accurately academic engagement, discipline, and inquisitiveness. The SAT and ACT merely supplement that material with more in-depth information on a student's cognitive skills.

Where does all this leave you, the anxious applicant, the puzzled parent?

My advice if you're applying to a test-optional school is to take the SAT or ACT only if you think your score might add context to your grades. Then, if you can, take the test at least twice. Given that most colleges use superscores anyway, you have nothing to lose. Worry less about your overall score and more about where your score places you in the range of the schools you're considering. Nothing is a sure bet, but your chances are better if your score is in the top quartile for the school and that's particularly the case for girls. A quick glance at the *U.S. News* rankings shows the middle 50 percent of test scores for a particular college. You should be above that figure, even if you have good grades and a solid curriculum to back up your scores, if you want to truly compete in the applicant pool of a top college.

The test score is the one significant metric applicants still have some control over during the college search. After all, it's too late for a do-over of grades from sophomore year. And the courses teenagers take their senior year of high school are largely the result of their course schedule from back in eighth grade.

Chris likes to tinker with computers. He also loves American history. His dream, he told Michelle Bailey one day in the fall of his senior year, was to major in computer science but also take a healthy dose of history classes.

But like other passengers in the college search I met, Chris had scant information about what it meant to major in something. Nor did he understand what it entailed to study computer science at a small liberal arts college, where he couldn't declare a major until his second year after taking a general curriculum across subjects.

A generation or two ago, Chris wouldn't even have considered a liberal arts college to study computer science. Those small campuses used to pride themselves on majors in the humanities (English and history), social sciences (sociology and economics), and the natural sciences (biology and chemistry). But since the Great Recession, students have shunned humanities majors in favor of vocational majors in computing, business, and health. The rising cost of college has made higher education more of a trans-action for this generation, who see a college degree primarily as a means to a job. Less selective colleges were the first to see this growth in computer science and professional majors as providing a job after graduation. But now this trend is the case even at top lib-eral arts schools. Over the eight years leading up to 2019, the share of humanities majors on top liberal arts campuses dropped from one-third to under a quarter.

For passengers such as Chris, not only is the contest to get into a brand-name college fierce, but so too is the competition to secure a spot in a popular major. At liberal arts colleges, Chris's major isn't much of a factor in admissions because the schools don't typically admit students by major. But many large universities do, particularly in high-demand fields, such as computer science and engineering. If Chris were applying to the University of Washington, for instance, he'd probably get in, but might not secure a seat in computer sci-ence because he didn't take the right set of math and science courses in high school. And once on campus he couldn't consider switching majors to computer science: UW and other big schools make it clear in their admissions materials that it's nearly impossible.

Because passengers focus on the college search later in their high school careers they miss the pre-game warm-ups to get ready. Looking back, Chris wishes he had met a counselor like Michelle Bailey a few years earlier. Perhaps he would have looked at enroll-ing in advanced courses outside of his high school. Maybe he would have taken the SAT more than once. Or he could have started his college search earlier so he wouldn't feel so rushed now.

A few weeks after his meeting, Chris tells his mom, Melissa, that he wants to apply to Gettysburg. She liked Gettysburg, too, but she also knows that its sticker price would be much higher than the two state schools she favored, Penn State and East Stroudsburg Uni-versity. She just didn't know how much higher until she and Chris sat down at their kitchen table to look up Gettysburg's tuition and fees.

"Seventy thousand dollars," Melissa says in her most reasonable voice. A single year for Chris at Gettysburg would cost $25,000 more than she earns in a year.

"A little over sixty-seven thousand to be exact," Chris corrects her. He already knew the figure. Chris found it while browsing Gettysburg's website a few days earlier when he emailed the college's football coach to see if he could get a spot on the team. The coach told Chris he was interested but didn't make any promises. Unlike many other athletes, Chris couldn't apply early. He needed time to compare financial aid offers from several schools.

"No matter where my super-intelligent, lovely, dreamer son likes to go," Melissa told me later, "we have to be realistic."

To placate his mom, Chris applied to Penn State and East Stroudsburg in October. Both schools accepted him within a few weeks. In early November, Chris took a road trip to see an old high school friend at Moravian College in Bethlehem, an hour from home. It was the Saturday of a big rivalry football game with nearby Muhlenberg College, and Chris thought it would be a good chance to check out the campus. His friend spent the day trying to persuade him to apply to Moravian. It was closer to home than Gettysburg. He could play football. And Moravian would give him a boatload of financial aid to land someone with his high grades and test scores. He could stand out in the classroom and on the football field.

Like other seniors I met who were passengers in the college search, Chris was being propelled by those around him: his mom, Michelle Bailey, and now his friend at Moravian. Chris and I spoke several times during his senior year. Whenever we talked, he was certain he'd land at a college somewhere the following year, but his path for getting there was uncertain and always changing. He was looking for the path of least resistance. He wasn't driving himself crazy like Nicole or Grace to find the perfect college at the top of some ranking. But he was also missing opportunities because of his passive approach. When Michelle suggested he apply to F&M because she knew they awarded generous aid based on financial need, he declined. He had his list of schools and was done adding to it.

In many ways, Chris and other passengers avoid the choice overload that tends to overwhelm drivers. The never-ending search for the right college by drivers not only requires time, effort, and money, but it also comes with high expectations and anxiety that, as we'll see, leads to self-blame if things don't work out. Parents of passengers shouldn't expect the circumstances of the college search to radically transform their child into a driver. My experience is that passengers are ambitious in their own way in that they often do end up making a good match. They want to participate in the college search, but on their own schedule. Your job as a parent is to gently nudge at the right times, not nag all the time.

In the month after his Moravian trip, however, Chris's enthusiasm about Gettysburg was fading fast. Maybe his friend was right. He at least needed to see what Moravian had to offer. In the last few weeks of 2018, Chris applied to the final three schools left on his list: Moravian, Gettysburg, and Lafayette. When I spoke with him in February, Gettysburg seemed to be in his rearview mirror. An acceptance had arrived from Moravian along with a letter outlining his financial aid.

"I haven't heard from Gettysburg yet," Chris told me, sounding disappointed.

And he wouldn't. Like most selective colleges, Gettysburg would send out its admissions decisions all at once in March. It can do that because it's confident it can fill a class from those invitations. Less selective schools, such as Moravian, were continually admitting students and spitting out aid letters because their yield was so low. They were forced to flood the zone with offers throughout admissions season hoping enough would stick by May 1.

Moravian gave Chris a sizeable chunk of money: $36,000 in discount coupons (what the college called scholarships) and another $8,500 in state grants and federal loans. Chris and his family would still need to come up with another $9,000. Even so, that was better than the $2,000 he got from the state school his mom was pushing. East Stroudsburg expected Chris's mom to contribute $16,000 toward the total price tag, about *a third of her yearly income*. Don't assume, as Chris's mom did, that the public college is always the cheapest option, especially in states known for high tuition at their public colleges, such as Pennsylvania, Illinois, Ohio, and New Jersey.

When I spoke to Chris in February, he seemed ready to commit to Moravian. Why not wait? I asked him. After all, he didn't need to submit a deposit until May 1 and by then he'd have an answer from Gettysburg and Lafayette. I was beginning to wonder if Chris would "undermatch." It's a term he had never heard before, but the idea has garnered plenty of attention and debate in higher education. It describes students who deliberately choose not to apply to or attend the best college they can get into based on their academic qualifications.

Slightly more than a quarter of high school seniors choose to go to less selective schools, according to one prominent study from the National Bureau of Economic Research. Chris is a textbook case of the reasons students decide to trade down. They might want to stay close to home. They might want to go to the least expensive college, which is particularly true of middle-class and poor students. Or maybe they are worried they won't be able to keep up with their classmates or fit in socially.

Sometimes students rebuff the most selective colleges because they get a lot of money or a free ride elsewhere. Students who are academically qualified to go to a seller end up undermatching to get money from a buyer.

Here was the choice Chris would likely face and why he was in danger of undermatching: Gettysburg is a top-50 liberal arts college; Moravian is ranked a hundred spots lower. At Gettysburg, Chris's SAT score would put him just below the average of incoming students; at Moravian he would be 250 points above. Gettysburg was a good match for Chris; Moravian would be an undermatch for him.

Why is undermatching a problem? Some of the most important learning that occurs in college comes from interactions with your peers. If you're surrounded by students who aren't engaged in their studies or campus life or are indifferent about graduating in four years, you might fall into that trap as well, no matter your academic achievements in high school.

The opposite also happens. Overmatching occurs when students end up at colleges that are above their league academically. About a quarter of students overmatch. Overmatchers tend to be from wealthier families who are often sought after by colleges that need full-pay students. Some top colleges are happy to take below-average students who can pay the entire tuition bill (or close to it) and parents are happy to pay to ensure their child attends a selective school. But one worry students should have in overmatching is that if they're a poor fit academically, they likely won't keep up in class once on campus and risk not graduating on time, or at all.

One view in the world of admissions is that the SAT and the ACT offer a critical balance for assessing students who come from high schools of widely varying quality. But that perspective isn't universally shared. There is a long-running and heated debate in the admissions profession over whether test scores are needed to compare high schools or should be used at all in the selection process.

Numerous studies show that grades by themselves are a better predictor of a student's success in college than test scores on their own. That's why many colleges feel comfortable dropping the SAT/ACT as an admissions requirement without jeopardizing academic quality. But studies also show that both metrics taken together are the best predictor of success—better than either measure alone. That's why other deans—led mostly by elite colleges and the leaders of the College Board and ACT—believe that test scores provide an added insight when evaluating students.

What everyone agrees on is that the architects of the SAT never intended it to be the high-stakes assessment for admissions it has become. As journalist Nicholas Lemann outlines in his book *The Big Test*, the SAT was first administered in 1926 to measure innate mental ability, or aptitude. Thus, its name: Scholastic Aptitude Test. In the decades that followed, the president of Harvard University saw the SAT as the great equalizer, a test that would allow Ivy League universities to diversify their student bodies based on intelligence rather than family connections (well, at least to a point). The SAT was narrowly tailored for elite universities to find smart kids in way-off places who didn't go to Eastern boarding schools.

But as the slice of the population entering college widened in the second half of the twentieth century, schools embraced the SAT and the ACT as a means of making distinctions among growing numbers of applicants. The tests became cemented in the admissions process when *U.S. News* chose test scores as an important ingredient in the college rankings. Colleges felt compelled to report high average scores in order to retain their place in the higher education hierarchy and keep applications flowing.

Alongside the SAT and ACT, another mainstay of the admissions process that has attempted to standardize the high school experience is the Common Application. When the Common App, as it's known, debuted in 1975, it was used by only a handful of schools. Today, the Common App is pervasive in competitive college admissions thanks to the Internet. Walk into almost any high school counseling office and you're likely to see a wall map of the nearly nine hundred Common App schools that dot the landscape in every state. In the 2018–19 application cycle, more than 1 million students completed 5.3 million applications using the Common App.

The Common App was built on the assumption that the high school experience is similar enough across the country that a form providing ten boxes for extracurricular activities, a selection of seven essay prompts, and five lines for honors could sum up a student's achievements. Perhaps when the application was created in the 1970s the lives of high school students were alike, at least among those applying to a select group of fifteen colleges. But the American high school experience that today's five-page Common App is supposed to reveal is anything but uniform.

For today's teenagers, the college application is a transaction, an exercise in counting up activities and checking off boxes on a list. It's a constant game of one-upmanship encouraged by the blank spaces on the application and the "brag sheets" that students complete for their high school counselors to use when writing a recommendation. Applicants change behavior based on what they think colleges want, often pushed by their parents. Students know they are trapped in a selection system managed by an application they don't approach as revealing the evolving story of their lives, but rather as blank spaces that must be filled in. They respond accordingly.

"Let us acknowledge the anxiety our words and policies cause," David Coleman, the College Board's president, told hundreds of college admissions officers, high school principals, and counselors at the organization's annual meeting in October 2018.

Coleman conceded that the College Board itself needed to reduce worry over the SAT and Advanced Placement. Research released at the meeting showed that a student's academic improvement in college leveled out at five AP courses. In other words, taking eight or ten AP courses doesn't really influence how well applicants end up doing in college, yet some admissions offices still tally AP courses as a sign of rigor. Coleman also took aim at the Common App, suggesting it reduce the number of extracurricular activities on the form to just three.

"We need to do more," Coleman said, "to stop the madness that has arisen around college admissions." It was a little rich coming from the head of a $1.3 billion operation that sits at the exact center of America's college madness.

Parents don't often have much choice about where their children go to high school. But what if you do? What if you can move to a better school district where your high-achieving offspring might just be average in a competitive high school? Or what if you can choose a charter school or afford a small private school where your child can stand out?

Research studies on what is known as the "big fish/little pond" effect have found that when it comes to getting into a selective college, students are better off being the big fish in a small pond. According to the research, applicants from the best high schools with legions of smart students clustered near the top of the class and a vast menu of rigorous courses available to them face tougher odds to gain admission to elite universities because so much is expected of them in the admissions process.

Does that mean if you're a parent you should pull your child out of the best high school unless they're an academic superstar? Not at all. As you have seen, a host of factors determine admission into a top college. My advice is that if you go to a competitive high school and aren't a star student be realistic about your college list. Understand who are the buyers and sellers on that list, especially if you can afford the tuition price. There are plenty of buyers looking to make their enrollment goal with average students who can pay the bills, and in the end, might be a better match for you than a seller.

Like it or not, admissions officers can't know much about an individual student, but they can know a lot about a specific high school. Chalk it up as another part of the admissions process that is (at least mostly) out of your control. Yes, knowing how it affects your application can help you strategize your college list. But also remember it's just high school, not your whole life. Enjoy homecoming, join student government, make friends, take classes that challenge you—and focus on the things you can shape in your college application. Which high school you go to is rarely one of them.

7

Finding Diamonds

Regular Decision

Emory University was founded as a small religious college in rural Georgia in 1836, but it owes its success today to a fizzy drink invented decades later: Coca-Cola.

In 1915, the founder of Coke gave the school a million dollars and seventy-five acres outside Atlanta for a new campus. Sixty-four years later, the company's longtime president, Robert Woodruff, who had built Coca-Cola into one of the world's most recognized brands, donated $105 million to Emory. At the time, it was the largest single gift to a university in American history. The gift, along with hundreds of millions of dollars that followed from the Woodruffs and their foundations, transformed Emory from a well-known regional university to one with a global reputation, growing selectivity, and a top-25 *U.S. News* ranking.

By the time I returned to Emory in early January 2019 to sit with admissions officers, they were facing the clearest result of their increased popularity: thirty thousand applications had arrived for regular decision, a 9 percent uptick from the previous year.

The university had already enrolled 653 students through two early admissions rounds. That was about half of its incoming class. That meant Emory needed to admit an additional 3,800 students for the 721 spots it had left. From here on out, admissions officials would be looking to reject about eight or nine applicants out of every ten they reviewed.

The fate of most students is sealed in the first evaluation of their materials. After spending five to ten minutes reviewing an application, admissions officers will either accept, reject, or in some cases put the student on the wait list—a decision that won't change before the applicant gets notified in March. A small group of applicants—probably around a thousand or so—will remain on the bubble, moving in and out of the acceptance pile almost until the time decisions are locked down days before they are sent to students.

Like other newcomers to the class of top universities, Emory is much harder to get into today for Generation Z than it was for their Generation X parents. Still, it's not as impossible as the numbers make it sometime seem. Because these regular decision acceptances are invitations, and not binding like ED, Emory must admit about three times as many students as it needs to fill the rest of its incoming class. The admit pool in every class is still made up of applicants who don't arrive with any admissions "hooks" and do everything right in high school: take the AP classes available to them, rank at the top of their class, score 1400s on the SAT, and have a deep and earnest commitment to a sport, student government, music, or the debate team.

But even for those bedrock applicants, the bar to get in seems to rise every admissions season. As Emory is flooded with more applications, admissions officers are forced to turn down more of the students they know full well are exceedingly capable of doing the work and would probably thrive at Emory. The applicants who truly stand out are not just seniors who "maxed out" on their high school curriculum and attained a top SAT score. It's the ones who have done all that but also have some sort of interest or talent that comes through in their list of activities, essay, or recommendations. Again, it's the depth and consistency of the story that the application tells about a student.

Just after nine on a cold January morning in Atlanta, Giselle Martin and Jetaun Davis begin reviewing applications in clusters by high school. Giselle is in charge of the Mid-Atlantic territory for

Emory, and one of the first applicants they evaluate is a student who wants to major in economics. His GPA is 3.67 (according to Emory's recalculation). The transcript shows a rising trend in grades after a C-plus and some Bs in the first two years of high school. He scored a 1570 on the SAT.

At first glance, the teenager is the type of solid applicant the admissions officers will see often today. What really makes this one stand out, however, are the details in his activities (two sports), essay (discovers bargain shopping while on a routine errand for his mom and turns it into an intellectual game), and recommendations (helped build a technology lab for the community center where he volunteered). "What in the world," Giselle asks, "how did he manage all of this?" He's marked ACCEPT (and will eventually enroll after turning down an acceptance from Princeton, an indication of the company that Emory now competes with in admissions).

Applicants like this one are fairly straightforward and easy calls for Giselle and Jetaun, much like those on the opposite end of the application spectrum who clearly aren't competitive in the pool. Where I see them and their colleagues get bogged down is with the applicants on the edges: those who are close to the admissions line, applicants who are "spiky" and excel in one particular area, or who have personal attributes that are important to Emory.

Early in their review, they land on an applicant from a high school Giselle knows well from her fall recruiting trips. Without even looking at the high school's profile, Giselle tells Jetaun that it offers the rigorous International Baccalaureate curriculum. But when Giselle flips through the student's transcript, she notices the senior hasn't taken any IB classes. The applicant has a combined SAT score of 1360—650 on the verbal portion of the exam and a 710 on the math—a good score, but one that still puts her in the bottom half of the typical students accepted to Emory. Her 3.95 grade-point average tells a different story. It puts her in the top half of the admitted class.

The three primary metrics admissions officers use are giving different signals to Giselle and Jetaun. The applicant has terrific grades but in a mediocre curriculum with a so-so test score by

Emory's standards. In all, it suggests to them a weaker chance for getting in.

For most applicants to most colleges, grades and test scores align. In other words, the test score makes sense with the grades on the transcript and vice versa. One study from 2011 of more than 150,000 students nationwide found that some 60 percent of applicants to college have test scores consistent with their academic performance in high school. The remaining students in that study, however, had a significant gap between the two metrics—either high test scores combined with low grades or low test scores along with high grades—much like the application Giselle and Jetaun are reviewing.

That applicant, as both a girl and as an African American, epitomizes the type of student whose grades and test scores are more prone to be inconsistent. Female applicants along with black and Latino students are likelier to have higher GPAs and lower test scores. Meanwhile, students—especially boys—who come from families making more than $100,000 and whose parents have graduate degrees are likelier to have lower GPAs and higher SAT scores (it's been well-established that SAT scores are highly correlated with family wealth).

What researchers find is that students with relatively low GPAs compared to their SAT scores often take more rigorous courses in high school. The reverse is true for students who have high GPAs, but low test scores. This is why the most important thing teenagers can do to improve their prospects at a selective college is to take the toughest courses they can in high school, not focus as much on prepping for the SAT. Once in those courses, aim for the best grades possible. It's usually better to get a B in a difficult class than an A in an easy course.

As Giselle digs into the transcript of the applicant with the 3.95, she finds the number is less impressive than it seemed at first glance, even though the girl is ranked sixth in her senior class. "This is a classic 3.95," Giselle tells Jetaun, "where you go undercover" by taking easier classes.

Even though the applicant is interested in majoring in math and statistics, she is taking only one math course in her senior year: pre-calculus. The student completed honors geometry and algebra in earlier years and earned As, but Giselle finds she hasn't taken enough math overall or "challenged" herself. "If she didn't want to do IB," Giselle said, "she should have beefed up in the math areas."

The recommendations from the applicant's teachers and counselor are short and vague. One letter from a teacher is addressed to "Dear Prestigious Academic Institution's Admissions Department." The counselor's recommendation essentially repeats the girl's résumé, and concludes by telling Giselle and Jetaun that the girl is "the ideal student for a highly competitive college or university with the ability to be successful in all future endeavors."

The letters are typical for a public high school where students usually don't meet with their counselor more than once or twice a year and teachers, especially the popular ones, are overwhelmed with requests for recommendations from seniors (hint: ask teachers during your junior year). Recommendation letters give admissions officers the opportunity to read between the lines of a student's application. The best ones give detailed information other parts of the application can't. They give specific examples and stories about how hard the applicant worked for a grade, how a student faced adversity in a course or in an activity, or how engaged the applicant was in learning.

When choosing a teacher to write a recommendation, consider the following among those you might ask: a teacher in a class where you had to work hard for a grade; a teacher outside the subject you want to major in to show your breadth of interests; or a teacher in a major subject area you had twice during high school to show your growth. Overall, admissions officers want to read a letter from someone who can adequately describe your weaknesses but also detail your potential.

The recommendation letter is yet another piece of the application where an applicant's high school can make a difference in admissions. When John Schwarz, the assistant director of MIT's institutional research office, was studying for his doctorate at Notre Dame, he analyzed more than 17,000 recommendation letters to a selective university for his dissertation. He found that the attributes of the letter writer, where they worked, and who they were writing about altered the ultimate content of the letter.

Overall, Schwarz uncovered that letters from nonreligious private schools were longer and provided information admissions officers found helpful—elaborating, for example, on course content or describing with narratives what made the student unique. Meanwhile, letters from traditional public schools devoted most of their space to "procedural elements, or elaboration of information contained elsewhere in the application, like extracurricular engagement or the applicant's course-taking," Schwarz wrote.

When Schwarz dug further into the background of the teachers and counselors who wrote the letters he made several provocative discoveries. First, math and science teachers at traditional public schools were less positive in their letters than their colleagues in English or social studies. Second, recommendation letters written by female teachers and counselors were more positive than those written by their male counterparts, even when they were writing about the same applicant. Finally, teachers and counselors, regardless of their gender, wrote both longer and more positive letters for female applicants than male applicants.

Recommendations rarely cause an application to be tossed aside on the spot, although I witnessed one case where a letter did. A counselor discussed at length a disciplinary action taken against a student for using a racial slur. The Common App added a student-conduct question to the form in 2007, and applications marked with some sort of school violation aren't unusual. But in this case what caused the admissions officers to pause (and eventually deny) was that the explanation from the counselor went on for several paragraphs. Colleges want to avoid admitting students who could cause problems on campus, and perhaps with this letter the counselor was signaling to the admissions office that the applicant wasn't worth the trouble.

Because many recommendation letters lack specific details, they end up neither helping nor hurting an applicant's chances of getting in. Admissions officers understand public school counselors oversee large numbers of students, and as a result, most recommendations are generic and short.

But even the extensive and detailed letters that arrive from private schools aren't helpful, either, especially if they are seen as excessive. Take, for example, the three-page, single-spaced letter from a well-known private school on the East Coast that led admissions officers to roll their eyes as they struggled to read it. Some letters are hyperbolic in their descriptions, such as the one private school that described its chorus as the *best in the world*. Those recommendations are about as useful to someone reviewing an application as the one paragraph, dashed-off note that shows a counselor barely knows the student.

The generic recommendations don't end up helping the applicant to Emory with the 3.95 GPA and 1360 SAT. Her window for getting in is quickly closing.

Giselle notes the girl took seven AP courses. But none are in math. Only one is in a science, and that was in AP Environmental Science, which many admissions officers consider the weakest of AP's science curriculum. Jetaun points out that the girl's essay is about her father, who died when she was in elementary school. "I relied heavily on the traits my father possessed and taught me in our short time together—focus, drive, and the determination to excel," the applicant wrote. "That inheritance he left me was everything I needed to succeed."

Giselle pauses. "It's heartbreaking," she says, before adding, almost in a whisper, "I can't do it." She adds a short note to the file: "We'll see much stronger from here." In many ways her comment describes the high school more than the applicant. She types DENY on the summary screen and lets out a sigh. There's no time to ruminate. The pair of admissions officers have at least another fifty applications to get through today.

It's applications like that one, Giselle tells me later, when she most feels the tension between the altruistic ideals that drew her to admissions work and the practical demands of Emory's institutional interests. The applicant's parents didn't go to college. Neither did Giselle's. Her father never made it past sixth grade; her mother went to work after high school.

Born in Cuba, Giselle moved frequently as a child before landing in South Florida for her last two years of high school. When Giselle broached the idea of college, her parents scoffed at the prospect. She hid her college search from her parents, using money from a part-time job in the local public library to pay her application fees. She told her parents the job was a volunteer gig. Giselle was accepted to Agnes Scott College, a women's college in Atlanta. Her parents told her she couldn't go. "They saw it as abandonment," she recalls, "that they were bad parents." Parental expectations and a family's identity and culture often keep first-generation students close to home for college, if they go at all. "I had responsibility for my younger sister," Giselle said. "Leaving would be a major loss to how my already financially stretched family was making do." Giselle pleaded with her parents, telling them they could visit family who lived near Atlanta. They wouldn't budge.

Wearing small oval glasses framed by short dark hair, Giselle recalls her own journey to college in the midst of selecting the next class for Emory. Her parents refused to take her to Agnes Scott for orientation and the start of classes. There would be no traditional drop-off with the family in tow. Giselle bought a one-way Greyhound bus ticket to Atlanta. The day before she was scheduled to leave, her parents changed their mind. "They drove me twelve hours," she says, "in silence." When Giselle's parents left her on campus, "They told me I'd be home in a week." She never looked back.

Giselle graduated from Agnes Scott in 1998 with a degree in

international relations, and then spent three years with IBM as a sales manager. It was a great job at a prestigious Fortune 500 company, but it wasn't a calling. She wanted to help high school students like herself get to college. In 2001, she switched careers, joining the admissions staff at Georgia Tech. A little more than a decade later, she moved to Emory.

It's nearly impossible for admissions officers to avoid viewing applicants through the prism of their own lives. Everyone has a soft spot for someone like themselves. Professional training, paired-reading, and committees are meant to root out bias, but that doesn't make the process necessarily fair, nor is it meant to. On one hand, admissions officers believe they need to account for years of systematic inequities in the American education system. But they also feel compelled to hand out the first honest piece of feedback a teenager has received in eighteen years filled with As and trophies.

Unlike doctors, teachers, or lawyers, there is no specific career path or special certification needed to become an admissions officer. The constant travel to far-flung high schools during the fall and the long hours of reading applications in the winter result in high turnover in a profession where the salary for someone just starting out is $42,000—a figure usually dwarfed by what the students they're recruiting will pay in tuition each year.

Most admissions officers fall into the position at first, often while looking for something to do before graduate school. Sales and marketing, however, are increasingly becoming popular routes into admissions. Jetaun was working as a manager overseeing market research at Yellowpages.com in 2013 when her alma mater, Notre Dame, was looking for someone to improve its online presence and revamp its approach to social media. Jetaun applied. She hoped a job in admissions would complement her aspirations of becoming a life coach. "I thought I could tell students how to be more competitive in applying to Notre Dame," she recalls.

But then she sat in her first admissions committee meeting at Notre Dame. "I saw how many awesome students didn't make the cut," she tells me one morning as we sit at Starbucks on the ground floor of the Emory admissions building. "It completely changed my mind about the advice I give to students. Now I tell them do the best you can, pursue your genuine interests, and let the chips fall where they may."

While admissions offices try to treat applicants from the same high school consistently, how they do so is rather inconsistent. I witnessed some readers review applications by school so they could more easily compare students; others preferred to jump around so they wouldn't get stuck in thinking about the opportunities offered by a single high school.

Consider the application that Jetaun and Giselle review from the same high school of the girl they just denied. This senior has slightly lower grades and test scores but the application grabs Giselle's attention for one reason: it's from an African American boy. None of the nearly dozen applications that Giselle and Jetaun had seen in the last hour were from black males. Emory is not alone in a dearth of applications from African American males. The gender divide on college campuses cuts across racial and ethnic lines, but it is widest among black students, where women outnumber men almost two to one.

This applicant's SAT score is also in the 1300s, but 50 points lower than that of his classmate. His GPA is also lower, a 3.69. He took one fewer AP course than his classmate, and like her, he didn't take any IB courses. He, too, writes his essay about overcoming adversity—his mom was diagnosed with cancer when he was fifteen.

On Emory's 5-point scoring scale, the pair of admissions officers give the applicant a 3 for his curriculum and a 2 for extracurricular activities—the same as the earlier classmate. But they give him two 3s on his recommendations and intellectual curiosity, compared to 2s the earlier applicant received. Again, the numbers are arbitrary scores based on vague measures, but in this case they're enough to get the applicant over the bar. He's in. Meanwhile, his classmate, who ranked some twenty spots higher in the class sits in the deny pile.

Like all things in admissions, applicants aren't judged by only one yardstick. At any one time, admissions officers are looking at individual achievements, applicants' work in the larger context of what is available to them, and finally the way each applicant fits into the needs of the overall class. That's why there is no single admissions formula: the ingredients are always changing depending on a school's needs in a particular year, or even at a particular moment in the selection process.

Most of all, admissions offices cherish what is rare. The two students were never pitted directly against each other, but it can certainly seem that way to the outside world. Decisions like these don't make much sense when they reach the hallways of high schools. The girl with the 1360, a 3.95, and seven AP courses is turned away. The boy with a 1310, a 3.69, and six AP courses is welcomed in. If the decisions stand at the end of the selection cycle, they will get chalked up as another example of just how inexplicable college admissions is.

The application of the male applicant is one case that is evaluated within the larger context of the incoming class rather than through the narrow view of a single high school. What's more, Giselle's familiarity with the high school gives her the confidence to admit a student that, at least on paper, looks weaker than a classmate. But in Emory's applicant pool of tens of thousands of applicants, there isn't as much difference between those seniors as it might seem to students and counselors within a single high school.

The beginning of January is the start of a ten-week sprint for admissions offices, from the moment when regular decision applications arrive to when final decisions go out. For all the advances in recruitment, enrollment managers haven't yet figured out a way to solve one intractable problem: how to add more days to January, February, and March.

For those three months, the home away from home for Emory's gatekeepers is a suite of offices tucked behind the spacious lobby where the university offers information sessions and campus tours for prospective students each weekday (the admissions engine is always humming). The private area is accessed only with a special key card. On this January morning, up and down the narrow hallway that extends half the length of a football field, admissions officers are evaluating applications behind closed doors. Several doors have yellow stickies. Scribbled on them: *Reading. Do Not Disturb.*

Compared to early decision, this regular reading round has a harsher tone and a faster pace. Watching the evaluations unfold offers a microcosmic view of the almost impossible decisions that admissions officers face at elite universities when so few spots remain just halfway through the selection cycle.

Some applications tug at the heart strings. One is from an undocumented immigrant whose father left the violence of his Middle East home soon after 9/11 for the only job he could get in America—at a fast-food restaurant. The applicant wrote in his essay that he accompanied his father to work one day only to find him behind the deep fryer. "I saw firsthand how exhausting the work my father did was," he wrote. At fourteen, the applicant was diagnosed with diabetes. But that didn't slow him down. As the oldest of three, he spent more than twenty hours a week managing the household, all while he took seven AP courses, earned a 3.75 GPA, and scored a 1400 on the SAT. But four Bs during his sophomore and junior year derail his application. "He has taken a strong curriculum," an Emory admissions officer writes in his summary, "but would like to see stronger grades for consideration."

He ends up in the growing pile of rejections.

Other teenagers are drowned in the sea of sameness that is the reality of the applicant pool at a top college. One senior whose parents are lawyers worked a summer job as a pizza delivery driver. It's *something* different. "You don't see that anymore," the admissions officer remarks. Even so, the reader finds the student lacking "a fire for anything." The applicant's 1440 on the SAT, 3.3 GPA, and solid activities—but missing leadership positions that admissions officers like to see—are not good enough.

He ends up on the wait list.

Throughout reading season, admissions officers at Emory and elsewhere describe applicants as *good kids*, *standard*, *steady*, and *kind*. Maybe there is more to each of the students, but the authentic version is hidden beneath layers of the curated portrait upper-middle-income students present to the admissions office, and the one low-income students don't know to present.

One place where applicants could stand out is in their essay, but most are unfortunately mind-numbingly similar. Teenagers have less than two decades of life to write about, and as a result, they often focus on the same things: overcoming an athletic injury, dealing with anxiety, depression, or their sexuality, or discovering themselves on a trip, with a fill-in-the-blank country such as Guatemala or Thailand.

The effort applicants spend writing their essays (and the fees parents pay to have them edited) is often inversely proportional to the time admissions officers devote to reading them. Admissions officers scan essays. When one grabs their attention, they'll have a closer read. Essays help lift candidates at the margins; they very rarely are the thing that gets an applicant in. The essays that stick out do so not because of *what* the applicants write but *how* they write it—with an authentic voice that gives readers a sense of what the student sees, feels, and thinks.

The essays that make an impression are often the ones admissions officers share over lunch breaks in the middle of reading season. One is about a girl who loves orange juice and who is worried about leaving home for college and missing family debates over pulp/no pulp. Another applicant wrote about her interest in the law after watching her parents fight hospital bills following a serious medical diagnosis she received in high school. The best essays are honest slice-of-life stories, both entertaining and serious, that tell admissions officers something they don't learn from another part of the application. They're essays that aren't trying to shoehorn seventeen years into 650 words.

For the Emory admissions staff to labor through hundreds of

files a day during the winter reading season, a chunk of applications needs to be moved quickly to the deny pile, in three or four minutes. But easy denials are not always clear from simply looking at the summary of academic metrics. Someone with high grades and test scores who probably would have been admitted in early decision is suddenly undistinguished in the regular pool.

A boy with a 1500 on the SAT from a "busy school group"—meaning one that sends reams of applications—is moved within four minutes to the deny pile after looking at junior year grades (lots of Bs, B-pluses), a rather run-of-the-mill résumé, and what admissions officers characterize as an essay with "surface-level thinking" about discovering the world through Google while recovering from an injury. Sure, it's a slice-of-life essay, but like everything in admissions, there are no rules.

A girl described as a "glue kid" who brings people together in the background is also shifted to the deny pile with a 1480 SAT score, an upward trend in grades after some Cs in her sophomore year, four AP tests with either a 4 or 5 score, and activities that include the varsity tennis team and acting.

It's not that any of these seniors are weak applicants; they just don't stand out in the larger pool or they're not what the university is looking for at that precise moment. Applicants and their parents "don't see and understand the whole pool like we do," Mark Butt tells me early on January 10, 2019. At that exact moment, Emory has 2,500 applications sitting in the admit pile. Admissions officers still have *another* 18,000 applications to review. Of that group, more than 15,000 will be rejected. "Without seeing the whole pool," Mark adds, "anyone on the outside can't see what stands out."

This is Mark's seventh go-round through reading season at Emory since he arrived in 2013. He is balding with a well-groomed beard, sports a perpetually cheerful demeanor that at times feels like a holdover from his self-described "rambunctious" youth in Canada. Mark's parents didn't go to college. His dad was in the military; his mom was an administrative assistant.

To keep him busy, his parents signed him up for skating lessons, and he fell in love with the sport. The University of Delaware was home to one of the world's leading training sites for figure skaters, so he landed there for college without ever visiting. Because he was on a student visa, he couldn't work off campus. He eventually found an on-campus job as a student tour guide. It was his first foray into the admissions world.

After college, he applied to the University of Pennsylvania's graduate school of education, but didn't have a way to pay for it. Disney on Ice was looking for skaters for a tour in Asia and Australia. Fourteen months on the road provided him the funds to pay for a master's degree in higher education management.

Admissions jobs for non-U.S. citizens were tough to come by. He found one college willing to sponsor his work visa: Ohio University. He traveled for thirty weeks a year to high schools and college fairs around southeast Ohio, West Virginia, and parts of Pennsylvania in a state-issued car, earning $28,000. "It was a great place to learn," he recalled. The work visa was transferable, and a few years later he moved to Johns Hopkins. There's where he first met Emory's admissions dean, John Latting. But working at a highly selective college meant senior admissions officers rarely left. So, Mark decided to jump to the other side of the desk: as a college counselor at a private high school. A place where affluent parents want their kids to go to hyper-selective colleges wasn't a "great fit for a first-generation immigrant," Mark now admits. Two years later he got the Emory job.

While applicants see a rejection as a judgment of their life's choices and accomplishments, Mark and his colleagues view a denial simply as weighing one institutional priority over another. It's why a rejected candidate for one school might be accepted at another even if the two colleges are similarly ranked. Every year, top colleges turn away tens of thousands of students who could succeed on their campuses. It's never clear who is the more qualified, the better fit, the truly deserving—or what any of that would really mean.

If it were clear to admissions officers who should get a spot in the class, and that test scores and grades were the only two measures of an applicant's worthiness, the next applicant in the pool at Emory would be a shoo-in for an acceptance letter.

It's just after 10:30 in the morning on the second Friday of 2019, when Lupe Monterroso, an admissions officer, opens the application. Lupe sets the timer on her iPhone. Seven minutes. When the alert goes off, it's a gentle reminder for Lupe and her reading partner on this day, Nicole Dancz, to move on.

As Lupe pores over the student's transcript, she does a double take. She's not familiar with this high school and the senior class is much bigger than she's used to seeing, around a thousand students. And this applicant ranks number three. Yes, that's right: *third* in a class of a *thousand* students.

The girl has taken more than a dozen AP courses and earned nearly a 4.0 GPA. Her lowest grade in high school was a 91—four years ago in ninth grade (a year Emory doesn't even count in its recalculation formula).

The applicant's SAT score? A near-perfect 1570.

Lupe turns down the soothing music playing in the background on her desktop computer and looks to Nicole. She asks for an evaluation of the applicant's extracurricular activities. The grades, curriculum, and test scores are among the strongest they will probably see on this day. If the selection process were conducted by a computer programmed to look only at the numbers, this student would be an automatic acceptance. But Lupe is reminded of something their boss, John Latting, tells them often: academic metrics are important, but they are not everything.

Nicole gives a run-down of the applicant's extracurricular activities: band, national honor society, tutor. Solid activities, but more like a checklist than a deep commitment to any of them. Nicole notes that the girl wants to be a doctor, but "lists no activities related to pre-med." Lupe suggests scoring the student a 3 out of 5 for activities. Nicole calls it a "weak 3." She wants to knock it down to a 2.

Given the size of the senior class, the recommendations are short and brief. "Nothing usable," Nicole says. She turns to the essay. The applicant writes about conquering the slide on the playground as a child. The essay makes a solid argument—without taking risks you don't achieve success—but like so many essays, it doesn't provide any details that advance the application or provide particulars not supplied elsewhere.

"A missed opportunity," Nicole tells Lupe about the essay. "We didn't learn much about her."

Lupe and Nicole give the applicant a 5 rating for her curriculum; two 3s for her recommendations and intellectual curiosity; and just a 2 for extracurricular activities. Lupe types a few notes in the file, and then gets to the recommendation for where to route her application. "Great kiddo. Incredibly smart," Lupe tells Nicole.

Emory accepts almost half of students with credentials like this student's, but the application illustrates the vagaries of admissions: no special combination of attributes exists that guarantees acceptance. This is an applicant who has clearly excelled in academics, but seemingly at the expense of everything else in her life. She's a flat, one-dimensional student.

"I'm okay with deny." And that's where the girl with nearly a 4.0 and almost a perfect SAT score ends up.

PART THREE

SPRING:
Decision Season

8

Shaping a Class

The Final, Close Calls

On a rainy and raw Tuesday night in late February, as Davidson's vaunted men's basketball team is locked in a late season battle with the University of Dayton, Mike Mansuy is holed up in his office across campus. Mike oversees one of the toughest regions for Davidson's admissions staff—Pennsylvania and New Jersey—where the North Carolina school competes for talented students against a wealth of well-known liberal arts colleges in the Northeast.

On this night, Mike is the last one left in Grey House, the two-story Georgian brick building that houses the admissions office. He is taking yet another look at the pool of applications from one of the top high schools in his territory. He knows these seniors are extremely well qualified, but they also have a host of other choices closer to home. Admit too many of these students and too few show up, and Davidson's yield rate—one of the key metrics that make schools look prestigious—falls.

Early the next morning, Mike joins three colleagues to discuss the fate of his applicants as well as hundreds of others. Similar groups of admissions officers are meeting at the same time, all with the goal of slicing the regular applicant pool from 5,200 to under 1,000 possible admits. Eventually, Davidson expects to make about 715 admissions offers to yield around 160 students, who will join the 338 students already committed from earlier rounds.

Let's consider those numbers for a moment to show how even at a small college, such as Davidson, choosing a class requires very harsh math. More than 64 percent of the class is already enrolled from early decision. What admissions officers are evaluating now in February is *seven times* the number of applications received in early decision but with just *two times* the number of offers to hand out.

Mike, who has a boyish face and close-shorn hair, spearheads the deliberations for his team. Methodically and with a quiet discipline honed during his collegiate running days at Dickinson College, he moves quickly through the applicants. On this morning in particular, he and his colleagues need to move fast. One of the admissions officers in the room, Kortni Campbell, is scheduled to lead an information session for prospective students touring campus in less than two hours.

In ten minutes, Mike's group zips through a dozen applications to either affirm or change the recommendations of the initial readers. The volume of applicants for this round is too large to assess in a single group, as they did with early decision in December. The ultimate destiny of many applicants is determined in these small groups; only about one out of every ten applications will land in front of the full committee in early March.

In a tsunami of applicants who are qualified on the surface, what matters at this point are the elements that differentiate students, or if they are particularly good overall, the chances they will ultimately choose Davidson—what admissions officers call LTE (likelihood to enroll). It's an acronym used frequently in discussions during regular decision. The more admissions officers dissect an applicant's intentions now, the better they'll fare in April when multiple schools are competing for the attention of the students they accepted. It's another way a college's agenda—in this case keeping its yield rate up—shapes admissions decisions.

When an application comes up from a high school that hasn't had a student apply to Davidson in four years, an admissions officer asks what is motivating this particular applicant. The committee often turns to the "Why Davidson?" essay to look for clues. In this case, the essay is boilerplate language about Davidson that can be found in any guidebook. The senior was already in the deny pile.

He remains there. So do two applicants whose parents work at other universities and never visited Davidson (the assumption is they'll probably attend college where their parents work), as well as another senior who wrote about his aspiration to attend the same school as Steph Curry, the NBA superstar who played for Davidson. "It leaves something to be desired," someone says.

Around midmorning, Kortni presents the case of a girl from New England. The applicant has high academic ratings. She took both AP and IB classes at a competitive high school. While this applicant is near the top of her class, Kortni has some concerns about her list of activities. "It's hard to suss out what she cares about," Kortni says. "There's a lot of member, member, member, and not a lot of leadership." The group agrees to mark her as a TA (tentative admit) for now. She will get another look the following week when the full committee meets (where she is moved to the wait list and eventually goes elsewhere).

A few cases later, the group confronts a dilemma: a girl in the top 20 percent of her senior class is tied at the same rank with a classmate already accepted in early decision. "She's an 8/5," Kortni says. To an outsider, the numbers sound like an elementary math lesson in fractions. In this case, the figures are an applicant's "academic track," how Davidson measures the rigor of a student's schedule. The first figure is the tally of high school courses completed at the highest level; the second digit is the number of major subjects in which those courses were taken. An 8/5 is considered solid; the higher both numbers are, the more breadth and depth the student has.

The applicant's essay is about a sibling who died. "She knows the difference between pity and empathy," someone says. "She doesn't appropriate her sibling's story for her own." One admissions officer notes the girl "is just a really good person." It's a refrain I'll hear throughout the day. Perhaps it's a way for them to assuage guilt a little at turning down so many qualified applicants.

The group decides to keep the student on the wait list, but flag her as someone who could be pulled off if needed. Despite the best efforts of admissions offices to ensure their decisions appear consistent to counselors and students in a high school, sometimes other concerns outweigh that goal, especially in regular decision, where seats are sparse.

Next up is an international student who goes to high school in the United States. Though it doesn't do so for domestic students, Davidson does consider financial need when admitting international students. The applicant can only contribute $3,000 toward Davidson's $66,000 price tag. Although the admissions officer responsible for international recruiting calls the applicant "impressive," she's too expensive. She is moved to the wait list.

Later on, Mike arrives at an application he had reviewed the previous night. In the Common App's ten spaces for activities, the senior provides details on two in particular: she's an instructor for an outdoor ropes course and a teacher's assistant in a summer class at school. The admissions officers around the table appreciate that the applicant took the time to explain her activities rather than rush through that section like so many students do.

The school counselor also mentions the girl's two activities in the recommendation letter. It's a rare moment when counselor and applicant are aligned—providing insight, however brief, into the specific passions and mind-set of a teenager in a process that often draws a blurry picture of an applicant. "She is totally unflappable," the counselor wrote about the student. The recommendation went on to describe how the senior rallied her classmates during a class trip where everything went wrong. "A real glue girl," someone says. The applicant is marked as an admit.

When the group senses an acceptance isn't certain, the discussion turns to whether the wait list or an outright denial is the better way to let the applicant down. Right before the group breaks for the morning, a girl with mostly Bs at a high school where Davidson is popular comes up for discussion. She occupies a spot on the wait list. Among applicants from her school, however, the girl's qualifications place her in the middle of the group. Someone asks if it's reasonable to think she'll ever get off the wait list. "It's a nod to the school" to even put her on the list, says one of the admissions officers.

Mike calls for a decision. "No reason to lead her on," says one admissions officer. The others agree. She is moved to the growing pile of rejections.

The home stretch for admissions is late February to early March. As the calendar turns and winter gives way to spring, admissions offices undergo their own transformation in seasons. The "rough" sort of the class is nearly complete. Those were the relatively easy calls, up or down. Now comes time for the "fine" sort of applicants sitting on either side of the admit line.

During these tense and hectic weeks, acceptances are set in stone. Think of it as finalizing the invite list for a wedding. Guests are moved on and off the list based on whether you think they'll show up or the groom's family has too many invites compared to the bride's.

Admissions officers ask questions about their invite lists, too. Do we have enough African American students or Latino students? Enough students who can pay the bulk of the tuition bill? Too many women in the class? Too many students from the Southwest or Northeast? Enough humanities majors?

The admissions profession calls this "shaping the class." This term describes the point in the selection process where selective admissions *is* the most unfair—especially if you believe that merit is based on a specific set of qualifications.

The applicant pool at this stage has been reduced to students who could prosper at that school—or at many campuses. These final decisions depend on what the class looks like or how much students in the admit bin will cost to enroll. This is the break point between fair and unfair, between a selection based on some measure of traditional criteria and one based on a variety of other factors: money, race, gender, and major.

Where applicants ultimately end up hinges largely on criteria beyond their control. But this is also the spot where an applicant's background can help push them over the line to an acceptance. Legacies, children of faculty and staff, and applicants under the watchful eye of a college's president or fund-raising office usually receive their biggest boost at this point.

Admissions officers loathe the shaping process. Some prefer to call it by the more unpleasant term Harvard uses: "lopping." Not only do they need to make difficult choices for often arbitrary reasons, but they are forced to jettison an applicant they favored during reading season. On the other hand, shaping offers one last chance to find a hidden gem to shift into the admit bin.

Just as the reading routine differs by college, so does the shaping process. Public universities with huge applicant pools and large numbers of incoming students typically use an ax rather than the scalpel smaller private colleges employ.

When the University of Washington finishes reviewing applications near the end of February, the team of readers have assigned three ratings to 45,000 applicants: academic, personal, and overall. Over five days, UW's admissions director, Paul Seegert, works one-on-one with another senior admissions officer to "batch admit" applicants. While the university reviews applications in a holistic fashion, it actually admits its freshman class using an old-fashioned number scale.

"Batch admit" is exactly what it sounds like: extremely mechanistic. Applicants are separated into clusters defined by their three scores. Each cluster has hundreds of applicants with the same set of scores. The most significant decision Seegert makes each year is where to draw the line among those clusters. That line is the difference between getting admitted, ending up on the wait list, or being outright denied. The cutoff depends on a variety of factors, but is governed by the number of applications and the strength of the overall pool. The cutoff also differs for Washington residents, out-of-state applicants, and international students, as well as those in two popular majors where seats are limited: computer science and engineering.

Seegert's goal is to calculate a cutoff point that produces the right number of admitted students to yield an incoming class of around 7,000 freshmen. In 2019, because applications were down among in-state students, the line was drawn lower than in the recent past. For that particular incoming class, it was easier for in-state students to get admitted than their counterparts the year before.

The shaping process at selective private colleges is less systematic. Admissions officers don't go back through the entire pool, but rather look for hints left by application readers or earlier committees about students who could be "pulled up" into the admit bin or "shaped out" to the deny pile. When they look at those students close to the line, they do so with a different lens—one aimed at a particular group of applicants that they might need more, or less, of.

At Davidson, the full sixteen-person admissions committee comes together for a week in early March to evaluate applicants flagged by the admissions dean, Chris Gruber. Each day, the committee focuses on a different batch of applicants: artists and musicians, deferrals from early decision, legacies, and children of faculty and staff.

This is where racial and ethnic diversity comes into play. Throughout the process, Chris has a sense of the geographic diversity of the applicant pool because admissions officers review by region, but he gets the clearest picture of how acceptances break down by race, ethnicity, and gender at this point. While Chris isn't given any "hard goals" for diversity by Davidson's president, he uses the shaping process to "self-correct" and ensure enrollments for various groups are at least on par with previous years.

During the five days of the shaping process, applicants on either side of the line are pushed and pulled between admit and deny. There's not one decision, but many. "Students see admissions as a report card on their life until now," Gruber told me, "but there are so many attributes that we're looking at in the end to build a community."

With just 2,000 undergraduates, Davidson is small, not much larger than many U.S. high schools. Located about 20 miles north of Charlotte, Davidson's picturesque campus sits among acres of lakes. Ranked in the top 20 of national liberal arts colleges, Davidson is unique among that group in that it has the intimacy of small seminar classes mixed with a Division I sports program. Its size and liberal arts tradition—with well-known programs in government, economics, and biology—is what drew Chris to the job in 2004 from the University of Richmond, where he also headed up admissions. Richmond was Chris's alma mater. As a freshman in 1981, he needed a work-study job to pay his tuition bill. There weren't many options. The admissions office was the best one, and it wasn't glamorous work. He helped an administrative assistant answer phones and sort materials that arrived with applications (it was all paper back then). He never intended the job to be more than collecting a much-needed paycheck.

After graduation, Chris moved back home to suburban Philadelphia, where he started a job as a salesman at a consulting company. At a party that summer he heard that an admissions counselor had left Richmond. He decided selling his alma mater was a better fit than selling a faceless consulting firm.

Chris has an angular, gray-flecked goatee and an oval face. He keeps up a jovial patter filled with dry humor as he trades admissions war stories with me over a drink following a Davidson basketball game. I can easily imagine him talking with prospective students and their parents when he visits high schools, something he still does even as he occupies the dean's office.

Chris is from the old mold of admissions deans, much like John Latting at Emory: comfortable in the role of judging an applicant's potential and crafting a class by poring over transcripts, essays, and recommendations and talking one-on-one to students and counselors. But that's only one of the many hats the modern admissions deans wear. Even at elite colleges, enrollment is the lifeblood of a campus and making the numbers work—keeping up yields, coming in on budget for financial aid—is critical.

In the spring of 2019, Chris's goal is to land on 785 acceptances by March 13, a week before decisions are sent out. Not all applicants land in the admit or deny piles. Many are shifted sideways to the wait list.

The "wait list" in admissions is a bit of a misnomer. Unlike a wait list at a busy restaurant when all the tables are filled, think of the wait list at a selective college as similar to an airline's practice of overselling seats, knowing not every passenger is going to show up. When colleges send out acceptances, they're never sure just how many will "yield"—how many of those admitted will take them up on the offer. Popular, brand-name colleges worry that too many students will accept their offers and there won't be enough room in the dorms. So, admissions deans often factor the wait list into their yield models. In other words, they admit fewer students knowing they'll likely pull at least a few off the wait list.

At most selective colleges, the odds of getting plucked from the wait list are long. Even so, a spot on the wait list offers a consolation prize of sorts to seniors, especially to legacies and students from high schools that send bundles of applications to a particular college. It sounds better to say you're waitlisted than outright rejected. When you're rejected, you have no idea how far you were from getting in. The wait list gives the impression you were somewhat close, even though you don't know how many students are on the wait list. Moreover, it's another way colleges serve their needs—by maintaining valuable relationships with alumni and school counselors. In one recent survey, nearly a quarter of admissions deans at private colleges said they put applicants with ties to the school on the wait list to avoid rejecting them.

By putting applicants on the wait list, colleges also have a ready pool of students to quickly fill seats without officially accepting them. Thus, admissions offices can keep a group of students connected to the college while also keeping their acceptance rates low.

For colleges, the wait list brings stability amid the uncertainty at the end of the admissions process, much as early decision does at the front end. For the Class of 2023, Davidson offered spots on the wait list to 1,530 applicants. To put that number in perspective that is three out of every ten students who *applied* in regular decision. The number of offers to be on the wait list is bigger than the *entire* freshman class it's supposedly waiting for. Davidson is not alone in offering so many spots on the wait list. On average, colleges place one out of every ten applicants on their wait list—and that number is even higher at top-ranked schools.

Schools offer so many spots on the wait list because only about half of applicants choose to stay on the list when given the chance. That's what happened in the spring of 2019 at Davidson: some 700 students agreed to remain on the wait list. On April 26—nearly a week before deposits were due from students who had been accepted—admissions officers started calling students on the list. Years ago, colleges would wait until deposits were due on May 1 to call waitlisted students. Now schools want to get a jump-start on their competitors. If they wait until after May 1, the best students on the wait list might already be committed elsewhere.

Colleges don't typically advertise the length of their wait list or how it is organized because they don't pull students from the list in any certain order. The wait list, like so much else in admissions, helps colleges fill their own priorities. If after the invitations have gone out a college realizes it now needs more English majors, more men, or more full-payers, for instance, they turn to the wait list.

In the end, from the seven hundred or so applicants who agreed to wait, only twenty-four additional students secured a spot in Davidson's Class of 2023.

There is a dirty secret in the shaping of a freshman class that few admissions deans like to talk about: money matters.

Let me explain. When I approached two dozen admissions offices about seeing inside their process for this book, one reason several declined was because they are what's called "need aware." That means at some point they take an applicant's ability to pay into account when deciding whether to accept them.

The vast majority of colleges consider an applicant's finances at some point, typically in the selection process or by shorting them on aid. Colleges might take the high road and claim they're "need blind" in making admissions decisions, but most of those schools give students only a fraction of the money a federal financial aid formula or the institution's own aid recipe determines a family can afford to pay for college. Those students are "gapped" in their financial aid packages because colleges don't have enough dollars to dole out to every accepted student who needs help. So, the schools either give aid on a first-come, first-serve basis, or to students they most desire.

How much families should pay for college all starts with the FAFSA (the Federal Application for Federal Student Aid), which generates what is known as the Student Aid Index (formerly known as the Expected Family Contribution). It's a number that shocks most families the first time they see it because it's often higher than they expect. What's more, some four hundred colleges—mostly private, selective schools—require families to complete another form called the CSS Profile to determine what the institution will give them in aid. The expected contribution spawned by the CSS is typically higher than the federal one because it captures the equity in a home and the net worth of family businesses, unlike the FAFSA formula. Either way, no matter what number the formula spits out, many families end up paying even more out of pocket.

Consider a family where the Student Aid Index is, say $10,000 a year. That student is offered a financial aid package from a school that covers only $50,000 of a $70,000 total bill. So the family who a government formula says can contribute $10,000 is charged $20,000—that $10,000 difference is the gap. Gapping is prevalent at American colleges, and the gap itself is growing as tuition and fees rise, family incomes remain stagnant, and most schools are unable to make up the difference from their endowments. The average amount students are gapped at a public college is $11,000; at private colleges, it's more than $16,000.

A few need-blind schools with huge endowments, including Emory and Davidson, promise to give students the money they need if they're accepted. Well, at least based on their expected contribution, which parents sometimes think is still too much for them to pay.

Even at need-blind schools, admission eventually can come down to money. Those colleges control how much they spend on financial aid by recruiting heavily in rich high schools and admitting in early decision a significant proportion of students who tend to be wealthier. And even when schools are need-blind, admissions officers still see the zip codes and the occupations of parents when reviewing applications.

Meanwhile, need-aware colleges typically provide financial aid that satisfies a student's requirements, without a gap, which is why they take an applicant's economic situation into account in the first place—the colleges have only so much money to give out. They think it's fairer to reject a student rather than accept them along with a $20,000 bill they can't really pay.

Lafayette College is a need-aware school and one of the few I found willing to show me how they make financial aid trade-offs in selecting a class. Located in Easton, Pennsylvania, right on the border with New Jersey, it was founded in 1826 and enrolls some 2,600 undergraduates. In 2019, *U.S. News* ranked Lafayette 39th among the best liberal arts colleges in America.

For much of the admissions process, "we lead with idealism," Matt Hyde, Lafayette's dean of admissions, tells me one morning as we sit in his office. But for several weeks during each cycle Matt says "practicality" takes over. "We have to craft a class with talent and diversity," he adds, "but I also need to deliver a solvent one."

Here's how Lafayette considers an applicant's financial need when selecting students in regular decision (it also follows a similar process in early decision). Lafayette's admissions officers review applications much as Emory, UW, and Davidson do. Lafayette, too, has a numbering scale across several categories, and students are judged initially on their academic and personal merits without having their parents' bank accounts analyzed.

But in the middle of February, a student's ability to pay begins to enter the admissions equation. From that moment until decisions are delivered near the end of March, Lafayette takes a much closer look at students in the pool with high financial need, a line that's recalibrated every year. In 2019, the line was drawn at $35,000, around half of the total cost of attending Lafayette for a year. To give you a sense of the task facing Lafayette's admissions officers consider this: some 2,200 of Lafayette's 8,500 U.S. applicants in 2018–19—a quarter of applicants—had financial need above $35,000. Roughly, that would mean a family with two children and an income of up to $175,000 a year would have that level of financial need.

During late February and early March there are several times where financially needy applicants might be swept out of the pool of tentative admits. The first is when admissions officers sort admitted students by high school. Students with an undistinguished academic rating and high need are moved to the deny bin or the wait list. Some of these admitted students, Hyde says, remain "in the conversation," but the vast majority of this group—about 250 applicants in 2019—are shifted out. Even then, if Lafayette admitted all the students left, not only would too many show up in the fall, but the college would have committed $58 million in grants and scholarships from a total financial aid budget of only $15 million.

Once those average, high-need applicants are mostly removed in the first cull, Hyde sweeps the admit pool a second time, taking the remaining high-need students out—at least temporarily. Until 2019, Lafayette followed a common practice among smaller schools of looking for needy students in the admit list and whittling their number down one by one to meet a budget goal. But such a practice right at the end of the selection cycle was bad for staff morale. Students whom admissions officers were passionate about admitting were ruled out indiscriminately.

With low- and middle-income students in a temporary holding area, the final two stages of Lafayette's need-aware process come into play. Hyde asks his admissions officers to identify their priority applicants from the holding area. These are not only the applicants the staff has come to love during their travels, but also students who have something to contribute to Lafayette's admissions agenda: whether that's enrolling more first-generation students or students of color or teenagers from regions that send few students to Eastern Pennsylvania.

During this part of the process, Hyde's staff is each allowed to pick one applicant out of every twenty in their region with high need. That results in about a hundred students being moved from the holding area back into the admit bin.

"It gives the staff a chance to feel somewhat good about a hard process because they get to choose students," Hyde says.

One of the priority applicants moved back into the admit pile in the spring of 2019 is an undocumented immigrant from New York who can't qualify for federal aid. She wants to major in engineering, and although her 1180 SAT score is below the college's average it's better than most of her high school classmates. Lafayette's admissions counselor who met the student said she'd "lie down in traffic for" her.

After the priority applicants like that girl are moved, the remaining students left in the holding area—some 775 of them in 2019— are shifted only if it makes sense "with the head and the heart," Hyde says, and with a unanimous vote of the admissions committee.

Even then, Hyde might need to cut some tentatively admitted students to make the budget. He has $7.5 million to play with in regular decision (the college has already committed the other half of its budget to early decision students). Hyde's statistical models tell him that he can make financial aid offers totaling $22.5 million in regular decision, knowing that the students who eventually show up will cost around the $7.5 million that remains.

As he moves students out of the admit pool, Hyde is careful to move students with varying levels of financial need. His models tell him that students who get huge financial aid packages end up enrolling more often than those with smaller awards or no aid at all. It's a balancing act in meeting enrollment and budget targets.

Among those who never make it out of the holding pen is an applicant from Pennsylvania who ranks fifth in his class of more than 600 with a 3.96 GPA and 1450 on the SAT. His financial need to attend Lafayette: $66,810. Another student kept out of the admit pool is a girl from the West Coast with nine AP classes on her transcript and a 1430 on the SAT. Her financial need: $57,000.

In the end, Lafayette rejected two hundred students the college tentatively accepted but couldn't afford. Those students "haunt me for months," Hyde told me. It's why Lafayette wants to join the small number of colleges that are both need blind and provide students the money they require. To do that, the college is slowly increasing enrollment to bring in more revenue, plowing some of the new dollars into financial aid. It's also raising millions from donors. But even as Lafayette pursues a need-blind strategy, the goalposts keep moving. Every year, Lafayette's costs rise and so do tuition and fees to keep pace, making that goal ever more challenging.

On March 5, about two weeks before Emory University is scheduled to deliver acceptances to the newest members of the Class of 2023, the admissions staff squeezes into a large conference room to hear from their chief, John Latting. Four months ago they had gathered to kick off reading season for thirty thousand applicants. Now they have reached the finish line, almost.

"Every applicant has a decision," John tells his staff to a round of applause. "Some," he adds, "are written in pencil."

At that moment, 4,959 high school seniors sit in Emory's admit pile. If the university were to send out those acceptances, it would result in a class of 1,660, about 300 students above the university's target (including 722 already enrolled through two ED rounds). The university's numerical models indicate the admissions staff needs to remove a thousand students from the admitted pile in order to end up with the right size class.

"It's going to be tough" to discard those students, John tells the staff. "Think not just about 'Is this a great student?' but what a great class looks like. It's about what we're looking for. That's what's going to determine who stays as an admit and who goes down a step or two."

As the admissions officers get ready to go to work within their regional committees, John cautions them not to evaluate applicants all over again. "Trust but verify," he says of the applications reviewed over the last few months. "What those earlier readers didn't have was the sense of the whole. Now we have that."

The elephant in the room is how to make the cuts while protecting what is rare in the class, specifically black and Latino students and men of all races and ethnicities. John never tells the staff to avoid moving students in any particular demographic, but the message is clear nonetheless. "The best class for Emory is a diverse class," he says. "If you don't seek that and don't defend that at this stage, it's not going to happen."

When it comes to the diversity of elite college campuses, students of color and first-generation students receive the most attention these days. But colleges are also struggling to maintain a gender balance. Two-thirds of colleges and universities report that they get more female than male applicants. Among the 135 most selective colleges, half of the schools admit men at a higher rate than women. Even with that advantage, men still represent less than 45 percent of students at American colleges. Schools worry about that number falling below 40 percent and changing the campus culture.

A decade-plus ago, the former dean of admissions and financial aid at Kenyon College wrote a popular essay in the *New York Times* laying bare the male preference in admissions. "The reality is that because young men are rarer, they're more valued applicants," Jennifer Delahunty wrote. The op-ed caused a firestorm in higher education circles, exposing what was regarded as an open secret in admissions: the selection process at top colleges *is* particularly tough on qualified women. That's especially the case in regular decision when colleges might need to make up for shortages of men from early decision, when women are more likely to apply knowing that ED could give them their best shot of getting in.

Gender is just one of many institutional priorities Emory's admissions officers juggle as they whittle down the admit pool in early March. On a Tuesday afternoon, five members of the Northeast team are jammed into Scott Allen's corner office tracking on a whiteboard the students admitted tentatively they are slicing out of the class. The applicant pool from the Northeast is among the strongest at Emory, so most students are shifted to the wait list instead of outright rejected, unlike in some other committees down the hall.

In the hour and a half after they broke for lunch, the Northeast group moves twenty-two students out of the admit pile. Among those is a girl with an A average and 1500 on the SAT who wants to major in pre-law. She ran track in middle school and made the varsity soccer team as a sophomore. One admissions officer finds the recommendations lacking because they focus on her personal qualities instead of what happens in the classroom. "I like her, if we have room," someone says. "Well, we don't," says Scott, giving a voice to the disappointment of everyone in the room.

They pull out a boy with 3 ratings on their 5-point scale in curriculum, extracurriculars, and recommendations, and a 4 in intellectual curiosity. Despite taking nine APs and scoring a 1400 on the SAT, the applicant has Cs in math and science throughout high school, resulting in a 3.42 recalculated GPA. "Math is not his jam," one admissions officer says, noting the applicant's enthusiasm for art history. "We don't have many boys interested in art history." But Scott points out that "math exists in everything at Emory," and reminds his colleagues that the applicant might come back up the following week in the final review of applications by high schools and majors (he ends up on the wait list and eventually enrolls at the University of Southern California).

As the afternoon wears on and the group gets deeper into the class, the number of students switched to the wait list slows down. They stall on a girl with a 5 curriculum rating, a 4 on intellectual curiosity, and two 3s on recommendations and extracurriculars. The number in Scott's mind is 194, which is how many cuts they have to make by the end of the week. "If we don't move her, I think we'll have a hard time getting to 194," Scott says. "We will run out of these files." They move her to the wait list (she eventually ends up at Barnard College).

Emory's admissions staff refers to their shaping process as "shape down," but also by its inverse, "round up." Shaping gives admissions officers a chance to lift someone close to the line over to the acceptance side. It's where applicants lost in the shuffle of reading season's fast pace are found again. One applicant moved to the acceptance pile here in early March is the African American girl whom Giselle and Jetaun had rejected two months earlier when they accepted a boy from the same high school with lower academic qualifications (he ends up enrolling; she doesn't). In admissions, the only definitive decision is the one sent to applicants in late March.

Shaping is the point where selective colleges can accept a few applicants with appealing qualities but with low SAT scores or a few bad grades knowing the decisions won't pull down the academic profile of the entire incoming class. Accept too many students with a 1200 score back in January and you might be lowering the class average for the rankings metrics. But now you can be confident the low SAT score won't harm the rankings so it's easier to accept her.

Late on a Wednesday afternoon in March, Mark Butt opens up the file of a girl in California. So far, the regional committee he's leading has moved twenty-nine tentative acceptances from their list. Their goal is to get to thirty-six by the end of the day. When Mark first calls up the file, it looks like one that could get them closer to their target.

At the top of the application dashboard in blazing blue type is her "Max Test" score: 1120 on the SAT. Below in red type is a hint for this committee left by the original readers: low admit.

Mark reads the notes in the file aloud. This girl's high school is in a poor neighborhood in California. "Strong rigor and good grades in context. Transcript is nearly all As." The curriculum rating on the applicant, 4 out of 5, is the highest of the four categories. Mark opens up the transcript for a closer look. One B in the first semester of sophomore English. Someone calls out the girl's mid-year grades, which arrived after the application was first reviewed. All As with a senior-year schedule that includes five AP courses. "This is a good," Mark whispers to himself. He was one of the application's original readers and sees the note he left for himself a few months earlier: "A rare winner from this region."

The girl's mother has a grade school education and a job in a warehouse. Someone in the room reads from the essay, where the senior writes about the privilege of having an older sister who encouraged her to apply to college. "Many kids in my community lack the support I'm so fortunate to have," she writes. In her last year of high school, she became a college mentor. "When talking to my mentees, I always tell them we have two choices: we can remain angry and ask why, or we can be inspired and ask why not?"

One of the admissions officers notes the average test score in this applicant's high school is only a 980. There is some concern among the group about whether she can do the work at Emory. Mark tells his colleagues that the girl scored a 4 out of 5 on the AP Calculus exam. That gives him confidence.

"Any questions?" Mark asks. "Keep as an admit?"

All hands in the room go up.

Two weeks later on March 20 at 6 p.m. Eastern Time, that girl's acceptance letter, along with 3,817 others, is released when Emory's president pushes a ceremonial red button in the auditorium where prospective students are first welcomed on their admissions visits. In the audience, the admissions staff celebrates the end of selection season with champagne, handheld confetti cannons, and balloons, all befitting a New Year's Eve party.

Afterward, John Latting rattles off a list of facts about the Class of 2023. Emory's acceptance rate fell to a record-low 15 percent (it was 30 percent four years ago, he notes). The median SAT score of admitted students was 1500. Unweighted high school GPA was 3.92. The admissions office processed 1.12 million documents, including 67,940 teacher recommendations and 76,095 student transcripts.

On a screen behind Latting, a colorful dashboard displays live visitor statistics to Emory's admissions portal and a real-time look at the university's social media feeds. Within minutes, video clips of students opening their decisions are appearing on Instagram. It's much different than in an earlier era in admissions when thick and thin envelopes would take days to reach students in their mail-boxes. But one thing remains the same: from this moment forward, the decision-making power in admissions for the first time in months has flipped from the college to the student.

In the following weeks, students with multiple acceptances will weigh their options as they try to pick one school by the May 1 deadline for deposits. Colleges will put on a full-court press in April to persuade students they are the right fit. Emory will hold three open houses in the coming weeks and also fly select groups of accepted students to Atlanta.

One of them will be the girl from California with the 1120 SAT score that Mark and his committee kept in the admit pile in early March. But in the end, it won't be enough to persuade her. Faced with multiple acceptances, she chooses the University of California at Berkeley.

9

Paying for College

The Best Class Money Can Buy

Every year, parents and students await both the coveted acceptances from colleges and the kicker that soon follows: the financial aid package.

That's when reality sets in.

Pinpointing the precise amount colleges need to give to the students they most desire—and preferably not a penny more—is a delicate balancing act. Schools want to offer enough money to lure students away from other schools where they were also accepted. But they need to collect sufficient tuition revenue to operate, too.

Figuring out that sweet spot is the job of *Moneyball*-inspired quants who have brought sophisticated statistical approaches from Wall Street and Fortune 100 companies to higher education. These experts in mathematics, computer science, and psychology often work far from campus at consulting companies that colleges hire to "optimize" spending on financial aid. It's a far cry from the origins of financial aid in the 1960s, when it was intended to help poor and middle-income students afford college. Nowadays, college leaders talk about pricing strategies like airline executives and retailers do.

Welcome to the world of "financial aid leveraging." Understanding how it works and who exactly has the "leverage" can help you in both your search for and final selection of a college. In the last decade, econometric modeling and data mining to find the best incoming class money can buy has been all the rage in admissions, especially at the colleges that are buyers.

One can see the influence that the business of enrollment management has had on the admissions function of higher education each fall when thousands of college and high school counselors gather for the annual meeting of the National Association for College Admissions Counseling. In a cavernous convention hall, hundreds of companies set up exhibit booths to peddle everything from marketing services to software for virtual campus tours. The hall is filled with firms that you never heard of but that help colleges figure out how much financial aid to give to you. It's a sector dominated by a few big players, such as EAB, the higher education consulting company that bought Bill Royall's firm for $850 million in 2014, and Ruffalo Noel Levitz, an Iowa-based firm that consults with more than a thousand schools. But it also has many mom-and-pop shops that have emerged in the forty years since the idea of enrollment management was first developed. That's the part of the market Brian Zucker occupies.

Zucker heads up Human Capital Research. He started the firm in 1990 with just one client. Today, Human Capital Research has seventy clients, including blue-chip institutions such as University of Richmond, DePaul University, and the University of Dayton.

From an office suite on the tenth floor of a small high-rise in Evanston, Illinois, not far from Northwestern University, thirty-two employees pore over numbers and tinker with statistical models. They help answer questions like this: Would that teenager from the Boston suburbs choose a particular college if the financial aid offer were sweetened by another $1,000? Would $500 be enough?

Brian Zucker lives in the world of data visualizations tools—colorful bar charts, line graphs, and bubble charts. All of them help his staff explain to campus enrollment chiefs and their presidents what is buried in massive government datasets and the key indicators schools closely track: admissions inquiries, applications, and yield. The consulting companies fold this treasure trove of numbers into complicated proprietary numerical models that tell colleges how much financial aid to offer in order to attract the students they most desire.

Consultants claim their model is the best and most accurate, but then one year it doesn't work and a college ends up short on undergraduates or gives out too much financial aid. That's when the consultants get fired, and a new firm with a slightly different model gets hired.

At the core of these models is a simple cell chart. Think of a piece of paper covered with square boxes, defined by factors important to the college: SAT scores, GPAs, family income, and financial need. Colleges design these charts based on what they want more of (full-pay students or high GPAs, for instance) or less of (low test scores and high-need kids). When financial aid officers offer money to an accepted student, the charts and the models they consult are critical to how much money to give out. Each cell in the chart includes a predicted yield, so colleges also know how many students are likely to accept an offer.

In the thick of finalizing financial aid packages for accepted undergraduates, consultants and enrollment managers are constantly playing with the parameters of their models to find the right mix of students in each box to hit a specific revenue target. The best models produce a class that maximizes revenue and is filled with the kinds of students the college wants. That means at many schools financial aid doesn't always go to the families that need it the most.

Let's revisit the idea we talked about near the beginning of this book. It's a simplification, of course, but I argue you can divide the universe of American colleges into two camps: buyers and sellers. The sellers, you'll remember, are the most prestigious places that could fill their classes many times over with students willing to pay the full price. The buyers (and most places are buyers) don't have their pick of the litter in the same way. They need to use discounting and other tools to attract the class they want. That's where this type of "leveraging" comes in.

Financial aid can sound like charity, but that's not the best way to think about it. Most colleges are forgoing revenue in one cat-egory—tuition—to use those resources in another—financial aid. As Zucker explained, the math is quite simple: instead of giving a $60,000 full ride to a poor or middle-income student and yield-ing one undergraduate, colleges split that scholarship into four $15,000 discounts that are offered to four wealthier kids who can bring some money to the table. If the college yields two or three of them as a result, it pulls in hundreds of thousands of dollars in tuition revenue over four years to pay for smart low-income stu-dents or other applicants that it desires. Do that several times over for an incoming class and you can see why leveraging works for the vast majority of colleges, the ones that don't have a billion-dollar endowment.

These are levers pulled by financial aid offices and their con-sultants that families never see yet determine who gets into a par-ticular college and how much money they receive in financial aid. Colleges don't reveal those financial aid strategies in the glossy brochures they send to prospective students. The true cost of a college remains unknown until the financial aid award letters—the result of months of behind-the-scenes work by the Brian Zuckers of the world—are delivered to accepted students.

High school counselors refer to October as "sucktober." It's a month when counselors are juggling a dozen critical tasks: wel-coming college representatives, processing applications for early decision students, and pumping out recommendation letters. April is probably a close second in terms of the busy season as students make their final decisions about where to enroll.

On a Tuesday morning in the middle of April, a steady stream of seniors—some with their parents in tow—drop by to see Diane Campbell, the college counselor at Liberty Common High School in Fort Collins, Colorado. The students visiting Campbell are weighing offers from multiple colleges. The conversations, how-ever, rarely focus on the academic merits of the different schools.

They're almost all about money, making Campbell's job at this time of year more akin to that of a financial advisor than a counselor's.

The students bring copies of their financial aid award letters, hoping Campbell can decipher what seems to be a secret code. Line up a selection of these letters from a group of schools and you'll quickly realize how each comes in a different format, uses difficult-to-understand abbreviations, and blurs the line between loans and grants. Unlike the government-required forms that spell out the details of a home mortgage, there is no common document that colleges must send to explain what you'll be paying and how.

The worst offenders suggest in these "award" letters that students are getting a great deal. Those seem scripted by the college marketing department rather than a financial aid advisor. One analysis of thousands of these letters found schools used more than 136 unique terms to describe the "Federal Direct Unsubsidized Loans"—common loans given to students that accumulate interest while an undergraduate is in school. Twenty-four colleges didn't even include the word "loan" in their description. Nearly 15 percent of letters included a Parent PLUS loan as an "award" without ever mentioning that parents need to apply for this loan separately and are responsible for paying it back. Perhaps most surprising is that only 40 percent of the letters actually calculated a bottom-line number that students would need to pay.

"This is maddening," Campbell says as she sits next to a senior considering Villanova University and goes line-by-line through the award.

The letter from Villanova includes two federal loans, an unsubsidized one for $2,000 listed simply as "UNSUB" and a subsidized loan for $3,500 called "SUB," but without any explanation of either (a subsidized loan means the student isn't charged interest while in school). It includes $3,000 in federal work-study, but again absent any description. To get that money students have to secure a work-study job (or two) on campus and it's unclear how many hours they would need to work to make $3,000 a year. What's more, families still have to cover the costs up front because the earnings aren't applied directly to tuition and fees. Normally, work-study jobs provide students with cash for living expenses. That is, if students can find a job. Often, there are way more undergraduates offered work-study than there are jobs for them, or students arrive on campus and realize they can't hold down a job and keep up with their academic work. In the end, work-study isn't really financial aid; it simply turns into another expense that students and parents somehow cover.

As Campbell moves through the letter, the senior becomes visibly more anxious. A line near the bottom lists a "Family Financing Option" for $38,182. One can only assume that means the family either has to find the cash or take out a loan. Perhaps most distressing is that the family financing option is one line *above* what is listed as the "total award" in bold type: $73,332. In other words, Villanova implies that it is *awarding* money to the student that actually comes from the family and the student.

When Campbell gets to the end of the letter, she flips over the page and then turns it back again. She's looking for the total cost to put the award in context. It's not listed anywhere. Campbell tells the student to call Villanova's financial aid office to ask about total costs and what the aid package might look like the second year of college.

Throughout the morning Campbell suggests to the seniors she counsels—who haven't even started college yet—that they make sure to ask about their sophomore year financial aid. Why? Because half of colleges practice what is known as front-loading—giving bigger grants to first-year students than to everyone else.

The practice is a classic bait and switch. Colleges attract students with a big discount the first year, and then once the students like the campus and want to stay to finish a degree, they get (or receive) less aid for the remaining years. To figure out if a college might be doing this, go to the federal government's College Navigator website to look at the average grant amount for first-year students compared with all undergraduate students. If there's a significant difference, that is a sign that you should at least ask about front-loading.

Later in the morning, a senior near the top of the class and her mother come to see Campbell. The student was accepted at Yale and is fresh off a visit to New Haven. She wants to commit to the Ivy League school, but now the question is how to pay for it. As a seller, Yale gives out financial aid based only on need. The senior received an aid package totaling $33,000, less than half of the university's $72,000 price tag. While Yale's financial aid formula might say the family can afford the difference, the girl's mother tells Campbell reality is different.

The girl has several other choices beyond Yale, including two schools that offered her full scholarships: Emory and Lewis & Clark in Oregon. But the senior seems much more interested in the Ivy brand than in her parents' bank account. "Ever since she was a little kid she wanted to go to an Ivy League school," the mom tells Campbell. "I never thought it was possible for her to get in."

The pressure that families feel to pay huge sums for what they see as the "right college" is real. Caitlin Zaloom, an associate professor at New York University, calls this phenomenon "cultivating potential" in her 2019 book, *Indebted: How Families Make College Work at Any Cost*.

In her research, Zaloom found that parents see their kid's potential as unrealized in high school and only the "best" college can provide the environment for them to explore and develop. In more than 160 interviews, parents told Zaloom they first considered how a college "suited their child's hopes" before grappling with the costs. "Parents made clear that they believed they had to suppress their own financial anxieties," Zaloom wrote, "so that they could allow their children's potential to take precedence."

The problem is that only the sellers among colleges have the money to provide enough in grants and scholarships to keep student and parent debt down. The much larger group of buyers encourages families to focus on the value of education rather than the actual cost. In the search for a college, the real cost of the purchase is revealed only at the back end of the process instead of at the front, unlike most big-ticket items we buy.

When teenagers start looking for schools, their quest is guided by academic and social needs as well as geography. Cost is a concern, of course, but families have only a hazy idea of what their tuition bill might look like. The college's sticker price listed on its website is useless since, at most schools, few people actually pay that figure. Exactly what a family's bill will be, however, isn't clear. At the most-sought-after colleges, financial aid offers don't arrive until after admissions decisions are released in March. From the moment the letters arrive, students and their parents have only about a month until the May 1 deadline to decide where they want to go—and most important, how to pay for it.

The seniors filing through Langley High School's college and career center in April are going through a mix of emotions. The last college acceptances for these students in northern Virginia arrived in the past few weeks. These acceptances are what they worked years for, and many have received invitations to some of the nation's top schools—Princeton, Stanford, and Wellesley. Yet there is a tinge of disappointment in their voices as they chat with the school's head college counselor, Hannah Wolff. Yes, they got in, but now their parents are finally facing the reality of how to pay for those dream colleges.

A girl with a loose-fitting gray sweatshirt who wants to attend Wellesley College in Massachusetts is Wolff's second visitor of the morning. "They only gave me $2,000," she laments, "and it's a $40,000 school." Already she misunderstands her package because tuition alone at Wellesley is $55,000. Wolff suggests she write to the admissions representative who visited Langley the previous fall for advice. "Be friendly," she reminds the student.

The teenager shuffles to a table a few feet from Wolff and pulls open her laptop to write a note, as another teenager waltzes through the door. "I just want to give you my news," the student says to Wolff. "I got into Princeton." Wolff gives the senior a high five. The arm is barely back at the student's side when he adds, "I need help with financial aid." The senior plans to return later in the day.

The conversations in Wolff's office about paying for college are not much different from those in Fort Collins, Colorado, and that's surprising given Langley's location. The leafy neighborhoods surrounding the high school are lined with well-maintained homes owned by two-earner families who expected their kids to go to whatever college they can get into. The median home price here is just shy of a million dollars. The average household income in the county is $115,000, almost twice that of Fort Collins. Only two counties in the entire country are wealthier.

Nobody sympathizes with these parents when it comes to paying for college. But even with combined incomes that reach well into the six figures, finding $50,000 or $60,000 *every year* for four years is not something most families can easily carve out of their household budget. Before the Great Recession, parents in neighborhoods like those around Langley might have complained about the rising prices of colleges, but in the end they usually paid whatever was needed to send their kids anywhere.

Now the conversation about college affordability has crept into these neighborhoods, too. No longer are these families willing to pay *any* price to go to just *any* college. Just look at the share of families who pay full freight at American colleges these days. In 2006–7, about 39 percent of college students paid the entire sticker price; today, fewer than 28 percent do.

The parents of today's teenagers didn't encounter the price competition between schools when they applied to college, and thus they largely underestimate it, to their disadvantage. The discounting arms race didn't begin in earnest until the 1980s, and even then, the aggressive practices widespread today were seen as something mattress stores employed, not eminent colleges.

Until the 1990s, financial aid officers from higher education's elite—including Harvard, Yale, MIT, Smith, and Amherst—

gathered together each spring to scrutinize the family finances of high school seniors who were accepted to more than one of the schools in the group. The point of this meeting, known as the Overlap Group, was to come to an agreement on how much the parents of an accepted student should contribute to their child's education. If all the schools offered similar financial aid packages, colleges believed, students wouldn't make a decision based solely on money. The U.S. Justice Department, however, found that cooperating on aid amounted to illegal price-fixing. Rather than engage in a lengthy legal battle, the universities eventually disbanded the group.

Over the next two decades, higher education's pricing war escalated. The result: *sticker prices* that seem remarkably similar but *actual prices* that vary widely and are largely hidden from prospective students. While consultants like Brian Zucker know what colleges actually charge, the consumers only discover the real prices after they're accepted and receive their financial aid package. The federal government requires colleges provide net-price calculators on their websites to help families estimate what they might pay there, but the results don't usually take into consideration merit aid that is a significant chunk of a financial aid award at many schools.

Two start-up companies, Edmit and TuitionFit, want to bring greater transparency to the financial aid process with websites that comb institutional data and crowdsource award letters. One senior who shared his award letters on TuitionFit and then accessed awards from other schools sent to students with similar academic profiles shows just how much prices can vary. The student was accepted to three schools, ranging in sticker price from $55,000 to $59,000. His actual cost after financial aid was factored, however, stretched from $27,000 to $41,000. Meanwhile, TuitionFit showed him packages similar students received from ten other schools with final prices that ranged from $14,000 at an in-state public university to nearly $41,000.

"People want to know a college's price when they start the college search," says Mark Salisbury, the founder of TuitionFit, who used to head up the data collection and analysis operation at Augustana College in Illinois. "But you can't shop for colleges by price." Both Edmit and TuitionFit allow high school students to look at the price of schools based on actual financial awards even before they apply.

An hour into the April morning at Langley High School, Hannah Wolff has already seen a dozen students who are agonizing over their college choices. A student who has patiently waited for nearly a half hour finally gets to see Wolff. He tells her that he's been accepted at three private colleges—Wake Forest in North Carolina, Case Western Reserve in Cleveland, and Brandeis in Boston—as well as the honors college at George Mason University, a public university nearby. "I like Case the best," he says, "but my parents, being so ambitious and all, looked at the *U.S. News* rankings and don't think it's well known enough."

Wolff asks the senior what he thinks about the honors college at George Mason. Public universities, such as Arizona State, Penn State, and Texas Tech, among others, are using honors colleges as a tool to lure top students. They promise essentially a private, liberal arts education to a select group of high-achieving students at the lower price of a public institution. While George Mason's price is attractive to his parents—$30,000 a year in all compared to anywhere from $46,000 to $50,000 after financial aid at the three privates—the senior says he wants to leave the state. Wolff shakes her head. She knows Virginia is full of good and inexpensive public colleges, but too many families dismiss them until this time of year when they get hit with sticker shock for out-of-state public colleges or private schools.

Judging by the questions the students are asking Wolff, it's unlikely the subject of price came up often in family conversations during the college search. These high-achieving students applied to top colleges. Either they didn't pay attention to eye-popping tuition figures listed on the websites of the colleges where they applied, or they assumed they would get a tuition discount. They were led to believe that if they got in, merit aid would follow because of their academic accomplishments.

But here's the problem: these students applied to colleges that are spectators to the merit-aid game. They applied to sellers, not buyers. Some sellers do have scholarship programs—for handfuls of truly outstanding students—but they don't tend to offer the well-publicized tuition discounts to students whose families have assets and the ability to pay. Those discounts are offered by less selective colleges downstream that use the money to lure high-caliber students away from top schools.

Many students from upper-middle-class families don't have financial need as defined by the government or institutional formulas but still need a discount. If that description fits you, be sure your list of colleges includes a mix of sellers and buyers. Getting aid at the buyers is easier if you can pay a good portion of the cost and are a strong student compared to their averages.

To put together a balanced list of buyers and sellers, families need to look at two numbers in particular. The first is a school's desirability as measured by its yield—the percentage of accepted students who end up enrolling. Students can only choose one school when admitted to two or more. Economists call this "revealed preference." The higher a school's yield, the less likely it is to spend money on merit aid to attract students.

The second number is the percentage of institutional aid spent on non-need-based aid. The higher the percentage compared to other schools on your list, the better chance you have of getting a discount.

Those two numbers—both of which can be found in the Common Data Set—are not perfect measures of your chances for securing merit aid, but they are a good yardstick to use.

To get a sense of the stark differences between schools on these measures, let's look at a few of the campuses Langley students were considering when I was there. The University of Michigan was a popular out-of-state option. But it has a healthy 45 percent yield rate and only 29 percent of its $226 million aid budget is spent on merit awards. Compare Michigan to another public university that aggressively recruits students in other states: the University of Alabama, which spends 64 percent of its $231 million in aid on merit scholarships and still yields less than a third of accepted students.

Plenty of prominent private colleges also fall into the camp of buyers as I've defined them. Tulane is one, spending more than half of the $153 million in aid it gives out on merit awards. So, too, is Rhodes College in Memphis (24 percent yield and 45 percent on non-need awards) and Case Western Reserve (18 percent yield and 38 percent on non-need awards). This doesn't mean getting into those schools is easy, but it does help you see a little behind the curtain of financial aid leveraging.

By the last week of April, seniors at Langley, Liberty Common, and other high-achieving high schools across the country know their time to decide on college is quickly disappearing. Their counselors can't do much at this point. They can't get them more choices. They can't get them more money. Even as one class gets ready to leave, Hannah Wolff and Diane Campbell have already started meeting with juniors and their parents about the next admissions cycle.

High school counselors serve as critical brokers and advocates for students in the college search process, yet at most public high schools they are overwhelmed with guiding students through anxiety and depression or the mundane task of course selection. Several studies and surveys have pegged the average caseload of a counselor as low as 230 students and as high as 460.

But the relationships forged between top public and elite private schools and admissions officers can often help in getting students on the margins across the finish line. During the Harvard affirmative-action trial, the university's admissions dean said students are sometimes admitted to keep a good relationship with a high school, a "100-year relationship" as he described it.

Among the high school counselors I met in researching this

book, those like Wolff and Campbell are the exception rather than the rule. Campbell is at a public charter school with eighty-six seniors. Wolff works in one of the wealthiest public school districts in the country. She is responsible only for college advising. Her school has a separate counseling staff for students' social and emotional well-being and course selection. She doesn't even need to write college recommendations unless asked. That gives her the flexibility to sit on an admissions advisory panel at the University of South Carolina and serve as part-time application reader at UC Berkeley, providing her students with further insight into the application process that counselors at less-resourced schools don't have.

For counselors, May 1 can't come fast enough. The day used to pass at most high schools without much fanfare. But in 2014, First Lady Michelle Obama turned the day into College Signing Day, a national event meant to mirror the pomp and circumstance that college athletes get when they commit to Division I programs. Participation in the event has grown from a few dozen schools to more than three thousand. In 2019, the event inspired 1.24 billion social media posts tagged #collegesigningday in twenty-four hours.

In Pennsylvania, Chris's high school had never before staged a signing day celebration. So few students went on to college, it hardly seemed worth the trouble. But Michelle Bailey, the College Advising Corps counselor at the school, believed that if she was going to change the culture, students had to see their peers being congratulated for their accomplishments.

Shortly after 10:30 a.m. on May 1, Michelle stepped up to the podium in the school's auditorium and looked out on the sparse crowd. Most of the senior class was undecided about what they would do after graduation. You could easily spot them: they weren't wearing college T-shirts like many other students. The second largest group of seniors was committed to one of the Penn State campuses. The university's mascot, a lion, showed up to congratulate them in person.

Then Michelle got to Chris, one of the stars of the senior class. "Gettysburg College," she said as Chris approached the stage wearing a blue-and-orange Gettysburg pullover.

The acceptance from Gettysburg had arrived a little more than a month earlier along with the financial aid package. It included $47,000 in scholarships from the college as well as state grants, work-study, and a federal loan. Chris and his mom would need to come up with $11,000, about a quarter of her annual income. On Michelle's advice, Chris appealed for additional aid. Gettysburg offered an additional $2,000. His mom found a second job to make up the difference.

At Gettysburg, Chris is an offensive lineman on the football team. His favorite class is calculus. But in the fall of his freshman year, he told me the transition to a liberal arts college has been rough for him.

At a state university or at a less selective private college, Chris probably would have declared his computer science major on the way in and jumped right into those classes first semester. At Gettysburg, like at most liberal arts colleges, he won't declare his major until the end of his sophomore year after taking courses across various academic subjects.

Given what his mom is sacrificing to pay for college, Chris had hoped Gettysburg would focus on making his education relevant to a job from the very start. It's not clear that in his truncated college search—where selectivity and financial aid trumped all—that he ever got a clear idea of what going to a liberal arts college was going to be like. I asked Chris if he planned to transfer. Maybe, he said. He didn't want to disappoint his mom or Michelle Bailey.

College is sold in the marketing materials and on the tours as a celebratory rite of passage. We spend so much money, time, and attention on choosing a college and getting into a college. Perhaps we could take just a bit of that and put it toward understanding how much college is going to cost, how we are going to pay for it, and what we might do once we get there.

10

Making the Final Decision

May 1

For colleges, April is like the end of a quarter for sales executives or Black Friday for retailers. It's when they must close the deal with students and parents who are weighing multiple offers. Getting families on campus in these frantic spring weeks is crucial. While we tend to think the campus tour happens at the *beginning* of the college search, about a quarter of all campus visits by students occur at the *end*—in the month of April. Of those visits, about half of families are stepping on campus for the first time.

That's why schools roll out the red carpet, playing host to what they advertise as "open houses" for accepted students but internally call "yield events." Research shows nothing influences a student's decision about where to enroll as much as the campus visit. We can buy almost anything online these days without seeing it in person, but we still want to stroll along the campus quad, sit in a classroom, and eat in the dining hall.

"As long as you're doing place-based education," says Jeff Kallay, "then the place still matters."

I'm walking with Kallay on a campus tour at a public university in New England. It's a Friday in mid-April. The school is one of hundreds that since 2006 have hired Kallay's company, Render Experiences, to remake their tour and train their student guides. On this day, he's a "secret shopper," hanging at the back of the scrum, black notebook in hand and iPhone ready to snap photos of anything unsightly that could scare away families: bagged trash waiting to be picked up, crumbling concrete, patches of barren grass.

By the time we head into the library, he's already filled three pages of his notebook and taken a dozen photos. "This is the fourth building we've been in," he says, shaking his head, "and we haven't gone beyond the lobby. That's not how these kids will live if they come here."

For generations the campus tour was like the plain-vanilla marketing teenagers used to receive from colleges in the pre–Bill Royall days. Until the Gen Xer Jeff Kallay came along to explain Millennials and then Gen Zers to college officials, tours conveyed information using guides who walked backward and recited facts and figures like an Alexa does now on our kitchen counter.

In 2001, while working for a higher education marketing company in Atlanta, Kallay read *The Experience Economy*. The book explained that companies are really hawking distinct experiences as much as services and products. How we feel about a product, our emotional bond, is the actual commodity for sale. Think Southwest flight attendants. Starbucks coffee. The Apple Store.

Kallay thought back to his childhood, growing up in Florida, and the days he spent at Walt Disney World, perhaps the premier seller of experiences. The park wasn't just a collection of rides and restaurants. Space Mountain, the 20,000 Leagues Under the Sea submarine voyage, Main Street, U.S.A. were all experiences that stuck in his mind. He estimates he's visited Disney's Florida and California parks 150 times in his lifetime.

For Kallay, who was a tour guide as an undergraduate at Lee University in Tennessee and later worked in admissions, *The Experience Economy* was a blueprint for how campuses could distinguish themselves. There was no easy way to compare the experience of attending one college against another. No magazines such as *Consumer Reports* or websites like Wirecutter for independent assessments. Sure, teenagers had the rankings but those largely looked at the quality of the students coming in the door. Other rankings looked at jobs and salaries after graduation. Picking a school for teenagers is about so much more, Kallay thought.

"It's about who you sleep with, who you eat with, your friends for life," Kallay told me. "It's a coming-of-age moment you can't put numbers on."

If Royall's marketing tactics were designed to fill the top of the recruitment funnel with prospective students, the campus visit designed by Jeff Kallay and his team, largely made up of former tour guides and admissions officers, would close the sale at the bottom of the funnel.

To do that, Kallay advised his clients to discard the old, fact-filled tours (that's what information sessions and websites are for) and abandon walking backward (less conversational and too slow). Instead he suggests shorter, customized tours (less "death march," more engagement) that focus on storytelling (lots of personal anecdotes about dealing with difficult roommates or pulling all-nighters) and authenticity (a signature moment that's Instagram-mable, say in front of a statue of the campus mascot).

"Our goal is that campus visits are better, that they are more guest-centric, and they are aligned with campus goals," Kallay says.

A few months before we met in New England, I joined Kallay for a training session of tour guides at a private college in Pennsylvania. There were ninety undergraduates and admissions staff in the room, a sign of how important the campus visit has become to colleges. The "campus visit coordinator" is now a full-time job at many schools. Along with student tour guides—or as they're now called, "ambassadors," which are mostly paid positions—they even have their own association (the Collegiate Information and Visitor Services Association) and gather for a national convention every year.

Wearing jeans and a sports jacket, Kallay, with a salt-and-pepper beard and thick, dark-framed glasses, works the room as part motivational speaker, part comedian, part consultant.

"What's the total cost to attend here?" Kallay asks.

"Sixty-seven thousand dollars," the group responds, almost in unison. Clearly, it was one of the many facts they had committed to memory.

"So, if you have a tour with four prospective students," Kallay says, "think about it: that's a million-dollar equation."

The campus tour has been called the "million-dollar walk" or the "golden mile" because of its importance to feeding the enrollment machine. The tour is another way that schools serve their own agenda in admissions by highlighting the bells and whistles they think separate their campus from the other schools students are considering. For colleges, it's a lot cheaper and easier to design a better tour than improve the undergraduate experience by hiring more full-time professors, adding career advisors, and building new classrooms and labs—all elements teenagers rarely realize they should care about while being herded around campuses.

Choosing a college is an emotional decision for families, and Jeff Kallay figured out that the college choice often comes down to what students think as they stroll around the campus center or see inside a dorm room.

"College, when it's all said and done, it's a bucket load of memories," Kallay told the tour guides. "You are selling experiences."

For Grace, the California Asian American girl whose dream it was to go to a private college in the East, Wellesley College was everything she had pictured from its website and brochures. It was Monday, April 8, and she was on campus for an open house for accepted students after flying all night on a red-eye flight from San Francisco with her mom. This was their first visit to the women's college, about twenty miles southwest of Boston. Grace had received her admission offer two weeks earlier.

That same week Smith College and three University of California campuses—Los Angeles, Berkeley, and Davis—also accepted Grace. Five acceptances to highly ranked colleges. Not a bad week.

The news from Dartmouth—her ED choice—wasn't as good. The early deferral turned into a rejection in regular decision.

Wellesley was now Grace's first choice. Her mom was still pulling for one of the UC campuses and their lower price tags.

During the open house, Wellesley's president talked with admitted students about how the college nurtures limitless dreams. Grace's tour guide was writing a book and developing a mobile app. She told me later that she imagined the friends she would make and the connections she could forge.

Women's colleges hadn't been on Grace's radar until an uncle told her about Wellesley, its emphasis on women's empowerment, and its strong alumni network. Her impression was solidified by an interview she had with a Wellesley alumna at the end of winter break. Of the half dozen alumni interviews she'd done, this one stood out. The woman seemed genuinely interested in Grace, her likes and dislikes, her favorite classes, her ambitions for the future. And Grace was attracted to the interviewer's easy confidence. Is that what it would be like for her?

But the euphoria of Wellesley's acceptance was followed by the disappointment of its financial aid offer. Grace didn't receive a dime. In my terms, Wellesley is a seller. Nearly half of the students who are accepted end up enrolling. It's prestigious enough and desirable enough that four out of every ten undergraduates pay its $75,000 annual price tag. As a result, financial aid from its $2.1 billion endowment is based mostly on need.

Grace's main objective in going to the open house was to visit the financial aid office and appeal for money. The staff member who met Grace told her the same thing her letter did: she didn't qualify for any aid from Wellesley. Maybe in two years, when her sister, a high school sophomore, went to college she might get something.

A few weeks earlier, when the financial aid letter had arrived from Wellesley, Grace and her parents had their most substantial conversation ever about paying for college. She found out that going to Wellesley would eat up the family's savings. There would be little left to pay college tuition for her younger siblings. "I shouldn't put the burden on my parents," she said. "I don't want to feel guilty about where I go to college."

By the time Grace arrived home from Wellesley, she had started to come to terms with the fact that the East Coast college wasn't an option financially. A week later she went to UCLA for an open house. For much of her senior year, Grace had rebuffed her parents' suggestion that she look more carefully at options in California. Now in Grace's head, UCLA was her only choice. Like Wellesley, Smith didn't offer her financial aid. UC's campuses in Berkeley and Davis were too close to home.

Although UCLA didn't give Grace financial assistance either, as a California resident, her cost there would be half that of Wellesley, around $35,000 a year. Her parents assured her they had saved enough money.

On the last Friday in April, Grace signed on to UCLA's website and submitted her $250 deposit to reserve a spot in the Class of 2023. Five days later, on May 1, she pulled up two other acceptances from Smith and UC Davis and selected "decline." Even though it was a formality, she couldn't bring herself to say no to Berkeley and Wellesley. She still felt regret; she still worried whether she had made the right choice.

"It's hard to let go of what you idealized," Grace told me later. "But that's what life is going to be like—you're going to want things and not get them."

In hindsight, she wondered whether she should have applied at all to a costly school that didn't offer merit aid. Grace's high school counselor had suggested schools known to be generous with money even if they weren't brand names. But Grace didn't want to listen to that advice a year ago. She was too focused on the idea of a "good college" because she believed ultimately that her success in life depended on it.

The anxiety about getting into a brand-name school starts with a single, fundamental principle believed by students and parents in top high schools: it matters *where* you go to college.

It's a bedrock belief I have wrestled with for more than two decades of writing about higher education. I didn't go to a highly selective college, yet I'm surrounded by people who did—and many of them maintain that the name on their diploma has had a significant impact on their success in life.

But CEOs and hiring managers tell me something different. When I wrote my last book, I spent time observing how executives from companies as large as IBM, Xerox, and Enterprise Rent-A-Car and as small as IDEO and Pinterest hire new college graduates. For the most part, I found that job applicants' experiences and their skills matter more in hiring than their alma mater or major. The advice in that book was that *how* students go to college—from choosing a major and courses to finding internships—plays a much larger role in life after graduation than *where* they go to college.

Consider this: every year, some 1.8 million twentysomethings graduate from a four-year college. Only 54,000 of them receive a bachelor's degree from what we'd consider a selective college. Clearly, employers have more than 54,000 good jobs they need to fill each year with college graduates.

That said, parents and students who obsess over getting into highly selective colleges aren't thinking about just any job after graduation. Rather, they're often focused on elite professions where graduates from top colleges typically land—management consulting firms, Wall Street investment banks, and white-shoe law firms. They're all filled with alumni from ultra-selective colleges. So, too, are the clerkships in the Supreme Court, the ranks of the national media in New York, the staff of Senate offices in Washington, and the CEO suites of the Fortune 500.

Elite colleges seem to lead to elite jobs, and in turn, elite money. Around half of *Forbes*'s list of the most powerful people, as well as half of America's billionaires, attended top schools.

The problem with these often-quoted statistics about selective schools is that they overlook the role that the individual student plays in their own eventual success—both the social and financial "capital" they bring to their undergraduate careers is very important. As we have seen throughout the book, top colleges don't take just anyone who applies. They accept smart students who exhibit promise—or who are well connected or come from upper-middle-class and wealthy families—and then unite them with top-notch faculty, research opportunities, ambitious classmates, and an extensive alumni network.

In other words, it's difficult to separate whether what happens to these students after college is the result of *who* they are or *what* they did while in college. The research on this question is divided as well, which is one of the reasons I have grappled with this question for so long. One camp of scholars concludes teenagers and their families are more responsible for what happens to them later in their life than we give them credit for. The other camp maintains that selective colleges matter.

One of the most famous and oft-cited set of economic studies on this matter comes from Stacy Dale and Alan Krueger. In 2014, the pair produced an update on their study from a decade earlier that examined the incomes of more than 30,000 adults who had graduated from thirty colleges and were now in their 40s and 50s.

In both studies, the two economists matched students of "seemingly comparable ability"—based on their SAT scores and class rank—who were admitted to the same colleges but made different choices. Some went to the most selective colleges, such as Stanford, while others chose to attend slightly less elite institutions, such as Penn State.

The studies compared the earnings for students with similar academic abilities who went to colleges of differing selectivity. What the economists concluded turned a long-held belief about the power of elite higher education on its head: the earnings of the two groups were essentially the same. A student with a 1390 SAT score who went to Miami University of Ohio but was also accepted by the University of Pennsylvania earned as much, on average, as the student with a 1390 who went to Penn.

The findings speak to the power of the individual. The average SAT scores of the colleges where the student applied were more likely to predict success than the school students actually attended.

The research by Dale and Krueger hasn't been without critics who say the studies would have shown a definite variance in student earnings if a much broader range of schools had been considered in terms of selectivity. But in reality, most well-positioned students rarely, if ever, consider such a large variety of schools. Their choices usually fall within a set of colleges that are strikingly similar in quality. It's more like students are comparing Honeycrisp and Gala apples, rather than choosing between an apple and Apple Jacks. That's what makes the fine distinctions that teenagers draw between top schools so maddening. The differences between what happens to the graduates of Rice (ranked 16th by *U.S. News*), the University of Rochester (ranked 29th), and the University of Illinois at Urbana-Champaign (ranked 48th) are subtle at best.

For forty years, top-ranked institutions have sold us on those distinctions, telling prospective students and their families that the brand name on the degree is what matters most when it comes to success after college. But in recent years, economists have been digging deeper into a stockpile of data from tax records and job postings. What they're finding is starting to shift the conversation around the question "Does it matter where you go to college?" For economists, it's a much more nuanced answer than before: majors and skills might count for more in the job market than the college itself. It makes sense. Employers hire for jobs requiring a distinct set of skills. Colleges as a whole don't signal that someone has those skills, but employers think a student's college major does.

Would-be college students now have access to those numbers that for years sat buried in government databases. In 2019, the U.S. Education Department released an update to the College Scorecard (collegescorecard.ed.gov), allowing students to take a more granular look at what graduates earn and how much debt they take on broken out by academic program, not just the college they attended.

It shows, for instance, that a computer science major from the University of Illinois earned $92,200 one year after graduation, just a few thousand dollars short of the same major at eighth-ranked Duke ($95,200). A history major from fourteenth-ranked Vanderbilt makes $26,500, about $3,000 *less* than one from Arizona State, which is ranked 115th (although the history student leaves ASU more in debt, according to the College Scorecard). An economics major from Tulane, ranked 44th, earns $41,100, about $2,000 *less* than one from Binghamton University, who also leaves school with about $3,000 less in debt.

In general, browsers of the College Scorecard will see that graduates of nursing, computer science, and information technology programs earn the most a year after college—almost no matter where they go—while psychology, drama/theater arts, and biology are the lowest paid (likely because psychology and biology majors go on to graduate or medical school, where the real money comes). One warning about the College Scorecard, however. The earnings embedded in the tool have their limitations: they only include graduates who took out federal loans, and, for now, first-year salaries.

But in this era of Big Data, consumer information about graduate outcomes at a microscopic level is only likely to improve. The Education Department has been working with private companies, including Google, to make federal data more accessible. And data analytics firms that study labor trends in real time are drawing more precise insights from scanning millions of online job ads and résumés—insights that every day are becoming available to college-bound students and their families.

One of those firms, Boston-based Burning Glass, has found, for instance, that marketing majors who have specific skills in SEO (search-engine optimization) and SQL (structured query language) earn nearly $20,000 more a year than those without those skills—no matter where their degree is from. Burning Glass also concluded that if liberal arts graduates gain proficiency in one of eight technical skills, such as social media or data analysis, their prospects of landing entry-level jobs increase substantially.

The bottom line: in your college search worry less about specific name brands and even majors and worry more about acquiring skills and experiences once you're on campus, such as finding an undergraduate research project or landing an internship. Remember: fewer than a third of college graduates work in jobs related to their majors.

In North Carolina, Nicole's carefully laid plans to attend a college at the top of the rankings began to unravel around the middle of March. By then, she had three acceptances in hand, one from Northeastern and two of them from local schools she had already vowed she wouldn't attend: UNC–Chapel Hill and NC State. On March 13, she got one more acceptance: the University of Washington.

But what Nicole was really waiting for wouldn't come until the end of March, on Ivy Day. That's when Dartmouth and Harvard and the other Ivy League schools all release their regular admissions decisions online simultaneously. She didn't expect to get into Harvard. That was a vanity application. Dartmouth, on the other hand, had been at the top of her list along with Penn from the start.

The news from Dartmouth, however, wasn't any better than the notice from Penn back during early decision. Nicole was rejected. Her 34 (out of 36) on the ACT, ten AP courses, and class rank in the top 10 percent of her top high school made her simply another high-achieving girl in the applicant pool of many selective schools. The day after the decision arrived from Dartmouth, she didn't want to talk. "She's a little fragile after the last wave of information," her mom wrote to me.

When we did speak a week later, Nicole had just returned from an accepted student event at Northeastern. "It wasn't great," she admitted. Perhaps it was the sting of Dartmouth's rejection fresh in her mind. Maybe it was her coming to terms with the co-op program and how different it would make the typical undergraduate experience as students cycled in and out of school to go to work. Or it might have been the accepted students she met who didn't seem of the academic caliber of those she had interacted with at Penn.

"This is just about me panicking," she said. "We all know I'm going to Northeastern."

For Nicole, how to pay for college was never the concern it was for Grace or Chris. Financial aid from Northeastern brought the price to $45,000 a year for Nicole. Her parents would cover the bulk of the bill and Nicole would pay the rest with earnings from a job and student loans. At the end of April, the question Nicole was asking herself was whether Northeastern was worth the price. She had become so enthralled with attending a college at the top of the *U.S. News* rankings that she never considered she'd end up somewhere else. So, she always thought she'd pay whatever it took to go to college because she thought tens of thousands of dollars would be going to Penn or Dartmouth, not Northeastern.

I asked her again about UNC–Chapel Hill. If she was worried about prestige, Carolina was ranked higher than Northeastern and it would be half the cost of Northeastern, every year for four years. She paused. She told me her high school had started compiling the annual list of where seniors are going to college. There were already forty seniors on that list headed to Carolina and it wasn't even May 1 yet.

"I can't stay in North Carolina," she told me.

On April 28, she paid her deposit to Northeastern. Thirteen months after she visited Penn filled with anticipation and hope, Nicole's search reached a conclusion much different than the one she had charted in her purple Moleskine notebook.

If you read through the volumes of economic studies about the benefits of going to a selective school, they largely focus on one outcome: money. But if you ask graduates of top colleges about their undergraduate experiences, you'll probably hear about something else: people. Whenever Nicole and I discussed her college search we usually ended up talking about the students and professors she hoped to meet at Penn or Dartmouth.

It just may be that the ultimate reward of a degree from a selective institution has little to do with what happens in the classroom. There's not much (or any) evidence that an Ivy League education is better than one from a college a rung down the ladder.

The reason parents drive themselves crazy to get their kids into Stanford or Harvard or Princeton is that they believe the life-shaping relationships that form in the dorms, on the athletic fields, and in the classrooms are what will give their teenagers entrée into society's highest echelons.

Sure, if you go to Harvard you probably have a greater chance of rubbing elbows with the founder of the next Facebook or the daughter of a Fortune 500 CEO. You also might have a better shot of getting into a top law school, landing a grant from the National Science Foundation, or earning a PhD from an elite university. But if you're a well-prepared student whose parents attended college, you'll likely find important connections and pathways to success at nearly *any* school on your list. As I've tried to make clear, just because you have the qualifications to get into Harvard, Stanford, Michigan, or Amherst doesn't mean that these sellers will accept you. Be sure to broaden your search and apply to a mix of private and public schools that are also selective—but not as hyper-selective—and take into account other factors such as the likelihood of graduating on time, affordability, and access to faculty, mentors, and advising.

Perhaps the biggest difference between hyper-selective schools and other institutions is the stream in which a student swims academically. At a top-ranked school, you'll step into a river of valedictorians, calculus geeks, and National Merit scholars. They'll pull you along, or in some cases wash you out. Smart students who, in tapping a given college, choose lower on the selectivity rankings will likely meet fewer classmates like them and have access to fewer resources such as labs, libraries, and professors. They'll have to swim upstream more often.

So I'm not saying that it doesn't matter whether you end up at the Rochester Institute of Technology instead of Yale, but the differences are a lot *less* stark than we like to believe. Does going to Yale help? Sure. But there are so many other factors contributing to your ultimate path to success that focusing exclusively on this one narrow stretch of it seems out of whack. Are you majoring in the right thing? Have you pursued the right internship? Did your parents let you "fail" enough as a teenager to build resiliency and the ability to navigate the uncertainty of a changing workforce? Do you know the right people at the firm where you're applying for your first job? In the end, college is a staging ground. It's one of many stops you'll make throughout life, but it's not the only one, and certainly not the last.

In the fall of 2019, Nicole was settling in for her first semester at Northeastern. Her favorite class was financial accounting. "The professor," she told me, "has a *real* job, in accounting," unlike professors at selective schools who mostly come from academic backgrounds. While she believed that an Ivy League institution would have challenged her more intellectually, she came to understand that Northeastern with its practical, job-oriented curriculum and co-op experiences would prepare her just as well for getting a job after college.

Nicole was already diving into her business major, where she was making friends through group projects. She joined a club sport, which was keeping her busy outside of class. She knew that Northeastern—like any college for any student—would only turn out to be as good as she made it. Although she didn't regret choosing Northeastern over Carolina, "sometimes I wish I was around people from my hometown or high school," Nicole told me. At Northeastern, "most people are from Massachusetts, New Jersey, or New York and so almost everyone knows someone from home."

Meanwhile, in Los Angeles, Grace has been pleasantly surprised to find a small college feel at UCLA. Her large freshmen-level lecture classes break into smaller discussion groups led by a graduate teaching assistant. "The discussions really are amazing because the PhD students are super smart and are very relatable to students," she said.

Although Grace told me she still would have applied to Dartmouth ED if she had to do it all over again ("for the lifelong connections and networks of an Ivy"), she now wishes she had explored UCLA more during the search instead of dismissing it until she had no other choice. "The professors I have are amazing at teaching, love what they're doing, and that makes me excited to go to class every day," she said. It reminds her of what she thought she would get at Wellesley.

"I really appreciate the vast opportunities that the bigger public school has offered," Grace told me. She joined two club sports teams and is applying for two environmental research clubs for the winter quarter.

It may not be the life on the East Coast that Grace pictured the previous fall when we met, but the college search for her—like that of so many of the three dozen teenagers I followed in my reporting—was a learning experience in and of itself.

The students I found who were happiest with the way things had turned out were able to maneuver through the unpredictability of life after their senior year by embracing a new school or two near the top of their list rather than remain entranced with the luster of the best brands as crowned by some magazine or website.

Few of the seniors I met in high schools across the country throughout 2018–19 were accepted into their first-choice colleges that were often among the most selective in the nation. But you know what? They didn't end up skipping college nor did they end up at Podunk U. In the end, they discovered that there is no such thing as a perfect fit.

A girl who got rejected early decision at Duke went to Carolina. Another denied by Columbia enrolled at Rice. A student who didn't get in early to Bowdoin went to Carleton. A girl who didn't get the financial aid she needed after getting in early at Brown ended up with a full ride to Boston University. A boy from Nebraska wait-listed at Grinnell got into the honors program at the University of Nebraska. One of the things that's missing in all the anxiety over the super-low acceptance rates at selective schools is that even those rejected from their dream school still end up at a place that's worthy of bragging about on the rear window of the family car.

Conclusion

Charting the Future

College admissions offices are tradition-bound places. Even as schools compete with each other for students, they still move in packs through the annual admissions cycle using a generic set of approaches—campus tours and direct mail, common deadlines, and strikingly similar rating scales for assessing applicants. Once every decade or so, a change will come along that rattles the system. The introduction of early decision in the 1950s. The direct mail boom of the 1980s. The transition to online applications in the early 2000s. The coronavirus pandemic in 2020.

But college admissions has largely escaped the kind of seismic shifts that have jolted other industries from Hollywood to retail malls to publishing. That's in large part because higher education as a whole is a heavily regulated industry. To gain access to the tens of billions of dollars in federal grants and student loans, colleges must be accredited by regional agencies, through which they essentially govern themselves.

Colleges and universities operate like a cartel. Nowhere is that more evident than when trying to gain access to their front door: the admissions office. High-profile schools, both among the buyers and sellers, set the rules of engagement, while colleges with fewer resources follow along. That was even true in the pandemic when a few schools shifted to test-optional and moved deadlines, and competitors adopted the same policies. Unlike in most other industries, a new entrant can't knock off established players. In admissions, there's no Netflix or Spotify pushing colleges to change as those companies forced television networks and radio stations to up their game.

But gradual changes in admissions are coming, driven by teenagers, the government, and colleges themselves.

Let's start with Generation Z, those born between 1995 and 2012. They will fill the pipeline of traditional students going to college through the end of the 2020s. Already, they are using tools to bypass the official marketing channels that colleges have long regulated. They scroll through topic pages on Reddit, such as r/applyingtocollege or r/SAT, without ever getting an email from a school or visiting its campus. They watch YouTube videos recorded by students talking about how they applied to college and showing what life is really like on their campuses. Take a look at Katherine Waissbluth, a Stanford undergraduate who has more than 50,000 subscribers to her YouTube channel, The Kath Path. Katherine's channel includes videos about a "Tuesday at Stanford," a "Day in the Life of an English Major," and the "Most Stereotypical College Essays." Some have more than 200,000 views.

If Gen Z is able to discover colleges through their own channels, they'll end up ignoring the gobs of traditional propaganda from colleges even more than they do already. They'll come to realize there isn't such a thing as a "dream college" or a "perfect fit," no matter how many times a college says that they're the one for you. Perhaps students and families will finally learn about the real place behind the façade of Bill Royall's marketing machine and see that college is what you make of it, not what some brochure or campus tour guide promises you.

At the same time, the federal government has opened up the floodgates to potentially even more aggressive sales pitches from colleges. For years, NACAC—the association of college admissions officers—held to an ethics code that banned schools from offering incentives to encourage students to apply early decision or from continuing to recruit applicants after the May 1 decision deadline.

But following an investigation by the Justice Department, NACAC was forced to scrap the rules in 2019. While colleges insisted that the guidelines were designed to protect students from being poached by schools with a vested financial interest in filling their classes, the government said the ethics code stifled competition and prevented students from getting the best financial deal.

Now that the restraints are off, colleges are likely to offer applicants perks—things like housing priority or special scholarships—if they apply early decision. Or schools will extend more financial aid in May, June, or July to lure those who were accepted but chose to go elsewhere. The result is likely to upend the traditional admissions calendar, and unfortunately, create even more anxiety among some students and parents.

Finally, colleges themselves are making other changes. Perhaps the biggest shift is the declining significance of standardized test scores. More than a thousand campuses had dropped the SAT/ACT as an admission requirement before 2020; another five hundred schools dropped the tests when the pandemic caused the tests to be canceled. It's likely that some will return to requiring a test score one day, either to bring surging application numbers back in line with the human resources needed to read them all, or because they believe the test score is a necessary signal amid all the noise of high school grades.

Still, many selective colleges will remain test-optional, looking to the experience of the University of Chicago. In 2018, Chicago became the most prestigious and highest-ranked university ever to go test-optional (it's No. 3 in *U.S. News* ranking). In the first year of going test optional, between 10 and 15 percent of applicants to Chicago didn't submit the ACT or SAT, about the same proportion who were eventually admitted without scores. Those who didn't send scores typically included supplemental materials—creative writing, research projects, or a clip of a performance—to bolster their application. "When they tied it all together," said James Nondorf, Chicago's dean of admissions, "I didn't need to see the testing to know that this kid was going to come here and be a rock star."

Other bigger changes to the admissions system are likely on the horizon, driven in large part by changing demographics.

After decades of fairly steady expansion in the number of high school graduates across the United States, the country is heading into a lengthy period of decline. The biggest drop-off will be between 2026 and 2031, when the children of the Great Recession reach high school graduation. Meanwhile, fewer high school graduates will be white or come from families whose parents went to college. Both the number of Latino and first-generation college-bound students are expected to grow substantially.

How the country experiences this next demographic shift will vary widely. The South and the West will account for nearly all the growth in the high school population through 2030. At the same time, the Northeast and the Midwest—home to the highest density of college campuses in the United States from Michigan and Ohio to New York and Massachusetts—will experience a steady and significant decline.

These pressures will impact buyers and sellers in starkly different ways, with consequences for students who plan to apply to both types of schools. Higher education in the United States is increasingly headed toward even more of a two-tier system, with accelerating polarization between the wealthiest colleges and the rest. With the pool of high school students shrinking, the students the top colleges enroll in the decade ahead will affect schools farther down the line.

In the wake of the coronavirus pandemic, buyers will become increasingly desperate to fill seats with tuition discounts—especially those near the bottom of higher education's hierarchy. Those schools will flood the market with even more marketing appeals to a wider range of teenagers, offering easier ways to apply and get in, while also struggling to balance what they collect in revenue from students with what they then give out in tuition discounts. For this set of buyers, fewer tuition dollars will mean less to spend on new dorms and classroom buildings, professors, and academic advising and career services.

Under such circumstances, prospective students need to be even more careful to avoid an undermatch because less-selective publics and privates won't be able to invest in services to keep undergraduates in school, get them to graduation, and help them secure a job afterward. The trade-offs schools will be forced to make—mainly increasing discounts to maintain enrollment—will eventually put them in a death spiral. Already, some schools are missing their enrollment targets every year. About a dozen colleges have closed each year since 2015—double the number at the beginning of the century—a trend that, along with mergers, is projected only to increase.

Meanwhile, sellers face a different set of trade-offs. Admissions has long been the lever top colleges pulled to improve their prestige and rankings. The campuses with the most enviable perch in higher education—the most highly ranked, or the super sellers, places like Harvard, Stanford, and Princeton—will continue to draw the best students using their vast resources. But those schools are few and far between. The group right below them—schools like Emory and Northwestern, still highly ranked but with billions in the bank rather than tens of billions—will be forced to spend more to keep up with the super selectives. Some will succeed, but others risk becoming more like buyers.

At the same time, sellers everywhere remain under pressure to diversify their student bodies. The question is whether these elite campuses will be willing to make the trade-offs necessary to enroll the significant numbers of low-income, first-generation, and minority students coming down the pike.

Will they recruit at high schools like Chris's or continue relying on programs that target the same small group of low-income kids with high test scores? Will they reduce the number of applicants they accept in early decision to open up more spots in regular decision? Will they reduce the preference they give in admissions to legacies and athletes, which would further their mission—and that of higher education in general—to promote social mobility? After all, colleges are not another set of private clubs but rather a public good that receive billions in tax breaks because of their role in serving broader society.

No matter what, history shows us that even as the admissions process changes, it continues to serve the agenda of colleges above all. It has to. Their needs for more full-pay students or more soccer goalies won't change even if the demographics of the country do. Elite colleges won't suddenly stop getting inundated with applications. In the end, the real purpose of admissions at a top college is that of gatekeeper—that is, to turn away the vast majority of applicants.

Beyond the changes bearing down on the admissions office in the near term, what if we imagined a more revolutionary overhaul?

One popular suggestion that comes up often is for a lottery, where names of qualified students would be picked at random until a class is filled. Others have urged developing a matching system, similar to the one for medical-residency programs that pairs the preferences based on rank-order lists each side submits. But establishing either structure for 3 million high school seniors would be a daunting task and one that probably wouldn't pass muster with federal antitrust lawyers because colleges would need to share information on students in ways that at least the government believes unfairly inhibits competition.

And so, the traditional process lives on. But for how long? The system is beginning to collapse under the weight of increasing applications, questions about its genuineness, and anger about a lack of fairness. Something has to give, especially as schools were forced to improvise their admissions process on the fly after COVID-19 upended the search for juniors in the spring of 2020—changes that could stick in the long run. So, what could the college search and the admissions process look like in the future? How might everyone involved in admissions together rethink the system we have today?

First, two suggestions for parents, students, and their counselors:

Take control over more of the admissions process. Assert the clout you have—decide for yourself what is important. Right now, it feels as if colleges get to press all the buttons: students essentially let colleges tell them what should matter in high school, and even in life. Turn the tables. After all, you're the customer. Colleges dictate the process because we allow them to.

The best way for students to gain leverage is to broaden their search beyond the super selective schools—the ones that have amassed great fortunes and generate so much attention that they must reject more than 90 percent of applicants. If you focus your search on what you want to *do* in college rather than *where* you go to college, you'll find schools that will provide a superb education at a reasonable price but that may not be wealthy or necessarily well-known. Just as Canada Goose makes a fine winter jacket—but not the *only* fine winter coat—Harvard, Princeton, Stanford, Michigan, and Williams don't have an exclusive claim on great educations.

Encourage students to drive the college search but allow for detours. A handful of the teenagers I followed during their senior year ended up at what they told me were their "dream" schools. When I checked in with them their first semester of freshman year, however, they were unhappy. They'd jumped through all the hoops to get in: the demanding classes, the high SAT scores, the legion of extracurricular activities. But for what—to do it all again in college? High school, like college, is a staging ground for the next phase of your life. Enjoy it while you can because you have little control over what happens in the admissions process. Allow for changeability throughout your search. It's okay to be unsure about what you want to major in and where you want to go. The students I met who ended up being most satisfied with their final choice were the ones who embraced the ambiguity of the process rather than got fixated on one or two schools. And, parents, let your child see the search as a learning experience. Stop using the college where *you* want them to end up as a trophy for your parenting.

And how could the federal government make the college search better? The fact is, it has enormous leverage that it can use more effectively:

Force colleges to recruit all applicants as if they're athletes. High school athletes upload their highlight reels to online recruiting sites so college coaches can easily find them. Once in the recruiting pipeline, prospective athletes are guided by coaches through the application process. It's a personal approach where students know if they're likely to get in even before they apply.

Colleges should bring elements of the athletic recruiting process to the *entire* application pool. Here's one possibility discussed by several admissions deans over the years: a national clearinghouse created by colleges or another entity, such as the U.S. Department of Education. Teenagers would upload samples of their work starting as early as their first year of high school, along with basic biographical information. At any point, students could choose to make their high school file available for admissions offices to see.

Over time, such a database could render the very idea of an application meaningless. Rather than wait for applications to arrive, colleges could search the student clearinghouse using specific parameters, much as they do when they buy names from the College Board for marketing.

But to even the playing field in admissions and bring more transparency to the clearinghouse process, both sides in the transaction need to see what the other is doing. Colleges should disclose what they're looking for. That way, students and their families can see if a specific college they're considering is, say, looking for students from Southern California, or from five specific zip codes in Florida, or for students who want to major in history, or for those interested in Catholic colleges. At the same time, students should list the other colleges on their search list and the places where they eventually apply. In this ideal setup, colleges could even disclose what they actually charge students with various family incomes and academic credentials, and families could list what they're willing to pay.

Sound far-fetched? Perhaps. The $9 billion admissions industry has a lot of incentive to *not* let that happen. But the U.S. government could easily force colleges to change if they want access to federal dollars.

But ultimately change is going to have to come from the colleges themselves. Here are four things they should do:

Eliminate binding early decision. October is the new January for seniors in pressure-cooker high schools, where ED tends to be more popular and only adds to the anxiety about choosing the right college. According to the Common App, the five days leading up to the ED deadline are now busier than the same period before the traditional January 1 deadline. For too many teenagers, ED has turned into little more than a strategy, a trick to help them get into a super selective school. They don't necessarily love the college; they just love their chance of admission.

Early decision—with its application deadline two months into a student's last year of high school—rushes a process that should be a journey of discovery and reflection for teenagers and their families. Early decision leaves students with the impression that there's only *one right college* for them.

To be sure, some teenagers know exactly where they want to go to college in the fall of their senior year. For those students, early action (without a binding commitment or limits on where else they can apply) or rolling admissions offer the opportunity for an earlier notification without forcing them to make a decision until the spring. What it doesn't do is give schools the insurance they want of locking in a significant portion of their incoming class in December. Thus, scrapping early decision would swing the pendulum in admissions ever so slightly back in the direction of applicants.

Redesign the application to focus on what really matters. Schools typically know that two basic measures indicate whether students will succeed on their campuses: high school courses and grades. That's why nothing usually carries more weight in admissions than those two elements.

After those two factors, there is a steep drop-off in the emphasis given to other parts of the application: essays, counselor and teacher recommendations, and extracurricular activities. Fewer than 15 percent said those factors are of considerable importance, according to an annual survey by the National Association for College Admission. Forty percent said they carry "moderate" weight. One reason is the unreliability of key elements of the application, said John Latting, Emory's admissions dean. "Activities are embellished, recommendations lack negative comments, and the standard now is multiple editors for essays," he said.

Admissions readers I watched over the course of a selection cycle generally glanced at parts of the essays and recommendation letters and scanned the list of activities. It's the only way they can wade through each year's rising pile of applications without adding more staff or days to the calendar.

This is not to suggest colleges pare back requirements to make the application easier and faster to complete or fixate only on grades and test scores. It's about making the application better.

Take the essay, for example. Essays are one reason why private admissions counselors can charge an average of $200 an hour or upward of $10,000 to help families through the admissions process. Students at wealthy and suburban schools often start working on their essay during English classes in their junior year or attend school-sponsored workshops over the summer. They might write a dozen drafts or more in the six months before they submit their application.

Think about it: what college course or job will give them that much time to write 650 words? If colleges want to understand how students express themselves in an essay (and without any help), require them to drop by some sort of assessment center—a counselor's office or college campus, for instance—and write an answer to a randomly generated question in a specified period of time.

On the application's list of activities, give space for fewer of them and then ask students to write about their most meaningful commitment, so they don't just see activities as prizes they collect in high school.

If parts of the current form are less meaningful, colleges should ask students for evidence of their potential beyond the usual polished checklist. Some schools, including Yale, allow students to submit images or audio and video responses. The Common App said 80,000 freshman applicants who used its application in 2018–19 submitted multimedia portfolios of their work.

Of course, a powerful force in keeping the status quo is the Common App itself. As it has grown from a paper application in the 1970s shared by a handful of colleges to an international juggernaut used by hundreds of colleges, so too has its control of the information an application requests. It sets the rules. To truly rethink the application, colleges would need to force changes to the Common App or cut ties with it.

That's a trade-off many colleges are unwilling to make given that the Common App helps flood the top of their application funnel with prospective students. But it's a choice that would tame the application monster they created. It could result in applicants who are truly interested in a college and would tell a more authentic story than the one currently produced by students who simply cut-and-paste their college applications together.

Expand the field. The reason college admissions has turned into a race to be won is that angst-ridden teens and their parents believe higher education is a scarce commodity. It isn't. Only seats at the most selective colleges are.

In the United States, prestige in higher education is measured by how many students a university rejects. While the philosophy on Wall Street is that growth is good, within higher education the prevailing wisdom is that increased size comes at the expense of academic quality and reputation.

But that philosophy isn't shared across the globe. In Canada, for instance, the three most-prominent universities—the University of Toronto, McGill University, and the University of British Columbia—enroll nearly 150,000 undergraduates. That's more students than the top eighteen U.S. universities in the *U.S. News & World Report* rankings combined.

Even as the number of full-time undergraduates at U.S. colleges and universities has grown, enrollment at the nation's most-selective and elite institutions has barely grown at all. There have been a few, modest exceptions. Stanford enlarged its freshman class in 2016 by about a hundred students. Yale expanded the class entering in 2017 by about two hundred students, the first expansion at Yale in forty years. They should expand the size of their incoming classes even more, and so too should the rest of the Ivy League and other top universities. To prevent these colleges from simply recruiting more teenagers whose families can pay full tuition, the federal government can encourage schools to enroll students from a broader socioeconomic range by providing more federal dollars for each low- and middle-income student they take. Schools would no longer have the excuse to turn away such students because they can't afford them.

Prospective students should then follow the lead of these selective schools and widen their own playing field to include colleges that will actually accept them. There are plenty of good schools that take a majority of students who apply. A student can only attend one college at a time, so there's no reason to apply to seven top schools. Parents and counselors need to do better to show seniors that there are more colleges out there than just those listed on the first page of the *U.S. News* rankings.

Allow students, early in their college search, to see the total price they'd likely pay. Right now, too many students don't know the actual price tag of a college until after they're accepted and shortly before the May 1 deadline for choosing where to go. Even if colleges never adopt the idea of a national clearinghouse, they should at least release a searchable database of their financial aid offers every year. Then prospective students could look up previous applicants with a similar academic background and family income to understand early on in the search process what kind of aid they might get.

By knowing the total and true price of a degree, students could shape their list to take affordability into consideration rather than selectivity alone. The likely result of syncing the financial fit of college with the social and academic fit is a list that includes a wider range of schools because it finally includes a critical data point: what you'll actually pay.

In 1972, William Fitzsimmons joined Harvard's admissions staff as assistant director. The same year, Charles Deacon started as Georgetown University's admissions dean. By October 2018, when Fitzsimmons took the stand in a federal courtroom to defend the university in a discrimination lawsuit, he had served as Harvard's top admissions official for more than thirty years.

Deacon watched the trial from afar. Both men are now in their seventies and among the longest-serving admissions deans in higher education. Their connection goes beyond their lengthy tenure, however. Both grew up with parents who didn't go to college. Now, they are the gatekeepers at two of the most selective, brand-name universities in the world, passing judgment on children of the rich and powerful, many with deep connections to the campuses. As young admissions directors in the 1970s, "Fitz" and "Charlie," as they're both widely known, started traveling together on joint recruiting trips and remain good friends decades later. In a profession that skews young, is obsessed with numbers, and is driven by marketing, the duo represent a very different era in admissions.

A few weeks after the testimony in the Harvard trial ended, I went to Georgetown's campus to visit Charlie Deacon. Deacon has a tuft of snow-white hair, a craggy face, and a gentle manner. He isn't one for the tools and tactics of the modern admissions business. Georgetown doesn't accept the Common App. "We're not looking for 40,000 applications," Deacon told me. "The whole thing is impersonal." He wants students to "compete" for a spot at Georgetown. And Deacon doesn't care for measures of demonstrated interest or early decision. "It doesn't matter how much you want to come," he said, "as much as we want you to come."

The most important thing for too many admissions offices, he said shaking his head in disapproval, "is not who you get, but that you get the right number."

In other words, admissions is now a sales job.

Deacon's approach is that there are "30,000 to 40,000 top kids out there" with A averages and a 1300 or better on the SAT. "That's 40,000 people in the entire country," he said. "These top ten, fifteen schools are essentially sharing that pool. And my view is that we get our fair share."

He paused. "Most everybody else in that group," he added, naming several top schools but instructing me not to write them down, "cares only if they get the *best* of them."

What does *best* even mean when evaluating the wave of applications that arrive at selective campuses each year? Deacon tells me a story that I'll hear a few more times in my reporting: if a top college mistakenly rejected a thousand students it wanted to admit and accepted a thousand who were close to the line but it wanted to deny, few people would notice.

As I was leaving, I asked Deacon if he had any advice for how I could better understand why we ended up with the admissions process we have today. He suggested I read a book that several others recommended as well: *College Admissions and the Public Interest* by B. Alden Thresher. Like Deacon, Thresher was a top admissions dean for decades; he spent twenty-five years at MIT.

The book, published in 1966, is now out of print. But in 2017, MIT published a free electronic copy on its website. Despite its age, the book remains remarkably relevant to the modern world of admissions.

The introduction to the electronic edition noted that Thresher called the book *College Admissions and the Public Interest*—as in the welfare of society—not the *Public's* interest, which is narrower. The title is a nod to the long view that Thresher takes throughout the book. It also serves as a useful reminder to applicants and their parents that the admissions process is not designed to be in the best interests of a single member of the public (meaning you, the applicant), but in the best interest of society as a whole.

I found Thresher's wider perspective refreshing. I'd just spent a year with teenagers and their families who believed a single admission decision was a verdict on their life. Admissions deans rarely take the long view, either. They're constantly worried about the year ahead, making their next class, meeting their financial aid budget, and fulfilling an ever-growing list of demands given to them by their presidents and boards.

Yes, admissions, even at its best, is an imprecise process. It's an educated guessing game played with rules that are constantly shifting based on a college's agenda. It's why teenagers—whether they're at the beginning, middle, or near the end of their college search—should constantly remind themselves that they can steer the process, but they can't control the ultimate outcome.

An observation Thresher makes on his opening page stayed with me long after I finished the book: "One cannot tell by looking at a toad how far he will jump."

It's one of the most quoted lines in the book for a reason. There is no admissions officer—no matter how experienced, no matter how much information they possess, no matter how long they study the application—who can predict who will succeed at a particular school and how far they will eventually travel in life.

Appendix

Beyond the Rankings:
Finding Unsung Schools

As the number of applications arriving at selective colleges rises every year, more and more high-school seniors and their families are left to wonder whether they have a better shot at winning a Powerball jackpot than gaining admission to a top-ranked school.

Whenever I spoke to high-school students, parents, and their counselors, one question came up over and over again: What should we look for in our college search? What makes a "good" college?

I understand why families rely so much on the college rankings, because it's difficult in the course of the search to find "the right fit." But after nearly twenty-five years of writing about higher education and visiting hundreds of campuses, I've found that there are fewer differences than we're often led to believe between a school ranked in the top 20 and one ranked thirty or fifty spots lower.

So, how does one find those colleges off the beaten path or hidden farther down in the rankings?

I've identified four ingredients that are critical to spotting a good fit. My choice doesn't mean that everything else *isn't* important. But if you're going to dedicate your time and energy anywhere as you sort through dozens or hundreds of colleges, here's where I think you should focus your efforts.

(You can find most of this information in a college's Common Data Set, the federal government's College Navigator, or by asking the college. If they won't tell you, that should send up red flags. For a list of resources, click on *Who Gets In and Why* on my website, jeffselingo.com.)

1. Find a campus where you'll swim along with the stream academically, but make sure the school is also pulling you along to the finish line.

You want to look for a college where classmates will encourage and challenge you, one that's a good fit—not a campus where you'll wash out because you can't keep up and not one where you'll have to swim against a stream of students lacking motivation.

- **Pay attention to the retention rate, which measures the percentage of freshmen who return for their sophomore year.** The national average is around 81 percent. Most selective schools are above 90 percent, and many highly ranked schools are above 85 percent. A retention rate around the national average or below, however, indicates that students are struggling academically, grappling with how to pay for school, or are not satisfied with their experience.

- **Scrutinize graduation rates and see how they compare to predicted rates.** Fewer than 50 percent of students who enter college seeking a bachelor's degree complete that degree at the same institution *within four years*; 62 percent finish in six years. Many colleges also compute—but don't often advertise—their "expected" or "predicted" graduation rate based on their student demographics. Ask for that number to see whether the school is under- or overperforming on what's expected. *U.S. News & World Report* also publishes the predicted rate for many schools in its rankings.

- **Understand how graduation and retention rates differ for students like you.** There's one rate for the college as a whole, but the numbers differ by major, family income, and gender. For example, the national six-year graduation rate is higher for women than men (65 percent vs. 59 percent).

- **Ask if your major will still be around in a few years.** The COVID-19 pandemic has caused severe financial stress at some schools, and, coupled with an expected downturn in high-school graduates around 2026, colleges are scaling back their offerings and cutting faculty. Yes, some schools will go out of business (mostly small ones, with enrollments of under a thousand students and struggling to attract applicants). The bigger issue is that you might apply to a college that will later slash programs or delay investments in new buildings and services. Be careful about going to a cash-strapped college not known for the program you're interested in, or selecting a major that has low enrollments.

2. Search for schools where you'll find your tribe of students, get to know faculty members, and connect with mentors.

Whenever I ask college graduates what remains with them long after they leave campus, I always hear about people. We may forget what we learned in a politics or philosophy class, but we remember a professor, a coach, or an advisor.

- **Look past the list of professors with degrees from prestigious places and bestselling books.** Be more concerned about whether professors will make time for you after class or during office hours. The Gallup-Purdue Index, which has surveyed tens of thousands of college graduates nationwide, found that well-being in life after college had less to do with where students went to school and more with what they did while they were there. Among six experiences Gallup identified with well-being are three associated with faculty: a professor who makes you feel excited about learning, cares about you, and encourages you to pursue your dreams.

- **Seek out faculty members, coaches, or club advisors during the search whom you might encounter later on as an undergraduate.** Ask how they interact with students on a daily basis. Do you sense that they could be a good mentor to you? Research suggests that finding a mentor increases the chances you'll stay in school and find success after college. Having a mentor in college who encouraged students to pursue their "goals and dreams" was found to be the strongest predictor of well-being out of the six experiences that Gallup asked about. But here's the problem: only 14 percent of graduates recalled having a professor who made them excited about learning and encouraged them.

- **Don't look just for the nice dorms and the good food but, rather, the places on and around campus where a student can cultivate life-shaping relationships that often come down to chance.** You don't want to be a spectator to the college experience. You'll need to take advantage of the relationships that form on your dorm floor and in classrooms and through clubs and activities. One study on this subject by three social scientists—Laura Hamilton of the University of California at Merced; Josipa Roksa of the University of Virginia; and Kelly Nielsen of the University of California at San Diego—followed a group of female students (and their parents) from forty-one families at a midwestern university. The three researchers found that those who were deliberate in directing their college careers, and, for instance, got tutors when they needed them and even navigated the social scene looking for opportunities to build networks, were more likely to finish their degree.

3. Scrutinize campuses for the opportunities they provide for hands-on learning and for landing internships.

College is about *how* you go, not *where* you go. You want a campus that offers a vibrant array of extracurricular clubs and has a lively buzz around student activities.

- **Ask about the frequency of class projects and how easy it is to join faculty on their research, even as an undergraduate.** The other three elements on the Gallup-Purdue Index of what contributed to well-being were "experiential" in nature: a project that takes a semester or more to complete; an internship that allows the application of learning; and extracurricular activities. These "work-integrated" elements, when combined with the "faculty relationship" ones from above, happen for only 3 percent of undergraduates, says Brandon Busteed, who led the work for Gallup. So you won't see all of them at every campus on your list, but find as many as you can.

- **Inquire about activities that you're interested in but that might be outside your major or school.** How easily can you join them, and how welcoming are they? The summer after my freshman year at Ithaca College, I worked in the freshman orientation office. That job shaped relationships that I still have to this day with people who weren't journalism majors like I was. The same with the student newspaper. We had plenty of students who didn't want to become journalists, but the experience provided a lifelong network for all of us.

- **Even if the campus tour doesn't go there, visit the career services office or the dean's office at your school and look for internship listings or places where this year's undergraduates interned.** In the research for my previous book, *There Is Life After College*, I found that winning an internship is increasingly the best way—and sometimes the only way—to getting hired by some organizations. Today, employers at large companies hire as full-time workers around 50 percent of the interns who worked for them before they graduated, and in some industries, the share is closer to 75 percent. You want to intern during your college career at least once, and perhaps try to parlay the last internship before your senior year into a job offer.

- **Find campuses that will allow you to pivot. There's a good chance you'll change your mind about your major.** The U.S. Education Department says that about 30 percent of students switch majors at least once. Also, with the skills needed to keep up in any job changing at an ever faster rate, look for places where you can also get a good liberal arts education that helps you cultivate skills in problem-solving, writing, and critical thinking.

4. Calculate the return on your investment.

Remember, this is *your* college search, not that of your neighbor, your teacher, or your uncle. Find the right fit academically, socially, and financially.

- **Don't be seduced by the name brand without thinking about the money.** Forget about that scholarship your neighbor's kid got to some school; not every college offers a discount, and not every financial aid package is negotiable. If you can't easily write a $23,000 check for the average in-state public college or $51,000 for the average private school—and do that for four years—then be sure to have on your list the "buyers" I spoke about earlier in the book (see chapter 2). That's where your chances for merit aid are better. You can explore my list of buyers and sellers at jeffselingo.com/buyersandsellers.
- **Don't pick a major based on money.** The majors that you *think* will pay don't always. A few years ago when I wrote an article for the *New York Times*, I found that salaries within specific majors vary greatly. For example, the top quarter of earners who majored in English make more over their lifetimes than the bottom quarter of chemical engineers. Even English or history graduates who make just above the median lifetime earnings for their major do pretty well when compared to typical graduates in business or a STEM field.
- **Ask about graduate outcomes, but don't depend only on the survey of new graduates.** Nearly every school does a "first destinations" survey, asking their graduates six months after commencement if they're employed or in graduate school. It's from that survey you'll usually hear about how 90 percent or more are employed or in school (I've rarely seen less than a 90 percent figure). There are many problems with these surveys. They usually have low response rates (who wants to answer if they don't have a job?). They don't tell you if the student is underemployed in a job that doesn't require a bachelor's degree. And most schools never repeat the survey, so you have no idea what happens five or ten years later. Some col-

leges, like American University, have comprehensive websites that detail job outcomes by major. Also, check out the salary by field information on the U.S. Education Department's College Scorecard (collegescorecard.ed.gov).

In the end, when searching for a college there's a piece of advice I like from a professor at Lehigh University, Jeremy Littau, who posted this on Twitter after teaching his last class for a group of departing seniors in 2020:

> A good college provides space for asking questions about who you are and your place in the world. They challenge you to interrogate your values for the first time probably ever, to keep what fits and consider other ways of seeing. The vocation part flows from that inquiry.

Acknowledgments

It takes a village to write a book—this one particularly more so than my previous efforts. To thank everyone here who helped in some way isn't possible. You know who you are, and I'm eternally thankful for your assistance.

You would not be holding this book in your hands without the three campuses that allowed me access to their admissions process for an entire cycle: Davidson College, Emory University, and the University of Washington. Officials at all three schools could have easily turned down my request, like so many of their counterparts did. Yet they welcomed me into their offices and their personal and professional lives, submitting to my endless line of questioning and my constant presence during the busiest and most stressful time of their year.

At Emory, I'm grateful for Nancy Seideman, who appreciated the scope of my request and cleared the way to John Latting and Paul Mathers, whose approval was necessary. John and his team at Emory gave me extraordinary access and exhibited extreme patience during my visits to observe their selection process. I'm especially grateful to Mark Butt and Angela Holman for arranging and guiding my visits with such ease.

At Davidson, Mark Johnson helped plan my visits and kept my reporting on track, while Chris Gruber was always there to explain the intricacies of Davidson's selection criteria yet another time or provide context about the wider world of admissions. At the University of Washington, I'm thankful to Phil Ballinger for taking a chance on this project and grateful as well to Robin Hennes, Dave Sundine, Paul Seegert, and Melissa Aydelott.

I'm thankful to every single member of the admissions staffs on all three campuses for the time they spent sharing the passions and frustrations of their roles. I wish I could have included all of their stories so the rest of the world could see the devotion with which they approach their work.

Many campuses were unwilling to let me inside their admissions offices because they didn't want me to see how they balance ability to pay in making selection decisions. Lafayette College was one of the exceptions, and for that I'm thankful to Alison Byerly, Mark Eyerly, and Matt Hyde.

In the early days of reporting, three individuals in particular shaped my understanding of the admissions landscape and connected me to key contacts in the business. Thanks to Giuseppe "Seppy" Basili, Rick Hesel, and Bill Conley.

The college search is a stressful process for most students, and it comes during some of the most anxious years of one's life. Dozens of high school students and their families opened up their homes and lives to me. I'm especially grateful to the three students featured in the book for sharing their stories: Grace, Nicole, and Chris.

Many individuals and organizations helped connect me with students, their parents, and counselors and answered my queries, including Nicole Hurd, Diane Campbell, Hannah Wolff, Michelle Bailey, Maria Aguirre, Jim McCorkell, Teresa Valerio Parrot, Cynthia Hammond Davis, Christian Ekholm-Jacobson, Dave Monaco, Sam Suchala, and Lisa Clay.

I'm grateful to the administrators, educators, and journalists who schooled me on admissions, its history, and the tradeoffs inherent in the work. My thanks go to Jon Boeckenstedt, Eric Hoover, James Murphy, Robert Massa, Eric Maguire, and Jay Goff. A number of people and companies who serve the admissions industry helped me better understand the role of these outside players. They include Brian Zucker, Bill Royall, Pam Royall, Brett Frazier, Bob Morse, Enxhi Myslymi, and Jeff Kallay.

Multiple drafts of the manuscript were helped greatly by the fine eye and thoughtful editing of Sheila McMillen, Katie Salisbury, and Jack Hart. Special thanks to Scott Smallwood for all the time and effort he spent helping me sketch out the narrative, improve the prose, and visualize the data to make more sense of it. Scott is one of the most talented editors I've ever worked with, and I benefited from the time he had to dedicate to this project. For their assistance with my research, thanks to Mackenzie Fusco, Kelly Field, Peter Schmidt, and Jonah Newman, and to my assistant, Kiri Mohan. Finally, I'm especially grateful to Karin Fischer for her help reporting from the West Coast. As always, any errors of fact or interpretation are mine alone.

My agent, Gail Ross, once again prodded me to push forward on the idea for this book and helped shape the proposal, and her tough love got me to the finish line. I'm grateful to the entire team at Scribner, especially my editor, Rick Horgan. Rick kept reminding me of my audience and pushed my reporting and writing in new directions despite my initial hesitations and even protests.

Several friends, colleagues, parents, and other authors read all or part of this manuscript, and helped make it better: Jane Karr, Goldie Blumenstyk, Martin VanDerWerf, Emmi Harward, Larry Blumenstyk, Jim Larimore, Julie Lythcott-Haims, Beth McMurtrie, Andrew Palumbo, and Carin Blatteis. I'm also grateful to all the friends in my life who listened incessantly about this book and were patient every time I said we'll get together when the book is done. Well, now it's done.

I'm deeply grateful for the individuals and institutions that support my daily work, especially Michael Crow and Jim O'Brien at Arizona State University and Rich DeMillo at Georgia Tech. Michael Horn, my cohost of the *FutureU* podcast, also deserves a special shout-out because some of the ideas presented here first got their airing in our work together. I'm also thankful to serve on the board of trustees of my alma mater, Ithaca College, and grateful to the members there who help me see on a regular basis the wider impact of higher education on our lives.

And, finally, thank you to my family. My parents, Jim and

Carmella, sacrificed so much for their children to have a great life and education. Mom and Dad—I love you for that and for everything you have done. Thank you to Jamie and Dave for constantly putting up with your younger brother growing up, which gave me the confidence to be curious and ask questions. Your continued support is a source of inspiration. I'm lucky to have two of the best in-laws in the world, Gene and Sandy Salko, who will drop anything at a moment's notice to help out. Maria Orozco has been a member of our family since our oldest daughter was three months old, and with her love and care, I never have to worry about our children when I'm on the road reporting or holed up in my office.

I reserve my deepest love and thanks for my children, Hadley and Rory, and my wife, Heather. This is not the children's book Rory wanted or the work of fiction that Hadley wanted, but I hope that one day—maybe when they're in high school—they'll appreciate the time I spent away reporting this book. No matter what, their smiles, their laughs, and their questions were always the inspiration for me to get back home or shut down the computer at the end of the day. Finally, for Heather, you are a source of love and joy. You make me a better person every day, and this book is for you.

Notes

This book is the result of nearly two years of reporting and writing during which I interviewed scores of students, parents, high school counselors, college admissions officers, and others involved in the admissions process. Much of the source material and my interpretation of it is from those interviews. Where I relied on books, articles, or reports for statistics or information, I listed those sources in the text itself or in the notes below. Data about colleges and universities included throughout the book come from the federal government's Integrated Postsecondary Education Data System, known as IPEDS (https://nces.ed.gov/ipeds), or a school's report to the Common Data Set. References to *U.S. News* rankings come from the 2020 edition, which was released in September 2019.

Most of the events described in the book I witnessed firsthand. Where I wasn't present, I reconstructed scenes based on the memories of those who *were* there.

One note on the students throughout the book: I went to great lengths to protect their identities. In the case of the applicants to the schools where I was embedded in the process, identifying characteristics have been withheld or made intentionally vague so I could include key details from actual applications, such as test scores, GPAs, recommendations, and essays. For two of the three seniors I followed through the process—Nicole and Chris—I included only their first names. The third senior, Grace, asked that her real first name not be used. She was given a pseudonym, as were other students in the book who are identified by name. All other details of their lives are true.

Notes

Introduction: Steering the College's Agenda

8 *one-third of Fortune 500 CEOs:* Kittleman Blog, "Colleges that Produce the Most CEOs," *Kittleman,* Oct. 15, 2018, https://www.kittlemansearch.com /news-blog/colleges-that-produce-the-most-ceos/.

9 *students applied to* seven or more *colleges:* Melissa Clinedinst, Sarah F. Hurley, and David A. Hawkins, "2012 State of College Admission," *National Association for College Admission Counseling (NACAC);* Melissa Clinedinst and Pooja Patel, "2018 State of College Admission," *National Association for College Admission Counseling (NACAC).*

11 *Black students . . . account for about 6 percent:* Jeremy Ashkenas, Haeyoun Park, and Adam Price, "Even With Affirmative Action, Blacks and Hispanics Are More Underrepresented at Top Colleges Than 35 Years Ago," *New York Times,* August 24, 2017.

11 *enroll more students from the top 1 percent:* Raj Chetty, John N. Friedman, Emmanuel Saez, Nicholas Turner, Danny Yagan, "Mobility Report Cards: The Role of Colleges in Intergenerational Mobility," Working Papers 2017-059, Human Capital and Economic Opportunity Working Group.

12 *fewer than 20 percent of their applicants:* 2017 admissions data from Drew Desilver, "A majority of U.S. colleges admit most students who apply," Pew Research Center *FactTank,* April 9, 2019.

12 *enrolled at their* top-choice *college:* E. B. Stolzenberg, M. K. Eagen, E. Romo, The American Freshman: National Norms Fall 2018, Higher Education Research Institute University of California, Los Angeles.

Chapter 1: Selling a College: The Endless Pursuit of Students

21 *spend an estimated $10 billion:* John Katzman, "The Spending War on Student Recruitment," *Inside Higher Ed,* April 18, 2016.

22 *administrator split his time between admissions and academic duties:* The history of admissions relies heavily on Elizabeth A. Duffy and Idana Goldberg, *Crafting a Class: College Admissions and Financial Aid, 1955-1994* (Princeton: Princeton University Press, 1998).

22 *Ohio's Hiram College put it in 1961:* Ambrose J. DeFlumere, "Admissions Office Policy," *The Hiram Broadcaster,* Jan. 1961, 2.

23 *The service got off to a slow start:* Jonathan Harr, "The Admissions Circus," *New England Monthly* (Haydenville, MA), April 1984.

26 *selling 30 million names a year:* Harr, "The Admissions Circus."

26 *Michael Sexton, the former dean of admissions:* As quoted in Eric Hoover, "Captain Caperton," *The Chronicle of Higher Education,* June 30, 2006.

26 *60 million names . . . 5.2 million students:* Eric Hoover, "Application Inflation: When Is Enough Enough?," *New York Times,* November 5, 2010; College Board, "SAT Trends 2010," *College Board,* Sep. 2010.

26 *buy prospects from over a dozen sources:* Edward M. Gillis, "College and University Admission and Enrollment Management Practices for Undergraduate

Notes

Freshman Inquiry Generation: Report of Findings," *Harvard Summer Institute on College Admissions,* June 2016.

27 *purchase names of sophomores:* Ruffalo Noel Levitz, "2018 Marketing and Student Recruitment of Effective Practices," *Ruffalo Noel Levitz,* 2018.

29 *only 11 percent elicits some sort of response:* Gillis, "College and University Admission."

31 *Back in 1975, 60 percent of students applied to just one or two colleges:* Application statistics in this paragraph come from John H. Pryor, Sylvia Hurtado, Victor B. Saenz, José Luis Santos, and William S. Korn, "The American Freshman: Forty Year Trends," *Higher Education Research Institute,* April 2007.

33 *parents focus on selectivity and reputation more than cost:* Thomas A. Flint, "Parental and Planning Influences on the Formation of Student College Choice Sets," *Research in Higher Education* 33, no. 6 (1992): 689–708.

37 *Fifteen percent of California students travel more than 500 miles:* Jeffrey J. Selingo, *The Future of Enrollment: Where Colleges Will Find Their Next Students* (Washington, D.C.: The Chronicle of Higher Education, 2017).

37 *a "re-sorting" of students:* Caroline Hoxby, "The Changing Selectivity of American Colleges," *Journal of Economic Perspectives* 23, no. 4 (2009): 95–118.

38 *students' choices cluster around type of college (public or private) and brand:* Jonathan Smith, Matea Pender, and Jessica Howell, "Competition among Colleges for Students Across the Nation," *Southern Economic Journal* 84, no. 3 (2018): 849–878.

39 *most selective institutions . . . account for about one-third of* all *applications:* Clinedinst and Patel, "2018 State of College Admission."

40 *unending stream of superlatives:* Frank Bruni, "College Admissions Shocker!," *New York Times,* March 30, 2016.

Chapter 2: Defining Prestige: The Buyers and Sellers

50 less than *a B average and* scored under *a 1000:* Jennie H. Woo and Susan P. Choy, "Merit Aid for Undergraduates: Trends From 1995-96 to 2007-08," *National Center for Education Statistics,* October 2011.

56 *Malcolm Gladwell argued in the* New Yorker: Malcolm Gladwell, "Getting In: The Social Logic of Ivy League Admissions," *The New Yorker,* October 2, 2005.

61 *19 percent of students enrolled in the Princeton Review's SAT review course:* Early 1980s figure is from Nicholas Thompson, "Playing With Numbers," *Washington Monthly,* September 1, 2000; current figure from email from Suzanne Podhurst at the The Princeton Review.

61 *its structure and development continue into a person's twenties:* Francis E. Jensen and Amy Ellis Nutt, *The Teenage Brain: A Neuroscientist's Survival Guide to Raising Adolescents and Young Adults* (New York: HarperCollins, 2015).

63 *boost scores by as much as 115 points for twenty hours of work:* Catherine Gewertz, "College Board Reports Score Gains From Free SAT Practice," *Education Week,* May 8, 2017.

63 *Students who reported* feeling *adequately prepared:* Raeal Moore, Edgar

Sanchez, and Maria Ofelia San Pedro, "Investigating Test Prep Impact on Score Gains Using Quasi-Experimental Propensity Score Matching," *ACT, Inc.*, 2018.

68 *Freeland once described it, "tired and mediocre"*: Richard M. Freeland, *Transforming the Urban University: Northeastern, 1996-2006* (Philadelphia: University of Pennsylvania Press, 2019).

70 *president called the rankings "a beauty contest"*: Nicholas Thompson, "Playing With Numbers," *Washington Monthly*.

73 *player hitting .220 comes up as the MVP*: As quoted in Nicholas Thompson, "Playing With Numbers," *Washington Monthly*.

74 *"It was very mathematical and very conscious"*: As quoted in Max Kutner, "How to Game the College Rankings," *Boston Magazine*, August 26, 2014.

75 *You get credit for the number of classes you have under twenty*: As quoted in Max Kutner, "How to Game the College Rankings," *Boston Magazine*.

77 *Applicants pay attention to them*: "College rankings and college choice: How important are college rankings in students' college choice process?," *Higher Education Research Institute*, 2007; "College-Bound Students Use a Wide Variety of College Rankings Sources," *Art & Science Group LLC studentPOLL* 12, no. 3 (2016).

78 *spending by $112 million per year to jump into the top 20*: Shari L. Gnolek, Vincenzo T. Falciano, Ralph W. Kunci, "Modeling Change and Variation in *U.S. News & World Report* College Rankings: What would it really take to be in the Top 20?" *Research in Higher Education* 55, no. 7 (2014): 761–779.

Chapter 3: Understanding Merit: Look at All the Bs

87 *preserving the admission of white men*: Jerome Karabel, *The Chosen: The Hidden History of Admission and Exclusion at Harvard, Yale, and Princeton* (Boston and New York: Houghton Mifflin Company, 2005).

88 *intended it pejoratively*: Margalit Fox, "Michael Young, 86, Scholar; Coined, Mocked 'Meritocracy,'" *The New York Times*, Jan. 25, 2002.

88 *of the 26,000 domestic applicants for admission to the Class of 2019*: Students for Fair Admissions, Inc. v. President and Fellows of Harvard College (Harvard Corporation), Document 421-252: Report of David Card, PhD. United States District Court for the District of Massachusetts, Civil Action No. 1:14-cv-14176.

101 *rely on seven primary paths to selecting a class*: Gretchen W Rigol, *Admissions Decision-Making Models: How U.S. Institutions of Higher Education Select Undergraduate Students* (New York: College Entrance Examination Board, 2003).

106 *described as a "walking bundle of contradictions"*: Eric Hoover, "Harvard Trial Reveals What Deans Are Made Of: Contradictions," *The Chronicle of Higher Education*, Oct. 22, 2018.

107 *the "dean of deans"*: Fred M. Hechinger, "About Education; New Job for Dean of Deans," *The New York Times*, July 24, 1984.

109 *only 9 percent of American youths earned a high school diploma*: Claudia Goldin

and Lawrence F. Katz, "Human Capital and Social Capital: The Rise of Secondary Schooling in America, 1910 to 1940," *NBER Working Paper No. 6439*, Mar. 1998, https://www.nber.org/papers/w6439.

110 *physical characteristics of prospective students:* Karabel, *The Chosen*, 327.

110 *justifying a bias for prep school applicants:* Karabel, *The Chosen*, 407.

110 *top alumni fund-raiser for Yale wrote to the president of the university:* Karabel, *The Chosen*, 452.

110 *six states passed measures to ban affirmative action:* Hua Hsu, "The Rise and Fall of Affirmative Action," *The New Yorker*, Oct. 15, 2018.

111 *Asian Americans are seen as the "new Jews":* Daniel Golden, *The Price of Admission: How America's Ruling Class Buys Its Way Into Elite Colleges—And Who Gets Left Outside the Gates* (New York: Penguin Random House, 2006).

111 *study in 2009 by two Princeton sociologists:* Thomas J. Espenshade and Alexandria Walton Radford, *No Longer Separate, Not Yet Equal: Race and Class in Elite College Admission and Campus Life* (Princeton: Princeton University Press, 2009).

112 *An internal Harvard study:* Nell Gluckman, "How Harvard's Admissions Office Courts Donors and Low-Income Students," *The Chronicle of Higher Education*, Oct. 17, 2018.

Chapter 4: Playing the Odds: Early Decision

119 *only nine of the top 65* U.S. News: From an unpublished analysis of College Board data by James Murphy, a tutor, testing consultant, and writer.

119 *more selective the college, the larger the number:* Melisa Clinedinst and Pooja Patel, "2018 State of College Admission," *National Association for College Admission Counseling (NACAC)*, 14.

120 *managing their application pools in uncertain times:* For a definitive history of early decision see James Fallows, "The Early Decision Racket," *The Atlantic*, Sept. 2001.

120 *admissions director at Williams College wrote in a 1955 report:* Fred Copeland, "Admissions Report," *Williams College Archives*, Sept. 30, 1955.

120 *60 percent of Amherst's incoming class came in through early decision:* Christopher Avery, Andrew Fairbanks, and Richard J. Zeckhauser, *The Early Admissions Game: Joining the Elite* (Cambridge: Harvard University Press, 2003), 27.

125 *About one in five schools say demonstrated interest:* Melisa Clinedinst and Pooja Patel, "2018 State of College Admission," *National Association for College Admission Counseling (NACAC)*, 17.

125 *They found that applicants who visited campus:* James A. Dearden, Suhui Li, Chad D. Meyerhoefer, and Muzhe Yang, "Demonstrated Interest: Signaling Behavior in College Admissions," *Contemporary Economic Policy* 25, no. 4 (2017): 630–657.

126 *"I have a responsibility to my institution":* As quoted in Douglas Belkin, "New Front in College Admissions: Nudging Students to Decide Early," *The Wall Street Journal*, Jan. 2, 2019.

129   *The* Washington Post *declared in a front-page headline:* Nick Anderson, "Early applications surge at prestigious colleges. So does early heartache," *The Washington Post,* Jan. 5, 2019.

129   *students selects what they perceive as the "pragmatic" option:* Christopher Avery, Andrew Fairbanks, and Richard Zeckhauser, "What Worms for the Early Bird: Early Admissions at Elite Colleges," *KSG Faculty Research Working Paper Series,* August 2001.

129   *"time creep" that tends to come in a competitive selection process:* Alvin E. Roth and Xiaolin Xing, "Jumping the Gun: Imperfections and Institutions Related to the Timing of Market Transactions," *American Economic Review* 84, no. 4 (January 1994): 992–1044.

130   *average acceptance rate for ED is more than 10 percentage points higher:* Melissa Clinedinst and Anna-Maria Koranteng, "2017 State of College Admission," *NACAC.*

131   *essentially equivalent to scoring 100 more points on the SAT:* Christopher Avery, Andrew Fairbanks, Richard Zeckhauser. *The Early Admissions Game.*

136   *16 percentage points less likely during regular decision:* Gabrielle Chapman and Stacy Dickert-Conlin, "Applying early decision: Student and college incentives and outcomes," *Economics of Education Review* 31, no. 5 (2012): 749–763.

136   *willing to trade the ability to compare financial aid offers:* Matthew Kim, "Early decision and financial aid competition among need-blind colleges and universities," *Journal of Public Economics* 94, no. 5-6 (2010): 410–420.

136   *one in three come from families earning more than $250,000:* Jennifer Giancola and Richard D. Kahlenberg, "True Merit: Ensuring Our Brightest Students Have Access to Our Best Colleges and Universities," *Jack Kent Cooke Foundation* (January 2016).

137   *run out of money for regular decision admits:* Gabrielle Chapman and Stacy Dickert-Conlin, "Applying early decision," *Economics of Education Review.*

142   *less than half of applications to selective colleges arrive with a class rank:* From an unpublished analysis by James Murphy, a tutor, testing consultant, and writer.

Chapter 5: Finding an Edge: Athletes and Legacies

146   *We're talking about deception and fraud:* "Transcripts: Actresses Felicity Huffman, Lori Loughlin Among Those Being Charged in College Entrance-Exam Scheme; Authorities Hold News Conference on College Entrance-Exam heating Scheme," *CNN,* March 12, 2019, http://transcripts .cnn.com/TRANSCRIPTS/1903/12/ath.02.html.

148   *45 percent in basketball and 40 percent in football—are African American:* Demographics of teams in this chapter come from "NCAA Demographics Search," *National Collegiate Athletic Association (NCAA),* http://www.ncaa .org/about/resources/research/ncaa-demographics-search.

148   *compared with 52 percent of undergraduates overall:* "Enrollment in Undergraduate Education: Race and Ethnicity of U.S. Undergraduates," *American Council on Education (ACE),* https://www.equityinhighered.org/indicators

/enrollment-in-undergraduate-education/race-and-ethnicity-of-u-s-under graduates/.

148 *Nearly half the recruited athletes at Harvard come from families making $250,000 or more:* "Meet the Class of 2022: Makeup of the Class," *The Harvard Crimson,* https://features.thecrimson.com/2018/freshman-survey/makeup/.

150 *Nearly 8 million kids played high school sports in 2019:* NFHS News, "Participation in High School Sports Registers First Decline in 30 Years," *National Federation of State High School Associations,* September 5, 2019.

150 *just 150,000 or about 2 percent . . . received scholarships:* "Probability of Competing Beyond High School," *National Collegiate Athletic Association (NCAA)* http://www.ncaa.org/about/resources/research/probability-competing -beyond-high-school; "Scholarships," *National Collegiate Athletic Association (NCAA),* http://www.ncaa.org/student-athletes/future/scholarships.

151 *sixty swimmers, but can give out only the equivalent of two dozen scholarships:* NCAA Academic and Membership Affairs Staff, "2014-15 NCAA Division I Manual," *National Collegiate Athletic Association (NCAA),* August 1, 2014, http://www.ncaapublications.com/productdownloads/D115.pdf.

151 *George Mason University awarded . . . University of Cincinnati:* Brad Wolverton, "The Myth of the Sports Scholarship," *The Chronicle of Higher Education,* November 20, 2016.

155 *athletic prowess weighs heavily in the admission decision:* "The Place of Athletics at Amherst," May 2016, https://www.amherst.edu/system/files/media/Place OfAthleticsAtAmherst_Secure_1.pdf.

156 *Youth sports participation by top-earning families:* Derek Thompson, "American Meritocracy is Killing Youth Sports," *The Atlantic,* November 6, 2018.

156 *fastest growing high school sports:* "Participation Statistics," *National Federation of State High School Associations,* https://www.nfhs.org/ParticipationStatistics /ParticipationStatistics/. (2012–13 and 2017–18).

159 *ubiquitous in elite higher education:* Richard D. Kahlenberg, ed., *Affirmative Action for the Rich: Legacy Preferences in College Admissions* (New York: The Century Foundation Press, 2010).

159 *acceptance rate for legacies at Harvard was 34 percent: Students for Fair Admissions, Inc., v. President and Fellows of Harvard College (Harvard Corporation),* Document 415-1: Expert Report of Peter S. Arcidiacono. United States District Court for the District of Massachusetts, Civil Action No. 1:14-cv-14176.

159 *one-third of Harvard's freshman class:* "Meet the Class of 2022," *The Harvard Crimson.*

160 *nearly 25 percent higher chance of getting accepted than a non-legacy with the same SAT score:* James Shulman and William G. Bowen, *The Game of Life: College Sports and Educational Values* (Princeton, NJ: Princeton University Press, 2001): fig. 2.3, 41.

160 *Harvard tagged 1,378 applicants special circumstances:* Card, David. "Report in *Students for Fair Admissions, Inc., v. President and Fellows of Harvard College (Harvard Corporation),*" Boston, December 15, 2017, 34.

160 *"I created a guarantee":* Jennifer Levitz and Melissa Korn, "'Nope, You're Not Special.' How the College Scam Mastermind Recruited Families," *The Wall Street Journal,* September 6, 2019.

160 *"entry-level" gift for admissions is $10 million or more:* Dana Goldstein and Jack Healy, "Inside the Pricey, Totally Legal World of College Consultants," *The New York Times*, March 13, 2019.

161 *Officials at the University of Southern California traded emails:* Jennifer Levitz and Melissa Korn, "'Father is Surgeon,' '1 Mil Pledge': The Role of Money in USC Admissions," *The Wall Street Journal*, September 3, 2019.

161 *Northwestern's president admitted to the student newspaper:* Alan Perez and Gabby Birenbaum, "Northwestern President Schapiro says he reads applications of some legacy, donor students," *The Daily Northwestern*, April 24, 2019.

Chapter 6: Comparing Grades: High School Matters

168 *Eight in 10 college students who completed AP Calculus:* David M. Bressoud, ed., "The Role of Calculus in the Transition From High School to College Mathematics," *The Mathematical Association of America and the National Council of Teachers of Mathematics*, 2017.

168 *67 percent of freshmen at Harvard reported they took AP Calculus:* "Meet the Class of 2023," *The Harvard Crimson*, https://features.thecrimson.com/2019/freshman-survey/.

169 *About half of American teenagers now graduate high school with an A average:* Michael Hurwitz and Jason Lee, "Grade Inflation and the Role of Standardized Testing," in *Measuring Success: Testing, Grades, and the Future of College Admissions*, ed. Jack Buckley, Lynn Letukas, and Ben Wildavsky (Baltimore: Johns Hopkins University Press, 2018), 64–93.

169 *Other studies have reached similar conclusions:* Seth Gershenson, "Grade Inflation in High Schools (2005–2016)," *Thomas B. Fordham Institute*, September 19, 2018, https://fordhaminstitute.org/national/research/grade-inflation-high-schools-2005-2016.

169 *A study by three economists of 10 million–plus SAT takers:* Joshua Goodman, Oded Gurantz, and Jonathan Smith, "Take Two! SAT Retaking and College Enrollment Gaps," *NBER Working Paper No. 24945*, August 2018. The study was conducted when the SAT score was based on a total 2400 points, but the finding that multiple takes results in a higher score still holds under the new scoring system.

170 *improvement of 20 points on the math section of the SAT or 10 points on the verbal section:* Derek C. Briggs, "Preparation for College Admission Exams: 2009 NACAC Discussion Paper," *National Association for College Admission Counseling*, 2009.

170 *greatest variation in SAT scores . . . happens at the extremes in terms of selectivity:* Jonathan Wai, "College rankings might as well be student rankings," *The Conversation*, August 21, 2019.

170 *more in-depth information on a student's cognitive skills:* Warren W. Willingham, "Prospects for Improving Grades for Use in Admissions," in *Choosing Students: Higher Education Admissions Tools for the 21st Century*, ed. Wayne J. Camara and Ernest W. Kimmel (New York: Routledge, 2005), 133.

176 *test scores provide an added insight when evaluating students:* Paul Westrick, Huy Le, Steven B. Robbins, Justine M. R. Radunzel, and Frank L. Schmidt, "College Performance and Retention: A Meta-Analysis of the Predictive Validities of ACT Scores, High School Grades, and SES," *Educational Assessment* 20 (2015): 23–45; Saul Geiser and Maria Veronica Santelices, "Validity of High-School Grades in Predicting Student Success Beyond the Freshman Year: High-School Record vs. Standardized Tests as Indicators of Four-Year College Outcomes," *Center for Studies in Higher Education, University of California, Berkeley,* 2007; Emily J. Shaw, Jessica P. Marini, Jonathan Beard, Doron Shmueli, Linda Young, and Helen Ng, "The Redesigned SAT Pilot Predictive Validity Study: A First Look," *College Board Research Report 2016-1,* 2016.

179 *big fish/little pond:* Thomas J. Espenshade, Lauren E. Hale, and Chang Y. Chung, "The Frog Pond Revisited: High School Academic Context, Class Rank, and Elite College Admission," *Sociology of Education* 78, no. 4 (2005): 269–293.

Chapter 7: Finding Diamonds: Regular Decision

181 *In 1915, the founder of Coke gave the school a million dollars:* History of Emory from Gary S. Hauk, *A Legacy of Heart and Mind: Emory since 1836* (Atlanta: Bookhouse Group, 1999).

184 *60 percent of applicants to college have test scores consistent:* Krista D. Mattern, Emily J. Shaw, and Jennifer L. Kobrin, "An Alternative Presentation of Incremental Validity: Discrepant SAT and HSGPA Performance," *Educational and Psychological Measurement* 71, no. 4 (2011): 638–662.

184 *low GPAs compared to their SAT scores often take more rigorous courses in high school:* Mattern, Shaw, and Kobrin, "An Alternative Presentation of Incremental Validity," *Educational and Psychological Measurement.*

186 *altered the ultimate content of the letter:* Jonathan D. Schwarz, "Lost in Translation: Elite College Admission and High School Differences in Letters of Recommendation," (PhD diss., University of Notre Dame, 2016).

189 *starting out is $42,000:* Average of all institutions from 2018–19 Professionals in Higher Education Survey conducted by The College and University Professional Association for Human Resources (CUPA-HR).

190 *gender divide on college campuses cuts across racial and ethnic lines:* Lorelle L. Espinosa, Jonathan M. Turk, Morgan Taylor, and Hollie M. Chessman, "Race and Ethnicity in Higher Education: A Status Report," *American Council on Education,* 2019.

Chapter 8: Shaping a Class: The Final, Close Calls

209 *on the wait list to avoid rejecting them:* Scott Jaschik and Doug Lederman, "2019 Survey of College and University Admissions Officers," *Inside Higher Ed,* 2019.

210 *number is even higher at top-ranked schools:* Melissa Clinedinst and Pooja Patel, "2018 State of College Admission," *National Association for College Admission Counseling (NACAC),* 2018.

211 *average amount students are gapped:* Based on 2016 figures, latest available, as calculated by Mark Kantrowitz, publisher of savingforcollege.com and one of the foremost experts on student aid.

216 *half of the schools admit men at a higher rate than women:* Nick Anderson, "The gender factor in college admissions: Do men or women have an edge?," *Washington Post,* March 26, 2014.

Chapter 9: Paying for College: The Best Class Money Can Buy

225 *only 40 percent of the letters:* Stephen Burd, Rachel Fishman, Laura Keane, and Julie Habbert, "Decoding the Cost of College: The Case for Transparent Financial Aid Award Letters," *New America* and *uAspire,* June 2018.

227 *"children's potential to take precedence":* Caitlin Zaloom, *Indebted: How Families Make College Work at Any Cost* (Princeton: Princeton University Press, 2019), 156–158.

234 *the event inspired 1.24 billion social media posts:* Teresa Watanabe, "Michelle Obama, celebrities in tow, brings words of inspiration to students at UCLA," *Los Angeles Times,* May 1, 2019.

Chapter 10: Making the Final Decision: May 1

237 *about half of families are stepping on campus for the first time:* Jeffrey Selingo, "How to Find a College You'll Love," *Washington Post,* March 17, 2018.

243 *America's billionaires attended top schools:* Derek Thompson, "Does It Matter Where You Go to College?," *Atlantic,* December 11, 2018.

247 *work in jobs related to their majors:* Jaison R. Abel and Richard Deitz, "Agglomeration and Job Matching among College Graduates," Federal Reserve Bank of New York, 2014.

Conclusion: Charting the Future

255 *"a rock star":* As quoted in Eric Hoover, "An Ultra-Selective College Dropped the ACT/SAT. And Then What?," *Chronicle of Higher Education,* July 10, 2019.

257 *About a dozen colleges have closed each year since 2015:* Moody's Investors Service, "Sustained stress will drive more private colleges to alter business models or close," *Moody's Investors Service,* July 23, 2018.

262 *Forty percent said they carry "moderate" weight:* Melissa Clinedinst, "2019 State of College Admissions, Chapter 3: Factors in Admissions Decisions," *National Association for College Admission Counseling (NACAC),* 2019.

Index

acceptance, acceptance notification
  admissions portal and, 132
  colleges competing for
    commitments after notifying,
    220, 237–40
  financial aid award letters and,
    224–26, 228
  Ivy Day, 247
  LTE (likelihood to enroll) and, 202
  March notifications, 120, 182, 208,
    213, 215, 218, 219, 228, 247
  May 1 deadline for commitment
    and, 220, 228, 234
  multiple acceptances, 94, 220, 237
  multiple acceptances, choosing
    second or third picks, 243–52
  open houses and, 220, 237, 240–41,
    242
  real-time look, decisions online, 220
  rising bar for, 182
  "rolling admissions" and, 174
  See also College Signing Day
acceptance, increasing chances of, 11,
    270–74
  AP courses and, 270–71
  application essay and, 144, 193, 197,
    202–3
  college search and, 259, 271–72, 273
  demonstrated interest and, 125–26,
    203
  depth and consistency of application
    story, 182, 273
  extracurricular activities and, 196,
    203, 204, 270
  high school attended and, 178–79
  keeping grades consistent, 271
  multiple test retakes, 171

recommendation letters and,
    185–86
  rigorous high school courses, 184,
    270
  test scores for top college, 171
  See also college search; early
    decision (ED) admissions; regular
    decisions
acceptance rates, 5, 7, 9, 23, 68, 76, 77,
    88, 137, 201, 207, 209, 219
  average for ED, 130
  average four-year college, 12
  "buyer" schools vs. "seller" schools,
    50, 127
  for children of top donors, 160
  College Board publication of, 22
  college search and considering, 59,
    117
  elite or selective colleges, 39, 40,
    252
  for legacies, 159
  as reason for multiple applications,
    22
  See also specific colleges
ACT test, 168
  advice for best score, retake
    multiple times, 171
  COVID-19 pandemic cancellations,
    xvii
  early decision admissions and, 61
  Emory applicant and, 84
  multiple test taking, 170
  Nicole (student applicant) and, 60,
    61, 62
  test-optional policies and, xviii,
    255
  top-tier students and, 51

Advanced Placement (AP) classes, 83, 86, 89, 108, 167, 168–69, 182
  advice about choosing, 270–71
  Calculus, elite colleges and, 168, 270
  Davidson applicant review and, 203
  Emory applicant review and, 2, 83, 90, 102, 103, 187, 190, 191, 192, 194, 196, 219
  high schools, variations in course offerings, 167
  impact on college performance, 178
  Lafayette applicant review and, 215
  Nicole (student applicant) and, 167, 247
Advisory Board Company, 44
affirmative action, 11, 108–9, 110–11, 113, 114
Agnes Scott College, 188–89
Allen, Scott, 101–2, 217–18
alumni interviews, 241
American University, 275
Amherst College, 54, 152, 154, 229–30
  application pool, 156
  diversity goals, 156
  ranking, 154
  recruited athletes, 153–56
  slot system at, 155–56
application
  advice for getting into college and, 272–73
  black women vs. black men applying to college, 190
  calendar for, 52, 120, 133
  colleges accepting after May 1, 12
  depth and consistency of application story, 182
  for ED, 61, 106, 117, 129
  importance of demonstrated interest, 125
  importance of essays, 144, 193, 194, 197, 202–3
  importance of showing "fit" and, 86
  multimedia portfolios and, 263
  multiple submissions and loss of cohesiveness, 86
  no rules for evaluation of, 194
  online, 127, 253
  redesigning (recommended change for), 261–62
  rising volume of, 22–23, 31, 38, 40, 90, 91, 101, 104, 114, 115, 129, 181, 182
  "school group" applications, 91–92, 132
  selective colleges targeted by, 38
  "stealth applicants," 41
  surge in (2020–21), xviii
  as a transaction, 178
  women vs. men applying to college, and who gets in, 190, 216
  See also application pool; Common Application
application essay, 3, 10, 12, 32, 54, 85, 262
  changing requirement for, 262
  cut and paste mistakes, 86
  Davidson applicant review and, 141, 144, 202, 203, 208
  Emory applicant review and, 84, 89, 91, 182, 183, 187, 190, 192, 194, 197, 219
  Grace (student applicant) and, 113
  Harvard applicant review and, 112
  improving acceptance chances and, 144, 193, 197, 202–3
  Tulane applicant review, 125
  UW and, 114
  UW applicant review and, 97, 100
application pool
  at Amherst, 156
  at big selective public schools, 101, 206
  competition for admittance and, 92
  at Dartmouth, 247
  at Davidson, 201, 202
  ED and, 61, 92, 120, 124, 129, 135, 136, 138, 143
  at Emory, 7, 92, 182, 183, 191, 192, 194, 196
  failure to stand out and, 194
  high-need students and, 213, 214, 215
  at Northeastern, 74, 76, 217
  recommendations for, 260
  reducing, 201, 205, 206, 217
  regular decisions and, 182
  rising application volume and bigger pools, 15, 74, 127
  at selective schools, 37, 143, 171, 192, 256, 266

shaping process and, 207
sorted by high school, 163
students on the margins and, 183
at Tulane, 124
women in, 136
at UW, 114, 116, 207
Arizona State University, 231, 246
athletes, 10, 11, 87, 147–59
  advantage in admissions, 151
  common profile of, 157–58
  Division I schools, 149, 157, 208
  Division III schools, 149, 151, 157,
    158
  ED and, 137–38, 153–54
  Emory and, 92
  example, lacrosse player, Division
    III, 151–54
  how colleges recruit, 153
  Hudl online recruiting site, 152
  income level and, 156
  matching with a coach and, 152–53
  for niche sports, 149, 156
  number of black vs. white students,
    148
  "prospect days," 152
  recruiting process for, 260
  scholarships for, 150–51
  slot system and, 155–56
  talented applicants vs., 149
  youth travel teams and, 149–50
Atlantic magazine, Fallows article on
  ED, 127, 131
Augustana College, 230–31
Avery, Christopher, 131

Bailey, Michelle, 166–67, 171, 172,
  173, 234–35
Baltimore Convention Center, college
  fair, 47–48, 52
Barnard College, 218
Barron's Profiles of American Colleges, 39
"batch admit," 206
Bates College, 152
Bethesda Magazine, college acceptance
  list in, 58
Big Test, The (Lemann), 176–77
Binghamton University, 246
Boston College, 23, 69, 76
Boston University, 37, 75, 76, 252
Bowdoin College, 54, 252, 255

Bowen, Bill, 157, 159–60
  The Game of Life: College Sports and
    Education Values, 157–58
Brandeis University, 231
Brighouse, Harry, 94
Brown University, 67, 129, 133, 252
Bruni, Frank, 40
Bucknell University, 155
Burning Glass, 246–47
Busteed, Brandon, 273
Butt, Mark, 83–85, 89–91, 194–95, 218
"buyer" or "seller" schools, 48–52,
    119, 125, 127, 130, 256–57, 272
  acceptance rates and, 50, 51, 127
  college costs, 50, 256, 272
  college fair and "buyer" schools, 51
  compiling a college list and, 49, 179
  COVID-19 pandemic, impact on
    "buyer" colleges, 256
  financial aid and, 223–24, 227,
    232–33, 241
  making a class vs. crafting a class
    and, 49, 51
  merit aid and, 50, 51, 75, 118, 256, 272
  Northeastern move from buyer to
    seller, 67–69, 79
  quality of education not defined by,
    49, 51

California Institute of Technology
  (Caltech), 107
California Polytechnic State
  University, 106
California State University, 106
Campbell, Diane, 224–28, 233, 234
Campbell, Kortni, 140–41, 143, 202, 203
campus visits, tours, 12, 61–62, 67, 141
  advice for getting into college and,
    271
  in April, after acceptance, 220, 237,
    240–41, 242
  COVID-19 pandemic and, xviii
  demonstrated interest and, 141
  increased acceptance after, 125–26
  "prospect days" for athletes, 152
  Render Experiences and, 237
  selling a college and, 237–40
  spring break and, 62
  virtual tours, xviii
Carleton College, 252

Carnegie Mellon University, 51
Case Western Reserve University, 51, 231, 233
Chosen, The (Karabel), 109
Chris (student applicant), 14
 AP courses and, 167
 college costs and, 172–73
 college search of, 63–66, 167, 173–74
 College Signing Day and, 234–35
 financial aid and, 173, 235
 Gettysburg College and, 165, 167, 174, 175, 235
 high school attended, 165–66
 high school counselor and, 165–67, 172
 Moravian College and, 173, 174, 175
 as "passenger" student, 171
 transition to college and, 235
 understanding of "major" and, 171
Clinton, Bill, 25
Coleman, David, 178
Colgate University, 51, 54
college admissions, 5
 about the college, not the student, 10, 11, 182, 194, 195
 acceptance rates and, 5, 7, 9, 12, 22, 23, 39, 40, 50, 68, 76, 77, 88, 117, 127, 130, 137, 160, 201, 207, 209, 219, 252
 "back doors" of, 145
 as a business, 12, 21, 40
 colleges as "buyers" or "sellers," 48–51, 119, 125, 127, 130, 256–57, 272
 colleges as cartels and, 253
 COVID-19 pandemic and, xvii–xx
 data, statistics, and acceptances, 122
 Deacon's approach, 265–66
 demonstrated interest by student and tracking of, 124–26, 141, 165, 203, 271–72
 duality of, 48
 ease of getting into college today and, 12
 enrollment management and, 69, 119, 222, 223
 full-pay vs. low-income applicants, 210–15
 growth of data-driven results, 69–70

high school-college relationship and, 163–79
 high school visits and, 165, 166, 189
 history of, post–World War II, 21–22
 holistic admissions and, 86–89, 93, 96, 98, 100, 108, 109–13, 116, 170, 206
 institutional priorities or agenda and who gets accepted, xx, 9, 10, 27, 70, 195, 201–10, 257–58, 267
 LTE (likelihood to enroll) and, 202
 by major, 172, 205
 measuring potential and, 100, 122
 meritocracy and, 88
 modern infrastructure of, 22
 multiple applications as problem for, 22, 40
 "need-aware" admissions, 136
 no system, no single approach, 101, 191, 194
 officers, about, 189
 parental anxiety and, 7–8, 11, 12, 243, 255
 parental income and, 88, 137, 205
 perspective of officers, 85
 private college, full-pay vs. low-income applicants, 98–99, 136
 public colleges, in-state vs. out-of-state applicants, 99
 race, socioeconomic level, and, 108–12, 147, 205
 rising application volume and, xviii, 22–23, 31, 38, 40, 90, 91, 101, 104, 114, 115, 129, 181, 182
 "rolling admissions," 120, 174
 seats available, Canada, 263
 seats available, elite colleges, 263
 seats available, U.S. campuses, 5
 "selectivity," 22
 specialized language and acronyms, 85
 student "files" and, 85–86
 as subjective or arbitrary, 15, 190, 191, 194, 195–97, 204, 206, 267
 talented applicants and, 149
 "tips" or "hooks," 147, 149, 182
 traditions and, 21, 253
 transparency and, 111, 113, 116, 159, 170
 yield rates and, 122, 123, 126, 127, 141, 174, 182, 201, 209

as zero-sum game, 6, 155
See also application pool; athletes;
college admissions process;
diversity; legacy admissions;
specific colleges
College Admissions and the Public Interest
(Thresher), 266–67
college admissions process
average time per application, 104
CBE and, 104–6
comparing grades, 94, 163–79
ED and, 4, 47, 51, 83, 106, 117–44
first cuts, 2
first evaluation, 181–82
focus on different aspects of the
application, 106
home stretch, "fine" sort, 205–9
January to March, ten-week sprint,
191–97
paired-reading approach, 91
personal rating and, 96–100
readers for, 95, 101
"reading" applications, 101
regular decisions, 181–97
"rough sorting," 168
shaping or crafting a class, 1, 2–3,
94, 122, 201–20
standards applied in context,
105–6
traditional system, 104
See also Davidson College; Emory
University; University of
Washington; *specific schools*
college admissions scandal (Operation
Varsity Blues), 5, 8, 145–47, 148,
160, 161
college admissions system, changes
for, 254–58
application redesign, 261–63
expanding the field, 263–64
federal government's role, 259–60
recruiting all applicants as if they
are athletes, 259–60
suggestions for parents, students,
and counselors, 258–59
truth in pricing, searchable
database, 264–65
College Board, 15, 29, 107, 178
about, 25–26
BigFuture website, 33–34, 269

name selling (search business),
26–27
publication of acceptance rates, 22
revenues, 26, 27, 178
SAT and AP tests, 26, 178
Student Search Service, 23, 26
study on admissions, 101
test prep by, 62
College Confidential, 123, 132, 269
college costs, paying for college, 8,
221–35
average in-state public college
tuition, 49, 272
average private school tuition, 49, 272
"buyer" schools and, 50, 256, 272
College Navigator website for
average grant amounts, 226
college search and, 272, 273
as consideration in applying, 33, 35,
230–32
dream colleges and, 228–30, 241–42
East Stroudsburg's cost for Chris,
174–75
families pressured to pay huge
sums, 227
"Federal Direct Unsubsidized
Loans," 225
financial aid leveraging and, 221,
223–24, 233
financial aid offers, weighing,
174–75, 224–28, 235
Gettysburg's cost for Chris, 235
Moravian's cost for Chris, 174
need for transparency, 230, 264–65
Northeastern's cost for Nicole, 48
not qualifying for financial aid and,
241–42
parental income and, 229
Parent PLUS loan, 225
prestige and tuition, 78
sticker price vs. actual price, 230
subsidized loans, 225
tuition discounts, 35, 49, 50, 51,
151, 174, 223, 224, 226, 229,
231–32, 256
UCLA's cost for Grace, 242
Wesleyan's cost for Grace, 241–42
work-study jobs, 225–26
See also financial aid; scholarships,
merit aid

college fair, 47–48, 51
college marketing, 9, 15, 19–45
  as arbitrary, 29
  boosting application numbers and, 20–21
  campus visits, tours and, 237–40
  choice and information overload, 34
  College Board's Student Search Service and, 23, 25–26
  college costs and, 235
  college fair, 47–48
  college's website, tracking by, 41–42
  CRM system and, 42
  direct mail, 19, 21, 29, 31, 253
  direct marketing and, 23, 24–25, 33–34
  email and social media marketing, 9, 19, 21, 26, 30, 33, 42, 43, 47, 125
  enrollment management and, 69
  Gen Zers and, 41, 254
  high school counselor visits, 22–23
  name buying, 25–29
  reach or dream schools pushed by, 38
  repositioning campuses into national names, 37–38
  Royall & Company and, 20, 24–25, 43–45
  shift in attitude toward, 23–24
  students ignoring marketing, 29–30
  "viewbook," 20, 38
college-planning tools, 38–39
College Possible, 14
college rankings, 15, 53
  author writing about, 9
  ED and, 127, 128
  as factor in school choice, 78
  irony of, 79
  prestige and, 70
  private vs. public schools, 73–74
  quantitative measures, 70, 71, 72–73, 74, 77
  SAT scores and, 131, 177, 218, 255
  U.S. News & World Report guides, 9, 15, 59, 70, 71, 72–73, 74, 77–78, 269
  See also specific colleges
college recruitment, 20, 23, 31, 43, 44, 47, 191, 239
  amount spent on, 21
  athletes and, 8, 137–38, 148, 151, 153, 157
  California targeted, 36–37
  campus visits and, 239–40
  low-income and first-generation students, 137
  recruitment funnel, 21, 47, 153, 239, 263
  shift to selection, 22
  of sophomores, 27
  See also college marketing
College Scorecard, 245–46, 275
college search, 6–7
  advice for students, 259, 271–72, 273
  athletes and, 152
  BigFuture website and, 33–34
  brand name recognition and, 38, 54, 55, 243–45
  California students going out-of-state, 36–37, 75
  choice and information overload, 34, 174
  Chris's search, 63–66
  college costs and, 33, 35, 172–73, 227–28, 230–31, 264–65, 272, 273
  college search as a funnel, 54–55
  college search class, Friends School, 52–54
  compiling a list, 35, 39, 49, 54–55, 133, 271–73
  COVID-19 pandemic and, xvii
  difficulty of comparisons, 55
  "drivers" vs. "passengers" and, 52, 64, 67, 152, 171, 172, 173, 174
  ED as disadvantage in, 133, 139
  as emotional decision, 55, 67
  expanding the field, 264
  factors to consider, 249
  filtering and online search, 34
  finding the right "fit," 15, 32, 38, 41, 55, 63, 86, 158, 195, 220, 251, 254, 265, 269
  Grace's search, 31–36
  high school counselor and, 33, 34–35, 36, 163–64, 233
  high school quality and, 179
  Internet and, 132
  as a learning experience, 251, 259
  legacy admissions and, 159
  likely or safety schools, 35

most satisfactory results of, 259

Nicole's search, 59–63

number of students choosing out-of-state schools, 36–37

"overmatching," 176

parental job during, 174

post-college careers, earnings, and choice of school, 243–47, 273–74

prestige and, 56–57

reach or *dream* schools, 35, 38, 252

"re-sorting" of students, 37–38

"seller" vs "buyer" schools, awareness of, 49, 179

target or *foundational* schools, 35

type of college (public or private) and, 38

"undermatching," 175–76, 256

uninformed "shoppers" and, 48

wealthy vs. poor and working-class kids, 63

See also Appendix of this book; campus visits, tours; college marketing; demonstrated interest

College Signing Day (May 1), 234–35

campus visits, tours and choice, 237–40

choosing second or third choices, good results of, 243–52

college costs and choice, 241–42

elite schools and opportunity, 243–44

making the final decision, 237–52

post-college careers and choice of school, 243–47

Collegiate Information and Visitor Services Association, 239

Columbia University, 62, 79, 131

Committee Based Evaluation (CBE or paired approach), 91, 104–6

Common Application (Common App), xviii, 96, 102, 125, 127, 177, 178

boosting application numbers and, 75

early decision applications, 52, 129

ED applications, 2018, 129

Georgetown not using, 265–66

multimedia portfolios and, 263

Northeastern University and, 75

problems with, 263

spaces for activities, 204

standardizing high school experience with, 177

student-conduct question, 186

supplemental question, 125

Common Data Set, 126, 128, 232, 270

Cornell University, 40

COVID-19 pandemic, xvii–xxi

campus visits, tours and, xviii

college closings and, 257

college search impacted by, xvii, 258

extracurricular activities and, xvii

financial stress and, 271

high school grades and, xix

impact on "buyer" colleges, 256

impact on high schools, xvii–xviii

testing cancellations and test-optional changes, xviii–xx

trade-offs schools will have to make, 256–57

Crafting a Class (Duffy and Goldberg), 22

customer relations management system (CRM), 42

Dale, Stacy, 244–45

Dancz, Nicole, 196

Dartmouth College, 67, 112–13, 117, 162, 247

Dattagupta, Satyajit, 121–23, 125, 126

Davidson College, 4, 13, 62, 130, 138, 207–8

acceptance rates, 201

admissions committee, 207

admissions dean (see Gruber, Chris)

admissions process, 212

application pool, 201, 202

college costs and, 204

as Division I school, 208

ED at, 139–44, 201–2

final round for accepting students, 201–5, 207, 208–9

financial need and international students, 204

judging a high school and, 164

July Experience, 141

as need-blind school, 211–12

ranking, 208

wait list, 203, 204, 209–10

"Why Davidson" essay, 202–3

yield rate, 201

Davis, Jetaun, 182–97, 218
Deacon, Charles, 265
Delahunty, Jennifer, 216
demonstrated interest, 124–25, 141
  admissions officers visiting high
    schools and, 165
  advice for getting into college and,
    125–26, 271–72
  campus visits and summer
    programs, 125–26, 141, 203
  college tracking of, 126
DePaul University, 222
Dickinson College, 202
diversity (race, gender, and
    socioeconomic status), 11, 97
  affirmative action and, 108–9,
    110–11
  Amherst College and, 156
  athletics and, 147–48
  Emory and, 216
  federal dollars needed for, 264
  final round of student acceptances
    and, 207
  gender balance and, 190, 216–17
  high school quality and, 168
  personal rating and, 97–98
  selective or elite colleges and, 11,
    257
  "tips" or "hooks" and, 147
Duffy, Elizabeth, *Crafting a Class*, 22
Duke University, 32, 37, 133, 251
  acceptance rates, ED vs. regular,
    130
  ED application surge, 129
  graduate earnings, 246
  recruited athletes and, 157

EAB, 44, 222
early action (EA), 120, 121, 261
early decision (ED) admissions, 4, 47,
    51, 61, 117–44
  "ABC" system, 120
  advantages, real or perceived, 130,
    131
  advice: what to do if you're denied,
    133
  application deadline, 117
  application pool and, 61, 92, 129,
    135, 136, 138
  application review for, 106

Avery's study of, 131
benefits for colleges, 130, 137–38
binding commitment and, 121, 134
boosting yield rates and, 123,
    124–25, 127
change recommended for, 261
college's priorities and who gets
    accepted, 135–38
as controversial, 119
date student is notified, 121
demonstrated interest and, 124–25,
    141
denials, impact on student's
    decisions, 133
ED2, 121, 123
example, Grace's application to
    Dartmouth, 112–13
example, Nicole's application to
    Penn, 117–19, 129
Fallows article on history of, 127
fourth age of, since 2008, 127–28
full-pay vs. low-income applicants,
    136–37
incentives and, 254–55
increasing competitiveness for, 131
legacy applicants and, 141–42
Naviance used for, 143
negatives for students, 61, 129–30,
    136, 137, 139, 261
number of applicants, 120, 129
percentage of admissions, 128
recruited athletes, 137–38, 153–54
recruited low-income and first-
    generation students, 137
rising application volume, 129
rising popularity of, 61
rules for, 120, 134, 144
schools offering ED, 119
selective colleges and, 119, 127, 129
"seller" schools and, 130
testing performance and, 61
tips for early applicants, 138, 143,
    144
who applies, ED pool, 135–36
women and, 136, 216
See also Davidson College; Emory
    University; *specific colleges*
East Stroudsburg University, 172, 173,
    174
Edmit, 230, 231

Elfin, Mel, 72, 73
Elon University, 62
Emory University, xviii, 13, 90–91, 181
  acceptance letters released, 219
  acceptance rate, 7, 194, 219
  admissions dean (*see* Latting, John)
  admissions offices at, 191–92
  admissions portal, 220
  admissions process, 83–85, 88–92, 100–104, 108, 182–97, 212
  admissions staff at, 83–85, 101, 182–91, 194–96
  applicants on the edges and, 183–85
  application pool, 7, 92, 182, 183, 191, 192, 194, 196
  applications from a school group and, 91–92
  CBE or paired approach, 91, 104–6
  defining merit in holistic admissions, 89
  diversity and, 216
  as Division III school, 92
  ED admissions, 83, 126, 130, 136–37, 181, 215
  examples of application reviews, 3–4, 7, 10, 102–3
  example of athletic recruit applicant, 92
  example of ED applicant, 83–85, 90
  example of black female applicant, 184–85, 187–88, 190, 191, 216
  example of black male applicant, 190, 191, 218
  example of a holistic review, 88–90
  example of undocumented immigrant applicant, 192
  factors that predict freshman grades, 108
  facts about the Class of 2023, 219–20
  final round for student acceptance, 215–20
  holistic review, 88–90, 108
  low-income and first-generation students, 107, 218–19
  as need-blind school, 211–12
  Oxford College, 101
  ranking, 73, 90, 181, 218
  rating system, four areas of, 89, 96
  readers for applications, 101–4
  recalculating GPAs by, 103–4, 108
  regular decisions at, 181–97
  rejections by, 194, 195, 196–97, 217
  rising application volume, 90, 91, 101, 181
  scholarships, merit aid, 227
  scoring scale, 190
  "shaping down" session at, 1–4, 215–20
  students committing to, 220
  wait list, 193, 217, 218
  Woodruff donations and global reputation, 181
enrollment management, 69, 119, 222, 223
Experience Economy, The (Pine and Gilmore), 238
extracurricular activities, 3, 10, 12, 54, 89, 90, 92, 97, 99, 109, 112, 114, 125, 186, 190, 197, 203, 217, 259, 262
  advice about choosing, 270
  changing requirement for, 262
  Common App and, 177, 178
  COVID-19 pandemic and, xvii
  leadership and, 89, 94, 102, 204
  personal score and, 99
  sports as, 149, 157
  support for majors and, 3, 196
  sustained involvement and, 102, 196

Fallows, James, 127, 131
Federal Application for Federal Student Aid (FAFSA), 211
  Expected Family Contribution, 211
financial aid
  admissions decisions and cost of, 204, 210–12
  aggressive practices and, 229–30
  award letter from Villanova, dissecting, 225–26
  award letters, 224, 225
  as bait to attract students, 223
  college decisions on how much to offer, 222–24
  college rankings and, 78
  college's secrecy about, 49–50
  comparing offers, 224–28
  considering colleges and, 36

financial aid (*cont.*)
  ED and, 136–37
  enrollment management and, 69,
    222, 223
  FAFSA, 211–12
  front-loading, bait and switch, 226
  "gapped" students, 211
  Gettysburg's offer to Chris, 235
  international students, 204
  maximizing a school's revenue and, 50
  Moravian's offer to Chris, 174
  "need-aware" admissions, 136, 210,
    212, 213–14
  need-blind schools, 211–12, 215
  need for transparency, 264–65
  Northeastern's offer to Nicole, 248
  origins of, 221
  predicted yield and, 223
  pricing strategies and, 221
  selective colleges and, 36, 49
  "seller" vs "buyer" schools and,
    223–24, 227, 232–33, 241
  for sophomore year, 226
  who gets it, 223
  See also scholarships, merit aid
first-generation students, xx, 12, 88, 97,
    107, 137, 147, 188, 214, 256, 257
Fiske Guide to Colleges, 32, 269
Fitzsimmons, William, 265
Ford, Gerald, 25
Franklin & Marshall College, 166,
    167, 173–74
Freeland, Richard, 68, 70–71, 74–76,
    78–79
Friends School of Baltimore, 53
Furda, Eric, 7

Gallup-Purdue Index, 271, 273
*Game of Life, The: College Sports and
    Education Values* (Bowen and
    Shulma), 157–58
Generation X, xvii, 6, 127, 169, 182, 238
Generation Z, 41, 182, 238
  bypassing official college marketing,
    254
  expectations for college, 41
  information on Reddit and
    YouTube, 254
  as "stealth applicants," 41
George Mason University, 151, 231

Georgetown University, 58, 155,
    265–66
George Washington University, 74
Georgia Tech, xix, 189
Gettysburg College, 165, 167, 174
  admissions decisions, 174
  Chris (student applicant) accepted
    at, 235
  cost of, 172–73
  financial aid and, 235
Gladstone, Malcolm, 56
Goldberg, Idana, *Crafting a Class*, 22
Golden, Daniel, *The Price of Admission*,
    161
Grace (student applicant), 14
  AP courses at her high school, 167
  BigFuture website and, 33–34
  choosing UCLA, 242
  college costs and, 33, 35, 241–42
  college list, 35
  college search, 31–36
  ED application, Dartmouth,
    112–13, 241
  extracurricular activities and, 113
  five acceptances received by, 240
  marketing to, 32–33
  PSAT results, 32
  top college goal of, 32, 57, 241
  UCLA's experience for, 251
  Wellesley open house and, 240–41
grades (transcripts)
  advice for getting into college and,
    271
  class rank and, 142
  college acceptance and, 2, 10, 168
  Davidson College and, 142, 143,
    203
  elite or selective colleges and, 58
  Emory and, 84, 102, 103–4, 108
  grade inflation, 169
  high school systems and, 168–69
  merit aid and, 50
  as measure of cognitive skills, 170,
    176
  as predictive of college
    performance, xix, 168, 261
  rigor of high school curriculum and,
    xix, 89, 91, 94, 108, 168, 183–84,
    203
  school profile and, 91–92

test scores and, 184
Grapes of Wrath, The (Steinbeck), 45,
  45n
Great Recession, 256
  college affordability and, 229
  impact on colleges, 128
Grinnell College, 252
Gruber, Chris, 138, 139, 207–9

Hamilton, Laura, 272
Hampden-Sydney College, 20, 24
Hargadon, Fred, 106–7
Harvard University, xviii, 56, 257
  acceptance rates, 160
  admissions dean, 265
  admissions lawsuit against, 8, 13,
    111, 112–13, 159, 265
  admissions process at, 112
  AP Calculus and, 168
  crafting a class and, 112
  "Dean's Interest List," 160
  EA and, 121
  ED and, 120
  financial aid and, 229–30
  high school-college relationship
    and, 233
  holistic admissions and, 112
  Kushner admission and, 161
  legacy admissions, 159, 160
  "lopping" at, 206
  merit of applicants, 88
  number of domestic applicants, 88,
    160
  number of spots, Class of 2019, 88,
    160
  number of students turning down, 94
  prestige and, 69, 70–71
  "racial balancing" and, 112
  ranking of, 73
  recruited athletes and, 148, 155, 160
  shaping relationships as benefit of,
    249
Harvey Mudd College, 30
Hennes, Robin, 95, 96, 113–15
high school, 163–79
  admissions officers and comparisons
    of high schools, 164, 190
  admissions officer's familiarity with
    the school, 183, 187–88, 191, 204,
    233

admissions officers targeting
  specific schools, 163, 179
admissions officers visiting high
  schools, 165, 166, 189, 214
advice for getting into college and,
  178–79, 185–86, 270–71
AP courses and, 167, 178
"big fish/little pond" effect, 179
college counselors at, college search
  and, 33, 34–35, 36, 163–64, 233
college counselors at, financial aid
  and, 224–29, 231–32
college counselors at, "sucktober," 224
Common App and, 177
competitive schools, 179
"counselor calls" to "feeder" high
  schools, 163
curriculum and wealth of students,
  167
elite private schools and, 169
parental choices and, 178
rigor of curriculum, 89, 91, 94, 108,
  168, 183–84, 203
"school group" admissions, 91–92,
  132, 163, 182, 194
sports at, fastest growing, and, 156
"high school movement," 109
high school student applicants
  athletes and, 152
  changeability and, 139, 152
  declining population and changing
    demographics, 255–56
  "drivers" vs. "passengers," 52–55, 59,
    64, 67, 119, 152, 171, 172, 173, 174
  ED and, 61, 117–44
  junior year and, 9, 24, 27, 32, 35,
    52–53, 59, 60–61, 63, 64, 65, 121,
    185, 233, 258, 262, 270
  multiple applications, 22
  number of applications submitted
    by, 9, 12
  number of graduates each year, 5
  "overmatching," 176
  parents' income and, 53
  reticence about sharing school
    choices, 58
  "school group" and, 91–92, 132, 182
  senior year and, 23, 35, 54, 61, 65,
    66, 86, 96, 120, 121, 129, 165–66,
    167, 171, 173, 242, 261, 271

high school student applicants (*cont.*)
sophomore year and, 27, 61, 64, 138, 152
"undermatching," 175–76
as uninformed about college differences, 48
who ended up happiest at college, 251, 259
See also college search
Hiram College, 22
holistic admissions (or comprehensive review), 10, 86
affirmative action and, 113
ambiguities of, 96, 98
Asian American students and, 111–12, 113
"batch admit" vs., 206
Emory University, 88–89
judgment about potential and, 100
origins of, as "anti-Jewish" system, 109–10
public universities and, 116
questions of fairness and, 86, 87
"racial balancing" and, 112
telling a cohesive story and, 86
test scores and, 170
University of California and, 93
UW and, 96–100
Hoxby, Caroline, 37, 39
Huffman, Felicity, 146
Human Capital Research, 164, 222
Hyde, Matt, 212, 213

Iger, Bob, 6
Indebted: How Families Make College Work at Any Cost (Zaloom), 227
independent counselors, 14, 117
Indiana University, 59
International Baccalaureate (IB) courses, 83, 168, 183, 270–71
Internet data industry, 15
Ithaca College, 6, 9, 273
Ivy League schools, 30, 54, 73, 79
acceptance rates, 58
admissions discrimination and, 8
athletes at, 148
benefits of, 248–49
expansion needed, 264
Ivy Day (admissions notification), 247
Jewish students and, 109–10

legacy applicants and, 109
prestige and, 57

Johns Hopkins University, 9, 107, 195

Kallay, Jeff, 237–40
Kaplan, Rebecca, 84–85, 89, 91
Kaplan Test Prep, 62
Karabel, Jerome, *The Chosen*, 109
Kath Path, The (YouTube), 254
Kenyon College, 216
Khan Academy, 62, 63
Krueger, Alan, 244–45
Kushner, Jared, 161

Lafayette College, 167, 174
ability to pay and, 213–15
about, 212
admissions dean, 212
admissions process, 212
as need-aware school, 212, 213–14
ranking, 212
undocumented immigrant and, 214
Langley High School, Langley, Va., 228, 231, 233
Latino students, 11, 256
Latting, John, xix, 100–102, 103, 106–8, 195, 208, 215–16, 219–20, 262
legacy admissions, 3, 10, 87, 109, 110, 141–42, 147, 159–61, 206
alumni giving and, 160
See also specific colleges
Lehigh University, 275
Lelling, Andrew, 145–46
Lemann, Nicholas, *The Big Test*, 176–77
Le Moyne College, 47–48
Lewis, Michael, *Moneyball*, 122
Lewis & Clark College, 26, 227
liberal arts colleges, 48, 62, 101, 165, 167, 235
broadening of majors and, 171–72
ED and, 119, 128
humanities majors and, 171, 172
rankings, 70, 154
recruited athletes at, 148, 154
selective or elite, 54, 148
similarity of, 38
See also Davidson College

Liberty Common High School, Fort Collins, Colo., 224, 233
Littau, Jeremy, 275
Louisiana State University, 11, 30

Maguire, Jack, 23, 69
Mansuy, Mike, 142, 201–2, 204
Martin, Giselle, 182–97, 218
Massachusetts Institute of Technology (MIT), 28, 30, 229–30, 266
McGill University, 67, 263
merit, 83–116
    AP and IB courses, 83, 87, 89, 96
    applicant weighed against entire class, 94
    civil rights movement and, 110
    Emory University and, 83–85, 88–92
    extracurricular activities, 89
    grades and, 84, 88, 93
    high school curriculum and, 89, 91, 94
    "holistic admissions" and, 86, 93, 96, 98
    lack of clarity in meaning of, 93
    as mind-set of admissions officers, 93–94
    parental involvement, 86–87
    selective colleges and, 87
    as shifting, institutional needs and, 87, 92
    summer activities, 87
    test scores and, 84, 87, 88, 93
    University of California and, 93
    UW and, 95–100
    See also scholarships, merit aid
meritocracy, 88
Miami University of Ohio, 244–45
Middlebury College, 54, 58, 148, 152
Millennials, 41, 68, 75, 127, 238
Moneyball (Lewis), 122
Money magazine college rankings, 70
Monterroso, Lupe, 196
Moravian College, 173, 174
Morse, Bob, 71–72, 73, 77
Muhlenberg College, 59, 173
Mulhern, Christine, 39

National Association for College Admission Counseling (NACAC), 125, 130, 222, 254–55

National College Advising Corps, 14, 166, 167, 234
National Collegiate Athletic Association (NCAA), 148, 150, 153, 158
Naviance, 38–39, 143
    scattergram, 39
New York Times, Delahunty op-ed on male preference in admissions, 216
New York University, 37, 122, 124, 129
Nicole (student applicant), 14, 129
    acceptances received by, 162, 247
    ACT score, 59–60, 62
    AP courses, 167, 247
    college costs and, 248
    college visits, 61–62, 67, 161, 247–48
    in competitive high school, 57
    compiling a college list and, 59
    Dartmouth rejection, 247
    desire for a top college, 57
    as "driver," 59, 60
    ED and, 61, 117–19, 129, 131–33, 247
    Northeastern University and, 76, 247–48, 250
    prestige school and, 58, 62, 162, 247
    SAT scores, 60, 63
    stubbornness in searching, 59–60
    Tulane offer, 118
Nielsen, Kelly, 272
Nondorf, James, 255
North Carolina State, 32, 59, 62, 162, 247
Northeastern University, 67
    acceptance rates, 68, 76
    application pool, 74, 76, 136
    attractiveness to students, 79, 118
    college costs, 248
    college rankings and, 70–71, 76
    Freeland as president, changes at, 68–71, 74–76, 79
    getting to top 100 university, 71, 74–76
    median SAT of accepted students, 76
    merit aid and, 75
    move from "buyer" to "seller" school, 67–69, 79

Northeastern University (*cont.*)
  Nicole (student applicant) and
    financial aid offer, 76, 162,
    247–48, 250
  parental income and, 78
  Pell Grant recipients, 78
  tuition rise, 78
Northwestern University, 62, 67, 127,
    154, 161, 222

Obama, Michelle, 234
Ohio State University, 154
Ohio University, 175, 195

Pace, Chris, 101–2
Pell Grant recipients, 78
Pennsylvania State College, xviii, 154,
    172, 173, 174, 231, 234
  post-college careers, earnings, and,
    244–45
personal adversity or mental health
    issues, 96–97
personal rating or personal score,
    96–100, 112
Pierce, William, 41–42
Pitzer College, 54
Pomona College, 35
Posse Foundation, 137
prestige (of a school), 56–57
  cachet based on history and
    location, 69
  changes in, late 1970s, early 1980s,
    69–70
  college rankings and, 70, 74–78
  enrollment management and, 69, 119
  Nicole's college search and, 59, 62
  prospective students, mistake of, 79
  public flagships, 99
  tuition and, 78
  yield rate and, 201
Price of Admission, The (Golden), 161
Princeton Review
  385 Best Colleges, 269
  college rankings, 53, 70
  SAT review course, 61, 62–63
Princeton University, 31, 62, 257
  college costs and, 229
  EA and, 121
  ED and, 120
  elite high schools and, 58

  legacy admissions and, 159–60
  ranking of, 73
public colleges. *See* state (public)
    universities

QuestBridge, 137

recommendation letters, 89, 94, 178,
    185–87, 204, 262
  advice for and getting into college,
    271, 273
  Schwarz's study of, 186
Regional Admissions Counselors of
    California, 37
regular decisions, 181–97
  candidates at the margins and,
    184–91
  at Emory, 182–97
  essay, importance of, 193
  final, close calls, 201–20
  financial needs and, 204
  grades and test scores, 184–85
  as nonbinding invitations, 182
  recommendations and, 185–87
  rigor of high school curriculum
    and, 184–85
  See also Davidson College; Emory
    University
rejections
  about the college, not the student,
    10, 11, 182, 194, 195
  admissions decisions and, 174
  choosing second or third choices,
    good results of, 243–52
  disciplinary actions against a
    student and, 186–87
  Emory 2019 and, 181, 194, 217–18
  example, candidate at the edges
    rejection, 184–85, 187–88
  example, one-dimensional student,
    197
  example, too many B's, 192
  first evaluation and, 181–82
  high grades, high test scores and, 194
  Ivy Day and, 247
  March notifications, 120, 182, 208,
    213, 215, 218, 219, 228, 247
  rising application volume and, 182
  wait list vs., 204–5
  See also acceptance rates

Render Experiences, 237
Rensselaer Polytechnic Institute, 51
research universities, 13, 48, 51, 57, 74
Rhodes College, 233
Rice University, 37, 73, 129, 133, 245, 251
Roksa, Josipa, 272
Royall, Bill, and Royall & Company, 19–20, 25, 34, 40, 43–45, 238, 239, 254
  college clients, 20, 24, 25, 43
  college marketing innovations by, 19, 24–25, 45
  death of, 44
  sale of company, 43, 44, 222
  speed and use of College Board names, 27–29
  "student lifecycle" and, 44
Royall, Pam, 44
Ruffalo Noel Levitz, 222
Rutgers University, 61

Saint Ann's School, Brooklyn, N.Y., 169
Salisbury, Mark, 230–31
Sanoff, Alvin P., 9
SAT (Scholastic Aptitude Test), 58, 168, 176–77
  advice for getting in, multiple retakes, 171
  combined with campus visits, 126
  COVID-19 pandemic cancellations, xvii
  early decision admissions and, 61
  Emory University and, 92, 102, 103
  family wealth and scores, 184
  importance of scores, 176–77
  multiple taking of test and, 169
  Nicole (student applicant) and, 60
  Northeastern University and, 76
  superscore, 169, 171
  test-optional policies and, xviii, 255
  U.S. News inclusion with college rankings, 131, 177
scholarships, merit aid, 35, 36, 49, 130, 227, 230, 231–32, 242, 272
  as bait to attract students, 50, 75, 118
  "buyer" schools and, 50, 51, 256, 272
  figuring chances of receiving, 232–33

Northeastern and, 75
  tuition discounts, 35, 49, 50, 51, 151, 174, 223, 224, 226, 229, 231–32, 256
"school profile," 91–92
Schwarz, John, 186
Seegert, Paul, 206
Segura, Will, 1–4
selective or elite colleges, 54, 62
  academic level of students, 249–50
  acceptance and crafting a class, 94
  acceptance at, 8, 12, 38, 57
  acceptance rates, 39, 40, 127, 252
  admission of men vs. women, 216
  admissions changes coming to, 257
  admissions decisions date, 174
  admissions offer from, 50
  admissions policies, debates over, 110
  admissions process at, 101
  Asian American students and, 8, 13, 111–12, 113
  athletes and, 87, 138, 147–59
  on-campus programs for college search and, 159
  children of big donors and, 160–61
  competitiveness for admission, 5
  COVID-19 pandemic and admissions to, xviii–xix
  diversifying student bodies at, 11, 57–58, 110–11, 257, 264
  ED and, 119, 127, 129, 130
  elite high schools and, 58
  elite professions, money, and, 243–47
  financial aid and Overlap Group, 229–30
  financial aid limited at, 36, 49, 241–42
  full-pay admissions, 176, 264
  grades, test scores, and, 168
  high school-college relationship, 163, 164
  holistic admissions and, 10, 109, 111
  income level and acceptance, 11, 58
  legacy admissions and, 159
  legacy status and, 87, 109, 110, 147
  low-income and first-generation students and, 257
  marketing by, 30–31

selective or elite colleges (*cont.*)
merit aid and, 50
merit defined by, 87
murkiness of admissions process
and, 86
number of students turning down, 94
parental goals and, 109
percentage of all applications and, 39
percentage of black students at, 11
percentage of total colleges, 50
preoccupation with, 5–6, 31, 38
rejections and, 195
as "sellers," admissions officers as
gatekeepers, 48–49, 50
shaping relationships as benefit of,
248–49
sports programs, 149
sticker price vs. actual price, 230
test-optional policies, xviii–xix, 255
test scores and, 170
three major types of, 14
Thresher on, 30
U.S. presidents, Supreme Court
justices, CEOs attending, 8
what is an "elite" college, 56
what is a "selective college," 39–40
Seven Sisters colleges, 120
Sexton, Michael, 26
Shulman, James, *The Game of Life:
College Sports and Education
Values*, 157–58
Singer, Rick, 146, 147, 148–49, 155, 160
Smith College, 229–30, 240
Southern Methodist University, 74
Stanford University, 40, 54, 70, 257
EA and, 121
elite high schools and, 58
Latting accepted at, 106–7
post-college careers, earnings, and,
244–45
seats available, 264
state (public) universities
application pool, 101, 206
average gap amount, 211
expansion of, 1960s, 22
expansion of out-of-state students
and, 115
holistic admissions and, 116
honors colleges and, 231
increasing selectivity of, 99

not always the cheapest option, 175
number of students enrolled in, 98–99
percentage of American students
attending, 12, 99
public flagships, 98–99
rising application volume, 114–15
shaping process and, 206
states with high tuitions, 175
in-state tuition, 98
in-state vs. out-of-state applicants, 99
Stegner, Wallace, 45n
Steinbeck, John, *The Grapes of Wrath*,
45, 45n
Stetson, Lee, 23
Student Aid Index, 211
student lifecycle, 44
Students for Fair Admissions (SFFA),
111–12
Sundine, Dave, 98
Susquehanna University, 51–52

test-optional policies, xviii–xx, 45, 170
test-optional schools, 171, 253, 255
test prep, 12, 60, 61, 62–63
test scores, 10, 11
ACT vs. SAT, 60, 63
as admissions metric, 168, 255
alignment with grades, 184
as balance for high school quality, 176
college marketing and, 31
college's search requests and, 29
COVID-19 pandemic and, xviii–xix
declining significance of, 255
drivers' advantage, 60
early decision admissions and, 61
effectiveness of test prep and, 63
girls and, 171
grade inflation and, 169
less selective colleges and, 170
merit aid and, 50
multiple test taking, score and, 169
multiple test taking, who retakes
tests, 169–70
perception of preparedness and, 63
as predictor of success, 176
selective or elite colleges and, 170
superscore and, 169, 171 *See also*
ACT test; SAT
Texas Tech University, 231
There Is Life After College (Selingo), 273

Thresher, B. Alden, 30, 167
  College Admissions and the Public Interest, 266–67
Tiggle, Darryl, 53
Tufts University, 53, 75
TuitionFit, 230–31
Tulane University, 74, 118, 121–26
  application pool, 124
  Dattagupta at, 121–23, 125, 126
  demonstrated interest and, 124–25, 126, 165
  EA, ED1, ED2 and, 123–24, 126
  example, pressure to switch to ED2, 123–24, 126
  graduate earnings, 246
  merit aid and, 233
  rising application volume, 122
  as safety school, 123, 126
  as "seller" school, 125
  yield rate, 122–23, 126

University of Alabama, 154–55, 233
University of British Columbia, 263
University of California (UC)
  Berkeley, 73, 93, 106, 135, 220, 234, 240
  criteria for admission, 93
  date for applying to, 135
  Davis, 240
  expansion of, 1960s, 22
  "holistic admissions" and, 93
  Los Angeles (UCLA), xviii, 73, 93, 135, 240, 242, 251
  Merced, 272
  ranking and, 73
  San Diego, 74, 272
  Santa Cruz, 115
  test-optional policies, xviii
University of Chicago, 62, 67, 255
University of Cincinnati, 151
University of Colorado, Boulder, 58
University of Dayton, 222
University of Delaware, 195
University of Georgia, 158
University of Illinois, 175, 246
  Urbana-Champaign, 245
University of Miami, 28
University of Michigan, Ann Arbor, 67, 73, 157, 232–33
University of Nebraska, 252

University of North Carolina, Chapel Hill, 32, 62, 69, 133, 135, 162, 247
  acceptance rates, 59
  admissions lawsuit against, 8
  ED and, 135
  recruited athletes and, 157
  in-state tuition, 59
University of Notre Dame, 129, 189
University of Pennsylvania, 37, 62
  acceptance rates, 9
  athletes and, 152
  CBE and, 104
  dean of admissions on parents of denied applicants, 7
  early decision admissions, rate, 117
  ED and rankings boost, 127
  marketing and, 23
  Nicole (student applicant), ED application of, 61, 129, 131–32
  post-college careers, earnings, and, 244–45
  tuition cost, 175
  urban neighborhood of, 68
  Wharton School, 117, 129
University of Richmond, 208, 222
University of Rochester, 133, 245, 250
University of South Carolina, 234
University of Southern California, 37–38, 68, 217
  college admissions scandal, 161, 162
  yield rate, 122
University of Toledo, 41–43
University of Toronto, 263
University of Vermont, 67
University of Virginia, 51, 155, 272
University of Washington (UW), 4, 13, 74, 98, 247
  admissions deadline for, 95
  admissions handbook, 99–100
  admissions process, 95–100, 113–15, 206–7, 212
  application pool, 114, 116, 206
  "batch admit" and, 206
  budget concerns and out-of-state acceptances, 99
  campus of, Olmsted designed, 98
  committing to a major and, 172
  computer science at, 172
  Equal Opportunity Program, 98
  example, applicant review, 96–97

University of Washington (UW) (*cont.*)
 example, personal score, 100
 holistic admissions and, 206
 number of applications received,
  2019, 95
 personal score and, 96–100
 popular majors and, 206
 racial diversity and, 97
 rating system, three scores of, 96
 rising application volume, 114, 115
 Schmitz Hall, 114
 shaping process and, 206
 socioeconomic status and, 99, 114
 in-state vs. out-of-state applicants,
  99, 206
 U.S. News ranking of, 98
 yield and, 207
University of Wisconsin, Madison,
 74, 94
U.S. Department of Education, 273,
 274
U.S. News & World Report
 basis for college rankings, 72–73,
  74, 77
 college rankings, xix, 9, 15, 59, 70,
  71, 77–78, 98, 128, 154, 181, 231
 college rankings, SAT/ACT scores
  column, 131, 177
 graduation rates, 270
 on ED, 119
 Elfin at, 72, 73
 "mean range" of, xix
 Morse at, 71–72, 73, 77
 Zuckerman buys, 72

Vanderbilt University, xix, 127, 128,
 246
Villanova University, financial aid
 award letter, review of, 225–26

VIP applicants (children of big
 donors), 160–61, 206
Virginia Tech, 51
 wait list, 3, 182, 193, 203, 204,
  209–10, 217
 actual acceptances from, 210
 institutional priorities and, 210

Wake Forest University, 231, 255
Washington University in St. Louis,
 9, 28, 73
Wellesley College, 228, 240–41
Wesleyan University, 148, 159, 255
Whiteside, Richard, 40
William & Mary, 69, 133
Williams College, 54, 120, 148, 154
Wolff, Hannah, 228–29, 231–34
Worcester Polytechnic Institute, 255

Yale University, 28, 133, 250
 acceptance rate, 2019, 40
 admissions policies, 110
 admissions process, 1960s, 110
 application innovations at, 263
 cost to attend, 227
 EA and, 121
 ED and, 120
 elite high schools and, 58
 financial aid and, 227, 229–30
 legacy applicants and, 110
 ranking of, 73
 recruited athletes and, 157
 seats available, 264
Young, Michael, 88

Zaloom, Caitlin, *Indebted: How Families
 Make College Work at Any Cost*, 227
Zucker, Brian, 222, 224, 230
Zuckerman, Mort, 72